LY ME TO HE MOON
THE OFFICIAL 'UNOFFICIAL' VOICE OF...
SUE 42 Vs. BARNSLEY - DIVISION 2 SAT. NOVEMBER 3rd 1990
OW WAS IT FOR YOU?
THE BARROW SOCCER FANZINE
GIVE 'EM BEANS!
ESTD 1989
barrow Definitely the Soccer
AUGUST / SEPTEMBER 2025
WWW.GIVEEMBEANS.CO.UK
GRORTY DIC
THE WBA FANZIN
WITH PENETRATION
GRORTY DICK FANZINE
THIS IS AN ALL TICKET FANZINE
Y Front
An Alternative Independent Look At All Things York City
Issue #50 £3
50
Crying Laughing Loving Lying
City's Best Ever Side - Midfield
Against Modern Football
KILMARNOCK F.C. SUPPORTERS MAGAZINE
No.1
30p.
KILLIE KEN
Keeps you in the know
REBELS
WITHOUT A CLUE!
SLOUGH TOWN REJECT SUPERLEAGUE STATUS
NOT ON YOUR NELLY, KELLY
AN ALTERNATIVE VIEW OF DARLINGTON F.C.
MISSION IMPOSSIBLE
PRESENTS VIC REEVES BIG NIGHT OUT AT FEETHAMS
50p
FEATURING 'KEVAN THE COMEDY DUCK'
ISSUE No. 13 DEC 1990
LEYTON ORIENTEAR
300 NOT OUT
11 EDITORS 2 TITLES 39 YEARS 4 PROMOTIONS FOUNDED IN 1986
HE'S BACK
This is the man who launched the London Daily News IT FAILED
This is the man who launched Sportsweak IT FAILED
This is the man who backed the Commonwealth Games IT FAILED
AND NOW....
ROBERT MAXWELL IS
MAD MAX
AT A GROUND NEAR YOU SOON
NOW SHOWING AT
DERBY OXFORD READING WAT
OFF THE BAL
PRODUCTION
ISSUE 12 DEC 87/JAN 88 40P
AF729967

FANZINE

The story of football's alternative press

DANIEL GRAY

BLOOMSBURY SPORT
LONDON • OXFORD • NEW YORK • NEW DELHI • SYDNEY

BLOOMSBURY SPORT
Bloomsbury Publishing Plc
50 Bedford Square, London, WC1B 3DP, UK
Bloomsbury Publishing Ireland Limited,
29 Earlsfort Terrace, Dublin 2, D02 AY28, Ireland

BLOOMSBURY, BLOOMSBURY SPORT and the
Diana logo are trademarks of Bloomsbury Publishing Plc

First published in Great Britain 2026

A catalogue record for this book is available from the British Library

Library of Congress Cataloguing-in-Publication data has been applied for

ISBN: HB: 978-1-3994-3170-5; eBook: 978-1-3994-3172-9

2 4 6 8 10 9 7 5 3 1

Typeset by Lumina Datamatics Ltd

Printed and bound in Great Britain by Clays Ltd, Elcograf S.p.A.

FSC www.fsc.org MIX Paper | Supporting responsible forestry FSC® C018072

To find out more about our authors and books visit www.bloomsbury.com
and sign up for our newsletters

For product safety related questions contact productsafety@bloomsbury.com

To Kaitlyn,
who walks from the lamppost
to behind the goalposts with me.

ENDPAPER CREDITS

4000 Holes #1, Blackburn Rovers fanzine. Credit: Scott Sumner (1989, private collection of Peter Slater).

A Love Supreme #4, Sunderland fanzine. Credit: *ALS* (1988, private collection of Peter Slater).

Dial M For Merthyr #64, Merthyr Town fanzine. Credit: *Dial M…* (2026, author's collection).

Electric Blue #6, Manchester City fanzine. Credit: Noel Bayley (1990, private collection of Noel Bayley).

Fly Me To The Moon #42, Middlesbrough fanzine. Credit: Geoff Thomas (1990, author's collection).

Give 'Em Beans!, Barrow fanzine. Credit: *Give 'Em Beans!* (2025, author's collection).

Grorty Dick #1, WBA fanzine. Credit: *Grorty Dick* (1989, author's collection).

Killie Ken #1, Kilmarnock fanzine. Credit: Malky McCormick (1988, author's collection).

Mission Impossible #13, Darlington fanzine. Credit: *Mission Impossible* (1990, author's collection).

Off the Ball #7, general fanzine. Credit: *Off the Ball* (1987, author's collection).

Leyton Orientear #300, Leyton Orient fanzine. Credit: Dave Knight, Julia Nurse, Tessa Balka and Chris Taylor (2025, author's collection).

Rebels Without a Clue #4, Slough Town fanzine. Credit: Warren and Pleb (1993, author's collection).

Terrace Talk #5/4, York City fanzine. Credit: Nik Curry (1985, private collection of Peter Slater).

The City Gent Hillsborough Disaster Special, Bradford City fanzine. Credit: *City Gent* (1989, author's collection – kindly donated by Mike Harrison).

The Memoirs of Seth Bottomley #26, Port Vale fanzine. Credit: Mark Kelly/Baz (1993, kindly supplied by Mark Kelly).

View From The Allotment End #25, North Ferriby fanzine. Credit: *VFTAE* (2024, kindly supplied by Matthew Kempson).

When Saturday Comes #28, general fanzine. Credit: When Saturday Comes Ltd. (1989, author's collection).

Y Front #50, York City fanzine. Credit: *Y Front* (2025, author's collection).

CONTENTS

PART FOUR – TURN AND FACE THE STRANGE

TIMELINE

1940: First printed use of the word 'fanzine' according to the Oxford English Dictionary, deployed by writer Russ Chauvenet to describe homemade sci-fi fan magazines.

1963: *The Shamrock*, with the cover strapline 'A Magazine for Celtic Supporters', created by John Doogan of Edinburgh. Research by Peter Slater of the Football Fanzine Culture blog credits this as football's first fanzine.

1972: Foundation of *Foul* magazine, the earliest fans' eye view national publication.

1974: First issue of Carlisle United Supporters' Club London Branch newsletter published. Renamed *Hit the Bar!* during the 1993/94 season, in 2025 it was proclaimed to be Britain's longest-running football fanzine.

1979: *Cheers*, Meadowbank Thistle fanzine launched.

1980: Early eighties proto-fanzines *Floodlight* (Colchester United), *Soccer Scene* (Barrow) and *The Web* (Queen's Park) begin publication. Over the next few years, a handful of other new fanzines appear, including *Elland News* (Leeds United), *Fingerpost* (West Bromwich Albion), *In the Loft* (QPR), *Red Final* (Aberdeen) and *Wanderers Worldwide* (Bolton Wanderers).

1981: First issue of seminal York City fanzine *Terrace Talk* distributed. In Liverpool, culture fanzine *The End* established.

1984: First issue of *City Gent*, Bradford City fanzine, published.

1985: Bradford Fire (11 May) and Heysel Stadium Disaster (29 May). Sportspages shop opens in London.

1986: Creation of country-wide fanzines *Off the Ball* and then *When Saturday Comes*, plus influential Leyton Orient fanzine *The Leyton Orientear* and *AWOL* (Meadowbank Thistle), among others.

1987: *The Absolute Game*, Scotland-wide fanzine, established. More than 30 new club titles appear.

1988: The fanzine boom begins with more than 120 new titles launched.

1989: Hillsborough disaster (15 April). One million fanzines sold over course of 1988/89 season.

1990: Taylor Report published in January. World Cup in Italy.

1991: Launch of *Standing Room Only* on BBC television.

1992: Publication of *Fever Pitch* by Nick Hornby. Start of English Premier League.

1994: *Fantasy Football League* airs on BBC for the first time.

60p

The Official 'Unofficial' Voice of The Boro

FLY ME TO THE MOON

No.63 Vs. Southend United - Div. 2 Sat. 2nd Nov. 1991

LANGBAURGH BI-ELECTION SPECIAL

INTRODUCTION

I can identify the moment I discovered fanzines – at around half past three on Saturday 2 November, 1991, in the Holgate End of Middlesbrough's Ayresome Park ground. Although I had seen them on sale, I had never dared ask my dad to buy me one; I presumed that they were off limits, *Viz* to the official matchday programme's *Beano*.

Then, that afternoon, Boro's Gary Parkinson missed a penalty against Southend United. A copy of *Fly Me To The Moon (FMTTM)* was hurled in anger over my head and towards the mesh fence at the front of the Holgate, where we kids would gather, its fearsome spikes not long removed. I won a scramble between several fellow young supporters in ski jackets and a grubby, creased copy of *FMTTM* issue 63 was mine. It is in front of me again as I write, its claim of being The Official 'Unofficial' Voice of the Boro still bold, its references to £6 terrace tickets for a forthcoming away game and ClubCall otherworldly.

From the way it looked to the words I surreptitiously read in the car home, it seemed impossibly unruly and exotic. Christ, there were even swear words. From then on, somehow, I persuaded my dad that before each match, I needed the fanzine in addition to the programme. At away games, I began to accrue the fanzines of other teams. I was fascinated and gripped by these ragtag publications that you certainly could not buy in our village newsagent. Aged 18, I finally dared write something for *Fly Me To The Moon,* and I hold that fanzine almost entirely responsible for whatever my career as an author has become.

For many years I did not understand an awful lot of what I read – I was nine when I received my Southend gift and can only truly have comprehended Roofus the Boro Dog and other cartoons. Yet I was transfixed, often beguiled by fanzines' front covers with their charismatic logos and strange titles, their speech bubbles and jokes that I couldn't fathom but were probably brilliant. Unlike comics, *Shoot!* magazine and fixing an empty pop can to my Raleigh racer's back wheel so that it made a motorbike sound, I never grew out of them.

In my ignorant bliss, I knew nothing of the world that gave birth to fanzines. They sprang from a time of despotic club chairmen and intransigent administrators of the game who cared not a fig for the supporters and the derelict conditions in which they watched football. During that era, supporters were policed as if they were all potential terrorists. Stadiums that fans said were death traps proved to be so.

Violence by the few made the many a target group for government, police and tabloid alike. The stigma knotted itself into society – football supporters were something old ladies tutted about and the chattering classes viewed as some wild and witless subspecies. Whereas in modern times new acquaintances gladly foist their chosen team upon a stranger, back then followers kept allegiances quiet until they could be absolutely sure that they were in the presence of a fellow traveller. There should have been some kind of secret handshake. To be a football supporter was to walk around with muck constantly on your shoe.

Football clubs themselves were only a notch above this disdainful attitude. Many supporters watched games from decaying, gangrened terraces and then queued to buy marked-up pies gridlocked with whatever the abattoir floor had to offer. At the bigger clubs, attention was already turning away from the five-quid thousands and towards the wadded corporate hundreds. Glass-screened executive boxes began to appear in grounds.

Governed only ever as a problem, bullied by the police and slandered by newspapers, fans were shoved into a corner. Despite these conditions, they did not turn to despair and walk away, nor act angrily or violently as per the stereotype they were subjected to. They resorted to typewriters, glue and jokes about Colin Moynihan's height. Their fanzines – usually A5 booklets but frequently A4 too – were crammed with content ranging from biting analysis of the game's ills and remedies for their healing, to pie reviews and probably libellous cartoons of leading footballing figures. Having fashioned their product via sneaky use of the works copier or at a cash-in-hand printers, as cagouled warriors they went out in the rain to sell them and endlessly face the question: 'Is that the programme, mate?'

All of this was produced and enacted by fans, often young and always prodigiously creative. The size of the club they covered did not matter. In fact, many readers felt that the smaller and more unsuccessful the team, the better the fanzine. From Aberdeen to York City, and *AWOL* to *Zico Was a Punk Rocker*, they draped our nation in photocopied paper.

Where they had been silenced, now the terrace many had a voice. Fanzines offered a space to chide hypocrisy, mock the powerful and set an altogether different agenda for the sport's future. This was a samizdat press run by and for anyone who had ever burnt their tongue on away end Bovril.

Fanzines arose to rehumanise the football supporter. This would not just be through polemic and opinion, but through wit and art. Early creators took the DIY ethos of punk rock and music fanzines and added campaigning zest, agitation and sarcasm. There would be no focus group to determine a target market. Fanzines were written by football supporters, for football supporters; words from behind the goal, not the press box.

From these homespun origins flowered a movement that would change football fandom. Their story is also that of a game and country in a compelling, depressing, wonderful and darkly funny time. Attempting to recount it is a privilege.

Despite this punk ethos in which everyone worked for free – at first, anyway – fanzines achieved mass market sales figures. It was said that in the 1988/89 football season, more than one million copies of fanzines were sold in the United Kingdom.

Over the decades, close to 2000 different titles have appeared, some for only a couple of issues, some unceasingly until today. Here was an underground movement that achieved maximum visibility and acute influence.

With those numbers, no book could expect to offer a comprehensive, encyclopaedic account of the fanzine movement. There is no single, organised and catalogued archive as there might be with other mediums, reflecting the unofficial, ad-hoc nature of the enterprise. That said, in researching this book I have viewed close to 8000 different fanzine issues and spoken to around 45 editors and other contributors; enough, I hope, for an informed, entertaining portrayal of what happened and what continues to unfold.

Parameters are also required. For each of the themes covered in the pages that follow, an entire *book* of its own could be written. The British fanzine movement inspired publications across the world, but each nation's culture deserves a dedicated volume, so I have fixed upon these isles. Regrettably, even Ireland's once-bustling scene does not receive much attention.

Chronologically, I could have begun with the renegade publications that foreshadowed football fanzines, such as Celtic's *The Shamrock* (1963) and *Foul* (1972), although the latter does make a brief cameo. Ditto, during the writing of this book *Hit the Bar!* (1974), journal of the Carlisle United Supporters' Club London Branch, was proclaimed the longest continuously printed fanzine. However, in an undertaking such as this, clarity is required, and so my focus begins in the 1980s with the fanzines that inspired the mass movement that quickly mushroomed. At the other end, I decided upon closing just after the mid-1990s at the conclusion of a 'long decade'.

By then, a modern version of football had arrived – by way of illustration, for several issues in 1995/96, *FMTTM* became *Voando Para a Lua* in tribute to Middlesbrough (Middlesbrough!)

buying Brazil's best forward, Juninho – and, in parallel, fanzines drifted somewhat from their original intentions, punky writing and unpolished designs. In that first decade or so they were at their swashbuckling best and annoying great numbers of the right people. They were bright, spiky, sparky; ready to change the world. That said, this is no eulogy: around 70 print fanzines still exist in this country and Ireland. Their vibrant perseverance and the stirrings of a renaissance are covered at this book's tail end. The by-product of filtering what I have used and disregarding much of the late 1990s and 2000s is a vast computer file of regret marked 'Possible fanzine book sequel stuff'.

Typos in fanzines were almost obligatory, and occasionally a badge of honour. To avoid an infuriating use of [sic] – and because I don't really know what it means – I have corrected most of them. There are other pitfalls to explain away. Fanzine issue numbering and dating were often idiosyncratic – perhaps editors wished to chisel timeless objects, perhaps they just forgot. Some fanzines were published monthly, a few weekly and many just whenever enough written contributions had been received, or funds saved for a trip to the local printing firm. I have endeavoured to use given or calculated dates where pertinent or relevant, but without clogging the page too much. Any reader wishing to follow up a reference is encouraged to get in touch.

The issue of fanzine writers' names produces another quandary that reflects the art form. Sometimes at the head or foot of their articles full names are given, sometimes first names, sometimes pseudonyms and often no names at all. This means a lack of consistency, which I hope is not irritating. Anyone quoted via pseudonym or in unattributed form is encouraged to get in touch for remedying in future prints, especially as the passage of time hopefully means no fear of repercussions from football club, workplace or mum.

During the writing of this book, I heard from several editors variations on the phrase: 'They nicked our stuff, we nicked theirs.' Copyright was an alien concept in much of fanzine land,

and 'all rights reserved' disclaimers rare. That was part of the attraction. All the same, I have strived to make references as clear as possible and attribute everything correctly. Again, do get in touch if anything has been missed.

One frustration of the research process was that, despite best efforts, I was unable to interview many women involved in the movement. Although there was a scarcity of female editors during my period of focus – honourable exceptions included Julie Pritchard of *Balls* and *Brian* and Gerri Conroy of *The Dalymount Roar* – women were heavily involved with football fanzines. A 1989 survey of fanzine editors by the Sir Norman Chester Centre for Football Research found that 20 per cent of writing and production was performed by women – far from perfect but probably higher than the average newsroom of the period. Thankfully, plenty of those 20 per cent do appear here through their written contributions.

I wanted to write this book primarily to salute and celebrate the fanzine movement and its vast, explosive contribution to fandom in the UK. To look once more at old fanzines amid a modern world of tight, clean design, blazing screens and low attention spans makes them seem fascinatingly otherworldly. It presents a rich account of what we were thinking, wearing, eating and saying 40 years ago – a people's history of football, and of Britain. It sparks all kinds of nostalgic wonder for those who were there, and piques the interest of those who were not, but, upon reading this book, will wish that they had been.

'The history of York is the history of England,' said King George VI. Come there with me now, and hear of that beautiful city's focal part in England's *football* history too. . .

TERRACE TALK

YORK NOMADS SOCIETY

Volume 5 Issue 7

20p

PART ONE
ORIGINS OF THE SPECIES

CHAPTER 1: YORKSHIRE YARNS

I took off my white woollen Bradford City scarf.
Smoke-filled and stained.
I have not worn the scarf since.

– *THE CITY GENT*, BRADFORD CITY FANZINE

Chief Inspector Hartley marched two suspects into the dim interview room. A lanky, humourless man, he towered over the pair, both in their mid-twenties. They were instructed to sit at a table while he crumpled himself into a chair opposite and glowered. Then, the policeman produced his evidence: a 32-page, A5 booklet whose typewriter text resembled more a village newsletter than some incriminating dossier.

Hartley, renowned locally as something of a tinpot tyrant, picked up the offending item and landed on page eight. He turned it around so that his subjects might see and pointed an icy finger at the paper, tapping on its surface. With wrathful eyes, the policeman glared across at them. Now they could see him twice: once in reality, and once in the cartoon that had stoked his rage. Nineteen eighty-four had not long ended, but Big Brother was still watching.

The scurrilous document that Hartley held was an issue of *Terrace Talk*, the York City fanzine. His interviewees were Mike Kettlewell and Frank Ormston, the fanzine's founders, and

Hartley had been loaned the club secretary's office inside the Minstermen's Bootham Crescent ground to make his urgent enquiries. Established in November 1981, *Terrace Talk* was one of England's first club fanzines of the decade, a seminal organ from which so much else would flow.

The cartoon in question depicted Hartley and other members of the North Yorkshire constabulary in the aftermath of a recent fixture between York and Hull City. That evening – 29 December, 1984, recalls the unstintingly mischievous Kettlewell 40 years on – 'the police decided to keep the home fans in after the game so they could get the 3000 Hull fans away. But all they did was throw the gates open and there was a lot of damage done to windows and cars in the streets around the ground by those Hull supporters.' The cartoon, he continues, showed 'Hartley and his men, commenting "I think everything went really well", but then in the background there was this mob rampaging down the terraced streets, breaking windows, fires blazing!'

Encouraged by the York City board, Hartley had long pursued *Terrace Talk* and its sarcastic, iconoclast ways. At times there was a distinctly slapstick air about this persecution, the hapless local bobby being outsmarted by snarky teenage miscreants in a comic strip. If Kettlewell and Ormston stood selling their fanzines by a lamp-post in the Bootham Cresent car park, they would be moved on for causing an obstruction. However, relates Kettlewell, 'We were quite into civil liberties at the time. We found out that as long as you're walking along, you can have your magazines in your hand and you're not causing an obstruction. So we would walk up and down and get stopped every now and then to make a sale.'

Since its inception, *Terrace Talk* had dared to question aspects of the way York City were run. Following issue 1 – not much more than a folded sheet of scrappy paper – the club had instructed their solicitors to threaten Kettlewell with a lawsuit for libel. Further, the fanzine criticised the policing of football supporters, not just locally but across England. Interrogating and lampooning the previously untouchable suits who governed institutions such as football clubs and police constabularies was a heretical act. It was the stuff of perilous insurrection, of the imperious old order being undermined. Earlier in the 1984/85 season, the football club and Hartley's force had united to ban the sale of *Terrace Talk* at Bootham Crescent. York secretary Tom Hughes even visited local newsagents and asked shop owners to do the same, claiming that the fanzine was the work of hooligans.

Later in 1985, the club changed its ground regulations to ban *Terrace Talk* contributors from taking photographs at matches, and brought in new rules forbidding the sale of all printed material except for the official club programme. Also forbidden was 'Unnecessary noise', ostensibly a crackdown on loud transistor radios but one that, said an article in October 1985's *Terrace Talk*, could apply to 'anyone talking too loudly, especially if they're criticising the referee, the City board, the police or *Emmerdale Farm*'.

'Football clubs were very exclusively for the board to run,' reflects Kettlewell. 'They didn't want any fan involvement whatsoever, and they certainly didn't want any criticism. They were frightened of us pointing out things, things that they could do better. If we'd have had fan involvement on the board then we could have raised those issues internally, but we didn't have that outlet. So we made the fanzine.'

He and Ormston responded to the club's suppression with a protest campaign, launching a petition and slapping around bright orange stickers. There were two slogans, recalls Kettlewell, 'No Ban on *Terrace Talk*' and 'I Want to Buy *Terrace Talk*', 'and we plastered them all over York, and that actually made the press.' Where previously they had been allowed to peddle the fanzine inside the ground, the ban forced them into street selling. Increased visibility, though, reaped higher sales. 'So there was nothing that they could realistically do to stop us after that, because there were no breaches of the peace,' says the genial Ormston four decades later, 'We weren't advocating violence or anything like that. We were just selling it on the street.'

This apparently incendiary publication was produced not in the shady dungeon of some anarcho-syndicalist print collective, but – marvellously – in the York branch office of the Women's Institute, a splendorous Victorian mansion. Ormston's mother was at that time the caretaker there, a job that came with living quarters. 'I moved in with her,' he explains, 'and that gave us access to office machinery. I remember sitting at the desks with these huge typewriters, massive old-fashioned, industrial ones, and you really had to bash them to get any sort of impact.' Once the WI staff had gone home for the day or left for their evening engagements in village halls across the county, he and Kettlewell would set to work on the next edition of *Terrace Talk*.

Tipp-Ex primed for the disguising of mistakes, the pair would strike at typewriter keys, deploy stencils for headlines and then print fanzine copies on the Gestetner duplicator, a primitive form of photocopier in which ink splodged on to paper from a drum turned by hand. Contemporaneously, these colossal contraptions were being deployed by underground activists in Poland and other Soviet satellites for the production of seditious leaflets. For later issues, cardboard templates and Letraset would be deployed, and a 'dodgy printer who did it cash in hand' engaged. Soon, a thousand copies of each issue were being sold, meaning that often one-third of a Bootham Crescent home crowd was in possession of this insubordinate, lippy phenomenon. Kettlewell and Ormston's pages had rattled the local establishment, and their endeavours had not gone unnoticed by football supporters elsewhere.

They were reading *Terrace Talk* 30 miles away, in the West Riding. There, in the autumn of 1984, a small group of Bradford City supporters sat in the Duchess of Kent pub and passed around a copy of this impressive publication. The gang were members of the CTC 73, an independent supporters' club who organised cheap coaches to Bantams away games. *Terrace Talk* had originated as the bulletin of a similar group – the York Nomad Society, founded by Kettlewell and others in response to York City's dire official transport offering. Two of the CTC 73 troop – Brian Fox and John Dewhirst – felt duly inspired to create a publication still flourishing today: *The City Gent*.

Fox, Dewhirst and early contributors were motivated too by discontent with their club's official matchday programme. It was an opinion shared of programmes by supporters everywhere. At best, they offered little beyond dull reports of news already known and bland nostalgic meanderings. At worst, they were mouthpieces for distrusted or pious club owners. All were consistent in ignoring the views of supporters, especially if those views happened to be negative. For a century, local newspapers' letters pages had remained the sole forum for grumbles and scrutiny, if indeed editors were inclined to risk cosy relationships with chairmen. Enter *Terrace Talk*, *The City Gent*, a smattering of other titles (see Timeline on page VII) and everything that was soon to bloom.

While both Yorkshire fanzines shared travel club roots, there was one major difference between them. 'This publication has been produced with the full consent of Bradford City,' wrote editor Fox in issue 1 of *The City Gent*, published in late October 1984. '. . . We operate with the goodwill of Bradford City FC and cater for the genuine supporter – which does not include troublemakers.' Kettlewell, by contrast, recalls how a York City board member bought his own first issue, 'read it, scruffled it up, threw it away, and said, "Well, if I were you, I wouldn't have bothered."'

Bradfordian co-operation and togetherness would soon be required through the most unimaginably dire of circumstances.

That first issue of *The City Gent* had included an article on the contemporary state of Valley Parade and its recent 'years of neglect – crumbling terraces, a leaky roof and inadequate supporters' facilities'. It pondered whether a better home might be found at a redeveloped Odsal, the stadium of Bradford Northern RLFC. In fact, it would soon emerge that £400,000 of safety and modernisation work on Valley Parade was to commence after the 1984/85 season's conclusion.

While researching his imperious *The Football Grounds of England and Wales*, Simon Inglis visited the ground in 1982. Having rested on a seat in the main stand with its wooden roof, seats and floorboards, Inglis noted in the book – with terrifying foresight – that 'Underneath the seats are flaps which open to reveal piles of accumulated litter'. He would later write in an issue of *The City Gent* how 'One of the ground staff told me that it was easier just to sweep the litter under the stand and then clear it all out once in a while. How often this was done he didn't say. . .'

Seven months after the foundation of *The City Gent*, on 11 May, 1985, that litter caught fire with hideous consequences as Bradford fans celebrated winning the Division Three title in a fixture with Lincoln City. Fifty-six people died. The stand was due for demolition on 13 May. The observations of *City Gent* writers sketch the course of that dreadful afternoon from the supporters' viewpoint. They are every bit as harrowing as one would anticipate.

'By 2.30pm,' wrote Andrew Flett, taking up his place in the main stand, 'everything was as it should be . . . The same familiar faces are next to us. Roy, Barbara, Jeff. The man with the transistor radio permanently placed to his ear relaying other scores to us as he heard them.' Flett continued: '3.44pm and nearly half-time. A glance down to the far end of the main stand indicates that some "idiot" has let off a smoke bomb. Thin grey smoke. It will soon clear. Back to the match.' Of the same moment, David Pendleton recalled, 'I saw Mark Ellis dashing along the left wing. We had already noticed a wisp of smoke behind us but it was nothing. Then I saw the flames and heard the whistle and the ball was kicked by Jackson out of the ground, and it and the game went into eternal limbo.'

Both writers watched as that light smog congregated furiously into a black bellowing mass and, wrote Flett, 'flames seemed to take on the characteristics of a liquid, literally appearing to flow along the stand and underneath the roof swirling and changing direction as they went . . . By the time half the stand had been engulfed, the heat was already causing the skin of my face to tighten and the hair on my head to tingle.' Flett attempted to leave via double door exits at the back of the main stand but found them locked and fans bunched beside them – 'I take my white woollen Bradford City scarf and tightly press it to my nose and eyes to try and shield my face from the thick, acrid smoke. Why is the crowd not moving?' Eventually, he made his way on to the pitch, from where others were hauling their luckier fellow supporters to safety. From that vantage, Pendleton reported that, 'On the scorched grass were broken and abandoned favours, and in the horrendous stand I saw a man sitting perfectly still, ablaze from head to foot. And I saw another man climbing over the burning seats. He was a silhouette in black edged with red fire and dancing sparks. He moved in jerks like a marionette and at last fell into the furnace.'

Like so many there that day, Flett and Pendleton had no way of telling loved ones of their survival. Across the city, relatives who had heard breaking news of the disaster waited in ghastly anticipation of a policeman's knock. 'I arrived home sometime after 5.30pm,' wrote Flett, 'I don't remember the drive home. I took off my white woollen Bradford City scarf. Smoke-filled and stained. I have not worn the scarf since. Thirty years.'

Flett's recollections and those of Pendleton were committed to paper quite some time after the horrors of 1985, in anniversary editions of *The City Gent* published in 2015 and 1995 respectively. In the years following the fire, few mentions of it were made in the fanzine's pages. A short editorial message appeared in the first issue released after its devastating havoc:

> Although little reference will be made to the tragic events of May 11th in this magazine, all of us at *City Gent* and CTC 73 wish to extend our heartfelt sympathy to all those who suffered in the disaster. We hope that this magazine reflects a feeling of hope and optimism for the future, whilst our thoughts remain very much with the victims of the Valley Parade fire.

Four decades on, current editor Mike Harrison explains some of the reasoning behind this decision. 'Brian Fox's parents were injured and they had a nightmare summer, obviously. So when it came back, Brian wrote that message. And that's it, and fair play I think. To try and cover the fire sympathetically . . . it's almost better not to do it and to try and be part of the club and city's future.' As Fox wrote in the 2015 anniversary fanzine, issue 200 of *The City Gent*, 'Some have suggested that *The City Gent* might have got more involved in marshalling opinions about the fire or even campaigning for fuller investigation of its causes. I think this misjudges not only the mood of the time in Bradford, but also the nature of a fanzine.'

Instead, *The City Gent* acted as a unifier between club, supporters and city, for example by regularly promoting fund-raising for the local hospital's groundbreaking burns unit. It strived to be optimistic in a city already plundered by mill closures and recession, and to show how a football club could symbolise the spirit of a place and lead its rejuvenation. The team aided this cause: through the 1985/86 season, despite roaming between other clubs' grounds as Valley Parade was redeveloped, demonstrating immense stoicism they achieved a mid-table finish in the second tier. 'Everyone has emerged stronger after the disaster,' said a *City Gent* article in April 1986. 'For a few there is understandable bitterness but the club and the community are stronger for having shared the experience. The spirit on the field is also present on the terraces. The people of Bradford at last have something to shout about: the dreams can continue.' The piece concluded that 'Ultimate success is the most fitting memorial we can give to the 56 who perished'.

In the same 2015 article, Brian Fox wrote about what had occurred on that foul May afternoon. 'Some of you will recall the near-full-page photo on the front of the *Telegraph*

& Argus on 13th May,' he said. 'The elderly couple lying down in the goalmouth were my parents.' Both his mum and dad underwent numerous hospital operations – 'Skin grafts took, then failed, were redone and then took again. At any point in the first six or seven weeks either or both of them could have died.'

Those focused *City Gent* issues allowed for almost unbearably poignant further reflection from Mick Dickinson and David Pendleton, both at different times editors of the fanzine. Pendleton wrote of how, as he stood watching matches 10 years on, in quieter moments he sensed the presence of 'the fiery tumult of that May afternoon . . . hovering on the fringes, waiting around the next corner. On misty days it comes that much closer and, perhaps with the ghosts of the past, it watches us.'

In 2015, Dickinson explained that 'I saw some things I don't want to remember but can't not remember, that I did what I could to help where I could, that I lost my youth, and became cynical, that I lost my trust in any kind of future, that I came to fear fire and crowds, and that City became as necessary to my life as drink to a dying man'. Earlier, in a 1989 Hillsborough Disaster Appeal Special Issue of *The City Gent*, Dickinson had given an insight into the temporary effects of the fire on wider Bradford. 'The whole city united in grief,' he recalled, 'and for a short time even racism disappeared. Those who make the monkey chants on the Kop these days forget how the local Bangladeshi community helped the survivors of the fire in little, human ways by making cups of tea and providing blankets.' His sentiments chimed with those of John Dewhirst in the March 1987 issue of *When Saturday Comes* (*WSC*): 'the camaraderie of the terraces extended beyond football. It's difficult to describe the atmosphere that existed in Bradford during that summer – the idea of a Dunkirk spirit became quite tangible, and a community was united.'

Mick Dickinson's father, Frank, composed what was perhaps the most aching, haunting passages about May '85 and its mental scars. Ten years on, working at Valley Parade presented him with the opportunity to sit in its empty, modern replacement main stand and recall 'the lovable strut that melted; the Marston Ales sign that vanished; the copper's helmet that burned slowly for a long, long time; . . . the green grasses that withered away . . . I recognise the need to remember – but dread the requirement to do so. The third strut from the end of the old stand, nearest the Kop, is a cenotaph that stands in my mind. Once in a while I have to visit it. . .'

Even if Frank and Mick Dickinson and the other *City Gent* writers saw the pre-fire Valley Parade as a beloved second home, there existed little sentimentality in their writings for what the main stand in particular had become. The old ground, wrote David Pendleton, 'WAS a death trap, no matter how quaint, or homely. I still occasionally feel angered by the ineptitude of decades of boards who allowed Valley Parade to become a death trap, but it's tempered by the fact that the malaise was nationwide.'

It was a theme powerfully espoused by Adrian Goldberg, co-founder of *Off the Ball*, the first national fanzine since 1972's *Foul*. 'Much of our football folklore is a glorification of squalor,' he wrote in its December 1986 issue. 'In the name of "character" and "atmosphere", we tolerate windswept terraced cages and dilapidated obstructed stands. The fire at Valley Parade was the terrible outcome of that philosophy; but as has been correctly pointed out, "Bradford" could just as easily have happened at up to 50 other League grounds.'

A successful and always eloquent writer and broadcaster, Goldberg still perceives Bradford as the tragic consequence of how supporters were perceived and treated from board room to bobby on the beat. 'It was quite clear very early on that Valley Parade had been a preventable fire,' he says, 'and some element of it was created by how football fans were seen – that safety exits were padlocked and so on, because you couldn't trust football fans not to try and force down the door and force their way in.'

In the pages of *Terrace Talk*, *The City Gent* and others, supporters had been stirred to tell their own side of the story at last. Their fanzines and the gradual awakening of a fans' movement would be needed: English football's hellish May was only halfway through.

THE "CITY GENT"

SUPPORTERS' NEWS

THE PUBLICATION OF CITY TRAVEL CLUB'73 (BFD)

CTC '73

1st EDITION

NOVEMBER ·1984·

20 pence

CONTENTS: CES PODD'S LIFE WITHOUT CITY...

TREVOR CHERRY SPEAKS....a frank interview

What the Bantam Saw...the latest hot gossip

THE ALAN WOOD TEMPERANCE SERMON...CAMRA Guide

Plus much more...

CHAPTER 2: HEYSEL TO THE FSA

A woman stopped us in the street to ask if we had seen her son. No, we hadn't.

— *WHEN SUNDAY COMES*, LIVERPOOL FANZINE

On that same cursed afternoon of the Bradford fire, another fan died at a game. Ian Hambridge had travelled from Northampton to watch his team, Leeds United, play at St Andrew's, Birmingham City's crumbling home. As was a depressingly regular occurrence, savage fighting between some home and away spectators erupted. Under pressure from squashed fans a wall collapsed, crushing Hambridge to death. He was 15 years old. It was his first and last football match.

Four days later, on 15 May, Everton lifted the European Cup Winners' Cup in Rotterdam, vanquishing Rapid Wien of Austria 3-1. In spite of police and tabloid fears, it was a peaceful occasion. Scousers played football with Dutch police officers. Their behaviour was later praised by the local force. British newspapers could not find the space to mention this cordial jubilance.

In 1988, Dave Wallace, editor of the Manchester City fanzine *King of the Kippax*, recalled visiting Brussels on business in the final week of May 1985. He had talked with Belgian policemen, asking how prepared they were for the visit of Liverpool and Juventus supporters on 29 May for the European Cup Final at the city's Heysel stadium. Wallace recalled their laughter at the very idea of trouble, 'having just helped the Dutch police sort out the Everton supporters. When I pointed out that the game in Holland had been a completely different situation . . . they just shrugged their shoulders.' Later, he asked a Belgian colleague whether he would be attending the final. The answer was a firm 'no' – 'It's the oldest stadium in Belgium and crumbling,' he had elaborated, and 'There's 5,000 forged tickets.' Speaking to me in 2025, Wallace recalls the Belgian's warning that 'It's going to be a disaster' and adds, 'UEFA were told about this and they had a chance to move it to a different stadium and they didn't.'

At 5 a.m. on 28 May, 1985, Terry Forshaw left Anfield on a supporters' coach bound for Belgium. It arrived outside Heysel at 8.30 a.m. the next morning, just under a dozen hours before kick-off. Reliving the trip four years later via the pages of the Liverpool fanzine *When Sunday Comes*, he recalled morning drinking in the Brussels suburbs and friendly chatter with Juve fans. Forshaw would later have a photo developed that showed fans Red and *Bianconeri* posed together, their respective flags held aloft. He and his friends moved on to the city centre 'where the atmosphere was completely different' – all Liverpool, all singing together, the tone buoyant if drunken.

The mood had shifted to 'intense' when they arrived back at Heysel stadium. Some had appeared without tickets and shoved themselves inside. Forshaw was swept along in a shoal of people, not having had to show his ticket. 'Others,' he wrote, 'were climbing over the seven-foot wall that ringed the stadium. A few were climbing back out, selling their ticket outside and then climbing back in.' There was shared, genuine shock at the shabby, precarious condition of the ground, the foliage thriving on terrace steps and concrete underfoot 'crumbling'.

Then, continued the Liverpool fan, 'the fighting began. It was initiated on both sides of the fence and was over fairly quickly. Juventus supporters backed off and the domino effect of this caused a crush behind them that led to a wall collapsing.' Thirty-nine people were killed and, Forshaw said, 'it seems likely that none were involved in the fighting'. A further 600 were injured as impromptu missiles flew.

There too that evening was BBC radio presenter and Liverpool fan John Peel. Peel and his wife, Sheila, were given tickets by Kenny Dalglish and found themselves sitting with the players' families, looking down upon the deathly wall. In the pages of *When Saturday Comes*, Peel described waiting 'for a long time inside this glass door under the stand, trying to pluck up the courage to walk out', and expecting when they did so 'to get the shit beaten out of us, if not actually killed, because it was where they were piling up the bodies, just outside the door, and there were lots of very very upset Italians.'

Terry Forshaw's *When Sunday Comes* article catapulted readers on to Heysel's lethal terraces. There was a pause in the game, which he and other Liverpool fans presumed was caused by a Juventus pitch invasion – 'At the time the thought that anyone had died never even crossed our minds.' Then, incredibly, the match continued. Slowly, the dire realisation that something dreadful had happened crept across the stands and 'Liverpool lost 1-0. But it didn't matter. By then nobody was particularly bothered about the game.'

It was not until Forshaw and his fellow supporters boarded their bus that the terrors of Heysel emerged. 'No one could believe it,' he continued, 'The coach was totally silent. The game wasn't even discussed.' On the long drive home, their voiceless vehicle was stopped twice by police and then again at customs. There were lengthy delays as all supporters' coaches were searched for stolen goods. Then, 'At a motorway cafe people shook their heads and shied away from us. But all anyone wanted to do was to phone home to say they were all right.'

The coach arrived in Liverpool at 11 a.m. on 30 May. The lives of its passengers had turned a dreadful corner and yet they were the lucky ones. 'People were looking at us as if to say, "Why have you brought this shame upon us?",' remembered Forshaw, then 'a woman stopped us in the street to ask if we had seen her son. No, we hadn't.'

Over the following months and years, in explaining Heysel from a supporter's viewpoint Liverpool fanzines and those of other clubs pursued similar lines of argument. They vehemently condemned violence and those fans who had accessed Heysel without a ticket. Yet they also pointed to the typical, substandard conditions in which supporters were expected to watch their teams – Bradford had its wooden stand and its litter pile, Heysel its mortal infrastructure and flimsy entrances.

The *King of the Kippax* article called the violence inexcusable but held that 'the deaths were caused by mass panic and a collapsing wall . . . A parallel could possibly be drawn with the Bolton disaster of 1946, when the gates were stormed and subsequently collapsed causing the deaths of 33 people.' It also highlighted the fact that alongside the Liverpool fans arrested and tried (26 were charged with manslaughter; 14 convicted), there were 'severe recriminations for the police', with force chief Johan Mahieu also found guilty of manslaughter.

Fellow Manchester City fanzine *Electric Blue* described Heysel as 'falling to bits', bemoaned UEFA's 'complete lack of foresight' in hosting Europe's biggest game in 'one of the oldest grounds in Belgium' and sarcastically applauded the local 'masterstroke' decision to put tickets on open sale during matchday. That move had allowed Juventus fans to buy access to a designated neutral area (Block Z), divided from Liverpool supporters by only a featherweight fence. In his *When Sunday Comes* piece, Forshaw cited 'non-existent' organisation for supporters and an 'incompetent' police service who 'lacked leadership' and 'were unwilling to take on responsibility . . .' No major inquiry into the Heysel disaster was ever held. Alongside the violence of some attending supporters, investigations that did take place cited the crumbling state and unsuitability of the stadium to stage a major sporting event. Belgian authorities – including the police – and UEFA were also criticised for their negligent organisation, not least in their provision of Block Z with its flimsy dividing fence.

'Thinking of that day now still makes me angry,' continued Forshaw. 'Nobody should have died.'

Not all fanzines were sympathetic towards Liverpool supporters. Some referred matter-of-factly to their 'murdering' of the Heysel 39 – for example, Manchester United's *Red News*. In 1988, issue 1 of Millwall's *The Lion Roars* employed the same term. They later printed an understandably incensed reply concerning this 'disgraceful slur' from Liverpool fan John Milburn, who pointed out that 'No Liverpool fan is being accused of murder'. Milburn asked, '. . . from where have you derived your information? I know far better than you the facts of that tragic evening, and the day long provocation suffered by non-reacting Reds fans, who could never have foretold the consequences of their eventual actions.' Anger was also directed at Liverpool because *all* English clubs were now indefinitely banned from taking part in European competition.

In the summer weeks of 1985, with the fanzine movement not long born, it was left to *Terrace Talk* to join the dots between The Three Bs: Bradford, Birmingham and Brussels. Its August edition brimmed with a form of analytical fury. There were words for the 'gutter press' who had claimed that the Bradford fire was started by hooligans: 'Perhaps so,' said the issue's editorial, 'but not the sort of hooligans *The Sun* meant. No, this was the work of the variety of hooligan that has refused to spend money to keep grounds in good repair.' That same attitude applied on the continent in the negligence 'of the authorities who allowed a major final to be played in a stadium which wouldn't be allowed to open its doors in the UK', the latter phrase a deep indictment indeed.

Linking the May horrors explicitly and another deadly incident in South America, *Terrace Talk* continued:

> The fact remains that 39 people died in Brussels mainly because there was no way out for them when they fled in terror. This is precisely the same as happened at Bradford where the death

> toll is now 56. In the same month, 10 people were crushed to death at the Mexican Cup Final because the entrances to the Aztec Stadium were too narrow for the amount of people flooding in. Again, the single death at Birmingham came not at the hands of violent fans, but as a result of a crumbling wall finally giving way.
>
> All this adds up to 105 football supporters dying because so many of the people who run the game are more interested in accumulating cash than in spending it to increase the safety and well-being of their supporters.

Terrace Talk columnist Den Thomas took aim at the traditional media's reaction, with its 'endless commentaries and debates and a zillion column inches of letters and articles on the problems and solutions of Bradford and Brussels by trendy, know-it-all, "I went-to-a-match-once" journalists, "hang-the-bastards" politicians and arty farty sociologists.'

As Thomas knew, it was clear that few journalists, commentators or public figures would champion the causes of football fans, and their clubs certainly would not. After May – and even before – the agenda moved to discussion of how supporters could be controlled, regulated, banned, caged. An infamous and withering newspaper quote summarised the prevailing mood. 'That comment from the *Sunday Times*,' says Graham Ennis of Everton's *When Skies Are Grey* fanzine, 'which said it's a "slum sport played in slum stadiums" watched by "slum people" typified everything. No one cared. The stadiums *were* decrepit. If you went to an away game, you were treated almost as a criminal. You were herded everywhere. And if you did get to the game, then facilities were virtually non-existent in most grounds.' Even the allegedly sympathetic *Guardian* newspaper declared that we should 'Quarantine our sad, sick game'. All focus was on the minority who fought near football grounds and not the majority who braved tumble-down terraces and sad catering to see their teams offer occasional delight. Wider society saw a sport of fighters, not lovers.

Through fanzines like *Terrace Talk* and *The City Gent*, then, those fans began to write their own stories from a blend of necessity and howling anger. Ten months after that desperate May, they would be joined by *When Saturday Comes*, a national publication that became the cement between the bricks of the fanzine movement. On the evening of Heysel, *WSC* co-founders Andy Lyons and Mike Ticher were already working together, in the Kensington High Street branch of the Our Price record store chain. Their undertaking of a stock check prevented them from watching the game on television but, recalls Lyons now, 'The manager of the shop had the radio on and he was following what was happening and telling us. I remember him saying that the kick-off had been delayed, and then it sounded like people had died.'

Ticher adds that Heysel and Bradford 'did crystallise a lot of perhaps vague thoughts that we'd had before about starting a football fanzine. It didn't immediately make me think "I'm going to start a fanzine right now", but it brought a lot of things to a head. And not just for us, but in general. It was such a terrible time. It jolted people. Obituaries were written for football – it can't go on like this, it's dying on its feet.'

July of 1985 wrought Live Aid upon Lyons' and Ticher's London, though admittedly not many acts performing that day at Wembley were to their taste. An anonymous article in *Bolton Wanderers Worldwide* – another early fanzine – proposed that principles from Bob Geldof's campaign could be applied to football. Its writer suggested that Live Aid had helped restore Britain's reputation abroad after it was 'badly tarnished by events leading up to and including the Brussels tragedy' and demonstrated that people acting together could remedy government failures. The authorities had failed to stop violence around football stadiums, so perhaps now true fans of the game could be inspired to do so for themselves. 'We don't need their blanket discipline,' proposed the article, 'the only way we will ever solve the problem is by changing attitudes ourselves. . . We can do it. If you cried when you saw the old man engulfed in flames at

Bradford or the anguished faces of Italians pinned to the ground in Brussels then you know we can. We owe it to them. . .'

Those early fanzines required a campaigning ally, a spoken voice who could take their arguments out into the world – not a rabble-rousing Irishman, but a union rooted in collectivism. Enter the Football Supporters' Association (FSA).

Rogan Taylor is a Liverpool fan from Toxteth. A writer and academic in his fortieth year at the time of Heysel, in the summer of 1985 he was constructing an article about what would happen next to football supporters. It would be a piece 'advising supporters to get their act together, because they were getting ripped to buggery,' he told Leicester City's *The Fox* fanzine in 1990. 'I remember at the time thinking that if the Liverpool and Juventus fans had met in an alehouse and organised that game they couldn't have cocked it up any worse – so maybe we should be running it.'

Taylor telephoned Pete Garrett – fellow Scouser, friend and football anorak – to check a historical fact. In the course of the conversation, he explained the premise of his article and how he would be urging fans to 'form their own union'. Garrett insisted that he and Taylor do the job themselves as no one else would; 'then he came round and badgered away for a while and in the end we did it.' The FSA's initial aim, wrote Taylor in a *WSC* article, was 'representation for supporters at all levels within the administration of the game'. Only through this, he continued, could 'tragedies such as those that occurred in 1985 be avoided in the future'.

Through engaging with and joining their local FSA branches, rather than acting only in the interests of their own teams, fans would find common causes. They would confront wrongs as a solid, unified force and at the same time demonstrate that going to football matches remained an act of affection and a joyous pursuit. Together, they could push to influence the future of the sport they loved even though, as ever, nobody had asked for their opinions. Robert Nichols, since the early 1990s editor of *Fly Me To The Moon*, believes that the local branch system helped the FSA flourish. 'The FSA wasn't divided up by football clubs, it was by areas,' he says now. 'So that was quite a novel idea itself. In packed meetings above pubs you'd have a brilliant feeling of commonality between fans across the country which had never existed before. We cared about the same things and were working together, and it all went hand in hand with fanzines, which of course we sold and exchanged at these meetings.'

The FSA's cause was helped by the fact that, in Taylor, they had an articulate and sagacious media presence, measured in his responses and keeping a cool head when all around him others were losing theirs. 'You'd see Rogan Taylor on breakfast TV and feel part of something,' adds Nichols. It was baffling for the wider public – inculcated into prejudice by the way supporters were represented only as hooligans – to witness on television a football fan who had apparently read books.

Taylor and the FSA's values aligned immediately with those of fanzines, and the two quickly entered into a symbiotic relationship that grew over the next decade. *Terrace Talk* were immediately involved. 'It was the aftermath of Heysel,' recalls Frank Ormston, 'and I saw an article about this organisation that had been set up and I thought, "yeah, that's exactly what we need".' In the August 1985 issue of *Terrace Talk*, endorsement was explicit. If football was now a business, as the media kept saying, 'why do the authorities take so little notice of what their customers are thinking and saying? We're good enough to pay £2–£10 a week, but not good enough to have opinions of our own. For this reason *Terrace Talk* welcomes the recent formation of the FSA which intends to provide a voice for all supporters that the clubs, the FA, the League and perhaps even UEFA and FIFA will have to listen to.'

Further emphasising the primitive FSA/fanzine bond, Lyons and Ticher dedicated the back page of *WSC* issue 1 – published in March 1986 – to the organisation. In a glowing endorsement headlined 'Hope – I wish you'd believe me' (a Pete Wylie & the Mighty Wah! song title), they saluted the potential of the FSA 'for counteracting the calcified institutions and trampling businessmen who are driving football steadily into the ground' and sensed it could be 'football's future'.

With assistance from Taylor and Garrett ('a big ex-copper, so that was interesting,' recalls Mike Kettlewell), the *Terrace Talk* two became part of that hopeful future by founding what was the second local branch of the FSA, after Merseyside. The North Yorkshire FSA held its first public meeting in that same March of 1986, in York's Punch Bowl pub on Lowther Street. The gathering's main topic was, 'Why are people staying away from football?', with Taylor and Garrett included on the bill.

'Well over 100 people turned up,' says Ormston, 'It was absolutely heaving.' In what was an astounding early victory for the branch given the events of 1985, York City sent three representatives to speak – manager Denis Smith and his assistant Viv Busby, and, most surprisingly, director Brian Houghton. 'We are particularly pleased that three representatives are coming from City,' said an article in the February issue of *Terrace Talk*, 'as it shows they are willing to meet with the FSA in good faith as a body which has the best interests of the game at heart.'

Kettlewell and Ormston were there at Anfield for the FSA's first national congress, in August 1986, where 250 delegates agreed five main motions: the first opposed any 'superleagues' in England or Scotland 'without proper consultation with supporters' organisations'; the second condemned any use of football 'as a platform for racist or sectarian views' and pledged that the FSA would campaign against racism and sectarianism; the third committed the FSA to campaigning for better ground facilities, 'particularly for women and for the disabled'; the fourth called for international fixtures to be played across teams' respective countries so that fans everywhere were able to watch their national sides; and the fifth condemned safety arrangements at Wembley.

To that end, in a chilling prelude to events three years later, the congress heard accounts of the recent Liverpool v Everton FA Cup Final at the English national stadium. Crushes at gates G and H had summoned memories of Heysel – many fans gave up and went home or departed to view the match on their hotel room televisions. Some supporters had gained access to the game with forged tickets and others with none; some with genuine tickets had been told theirs were fakes. When fans did get through, they found overcrowded terraces and could see not even a flicker of action. One estimate gave the attendance figure at 112,000, more than 10 per cent over capacity. Rogan Taylor highlighted the great fortune of this being a fixture contested between the traditionally harmonious Merseyside clubs, reaping a spirit of co-operation rather than tension. 'If it had been any teams other than Everton and Liverpool,' he said, 'we would have been stacking bodies along Wembley Way. It would have made Heysel look like a Sunday School picnic.'

At the heart of everything for supporters, fanzines and the FSA remained the simple act of going to the match. By the mid-1980s it was often an unpleasant undertaking, yet in pursuit of pleasure and escape from real life – and out of stubborn devotion – still they went. That love of theirs conquered all.

DIAL 'M' FOR MERTHYR
ISSUE 16
50p
STILL FENCED OFF ... WHY ?
THE 'ZINE OF THE PREMIER CLUB IN THE VALLEYS

CHAPTER 3: TOILETS, FENCES AND FISTS

For too long supporters have been expected to part with their cash and their human rights at the turnstiles, to be greeted with food not fit for cockroaches, toilets second hand from hell, heavy-handed policing, antiquated stadia . . .

– *BALLS*, GENERAL FANZINE

Their love was not blind. Supporters saw with piercing clarity the residual faults of the places in which they watched matches. Even if not all football grounds were lethally dangerous, most were tainted by awkward views of the pitch, dire facilities and a brand of filth and squalor about which Victorian philanthropists would have commissioned reports. Indeed, some stadiums had scarcely been updated in a century. Often, going to the match was an act of bravery and a feat of endurance.

These decrepit conditions inspired many prime, sardonic fanzine words. It was as if – on some flawed level that sated a supporter's attraction to doom and melancholy – match-goers revelled in them. As *The City Gent*'s John Dewhirst wrote of his Bradford contemporaries in the early 1980s, 'there was almost an inverted snobbery in the toleration of adversity. Perhaps an afternoon on rain-swept terraces was to be a demonstration of one's machismo.'

Outside of urinal industry trade catalogues, until football fanzines never before had so many pages been devoted to lavatorial matters. There were grim, darkly funny accounts of bogs that leaked on to terraces and queuing in foul foot-deep swamps. In 1986, *Off the Ball* declared Reading winners of its first Bog Standard Award 'for services to alternative leisure pursuits'. Their 'open-topped (convertible) gents' in the away end provided 'pre-match and half-time entertainment with excellent views from the terrace above'. Two years later, the fanzine's co-founder, Steve Beauchampé, saluted Kidderminster Harriers' soon-to-be demolished toilet block with its 'corrugated steel walls that shimmered in the floodlights like a beacon to those in distress'. Cantering into his typically poetic stride, Beauchampé continued:

> Its flush measured six on the Richter Scale and could, if the wind was favourable, be heard over all of Worcestershire. At peak periods, there was more steam than in a Turkish bath, and, billowing unhindered from the topless john, it surpassed anything the nearby Severn Valley Railway locos could manage . . . Inside, it's as damp as the wreck of the *Mary Rose*. A reservoir-load of Banks's finest has been sandblasted against its walls down the years, and these torrents of abuse have taken their toll.

Beauchampé may well have enjoyed Sutton United's salubrious away offering, as described in the Waterlooville fanzine *Flippin' Heck Ref, That Was a Foul Surely*. With its 'rusty tin walls creaking gently in the breeze', the club had 'got around' their structure's lack of roof by 'painting one half of an umbrella on the side, no doubt to keep the worst off. Inside, dead leaves all but cover the floor and fill the troughs, while the odd scribble on the wall marks the passing of a previous pilgrim.'

Unstinting urinal reportage continued. Preston North End's Deepdale was denounced by two of its own fanzines. A *Win on the Plastic* writer decried having to 'wade through an open sewer to relieve myself whilst avoiding low hanging electrical cables. Mind you, I'm a football supporter so I deserve such things.' Then in *Tales from the Potting Shed*, a fellow Lilywhite wrote, 'the youngsters have to wade to the shallow end to avoid drowning and total strangers piss all over your foot because it's so bloody dark and then you find that there are no hand-washing facilities.' Staying in Lancashire, Sunderland's *Wise Men Say* described the away end gents at Blackburn Rovers as being 'cunningly disguised as a scale model of the Norfolk Broads'. Dunfermline supporters visiting Morton's Cappielow home were advised to take 'flippers and an aqualung for the toilets'. Down in London, West Ham United's *On the Terraces* simply noted that 'the state of the toilets is usually nauseating by half-time'.

The drowning potential in the Gents', however, was nothing when compared to the humiliations encountered by 1980s women supporters. In fanzines they could relay their experiences, often with quite marvellous levels of sarcasm. 'The initial problem is in finding them [Ladies' toilets],' wrote an author known only as Rachel in the Meadowbank Thistle fanzine *AWOL*, 'it usually requires a Ph.D. in Geography. I opt for the strong bladder.' Stories were many of away ends completely bereft of female facilities, and the ignominy of having to identify oneself to a steward and be guided to a Ladies' in the home stands. In Notts County's *The Pie*, the pseudonymous To Loos the Trek reflected that: 'I'm the woman who is usually standing with legs crossed talking to a steward or local bastion of law and order. It's not that I've got a thing about men in fluorescent waistcoats or blue uniforms, it's just that I'm trying to find out where the nearest ladies loo is.'

Through the pages of Blackburn Rovers fanzine *4000 Holes*, another writer offered advice for female toilet users at Ewood Park during the 1988/89 season. Her tips included, 'Make choice between broken toilet or broken window . . . Sit, raise right leg (left if preferred) to keep the door shut . . . Pull chain and run to avoid shower (if lucky) . . . Collect mushrooms off wall on way out!' In her regular 'Sarah Says' column for *The Leyton Orientear* fanzine, Sarah Tabor wrote of the need to be a 'contortionist' to use the Brisbane Road Ladies. 'I am only a size 10 and I have problems. The gap between the toilet door and the loo is so short that you virtually impale yourself on the door trying to open it.'

Both would have found solidarity with Syuzen Buckley of Hibernian's *The Proclaimer*, who described Hibs' Easter Road amenities as being 'built from left-over props from *Auf Wiedersehen, Pet*'. Buckley's greatest ire, though, was reserved for city rivals Heart of Midlothian, and their away end 'bog . . . an obvious Roman relic . . . An Aladdin's cave for all you insectologists out there. Mildew decorates the walls, as do fungi and dock leaves (which can substitute for the lack of Andrex, I suppose).'

Having waded forth and escaped lavatorial captivity, supporters were often struck by another blight upon what we now call the 'matchday experience': a soaring steel fence, affixed pitchside to the perimeter wall and requiring a periscope to see over. To watch a game through such a contraption was to see flickers of footballers darting as if in a zoetrope. Most fans moved up the terrace in order to peer over fences like nosy neighbours, though an unencumbered view of the whole pitch was impossible. A fence's aim was to prevent supporters encroaching upon the pitch. Since the late 1970s an increasing number of clubs had erected these barriers to stop pitch invasions, many later garnishing them with metal spikes. Fanzine writers did see one thing through these barricades – coming danger. As Queens Park Rangers' *In the Loft* – edited by 16-year-old Howard Prosser – asked of its club's new sunken away end fence system in August 1988, 'What chance would people have of escaping? Do QPR not think of the consequences?'

Some fences became notorious, repeatedly appearing in different fanzines. 'Like watching a game through a cheese grater' said *The Leyton Orientear* of Stoke City's infamous away end barricade. At Brighton and Hove Albion's Goldstone Ground, the away end fence 'Gave an excellent impression of a P.O.W.

compound', according to *Wise Men Say*. Leicester City's *The Fox* went further. 'The beast itself is an eight-foot high, double fence,' detailed a report of a fixture there in January 1989, 'consisting of wavy railings topped with lethal plastic rotating spikes . . . A shoulder-high fence would be quite adequate with these little bleeders on top. Sort it out Brighton, I didn't pay a fiver to see 40% of the playing surface.' Wimbledon's Plough Lane was noted for its obstructions, and in an ingenious melding of matters toilet and fencing, *WSC* noted that the only way to see the whole of the pitch from the away end was to stand on a urinal and peer through a small window.

Oxford United's Manor Ground similarly received numerous mentions, as typified in a 1988 article by Alistair Coleman in Arsenal's *The Gooner*: 'The first thing that grabs you as you enter the ground is the security fence. Even standing at the back of the terracing you can't see over it – the video camera is in the way . . . rumour has it that the Manor Ground will be used as a prisoner-of-war camp when the next war comes.' More succinctly, *The Preston Pie Muncher* called it a '15-foot monstrosity', and *The Fox* reported that the fence had 'been known to interfere with low-flying aircraft'.

Elsewhere, writing in *The Chelsea Independent*, Steve Edmonds summarised criticisms frequently made of Norwich City's Carrow Road. There, a 'shallow' away end and low roof combined to obstruct the 'entire 18-yard box', and fencing segregating home and visiting supporters 'hid both corners'. Edmonds continued, 'It was a remarkable piece of surrealist architecture. The clarity was devastating – a football stand from which you could see no football! I could suddenly see that the excessive amounts of wire and metal were vitally important to the artistic integrity of the piece.'

Another regularly maddening, perplexing experience was that offered at Highfield Road. A supposedly modern stadium, Coventry City's home nonetheless had visiting supporters watching from behind a fence inside a designated cage area. Writing in the March 1987 issue of *Off the Ball*, Steve Beauchampé described the experience as 'downright offensive and unnecessary . . . And they have the gall to request repeatedly over the Tannoy that visiting fans clear the gangways. Just where do they expect us to go? On the pitch? Back outside? Stand on each other's heads to form a double layer of fans?' Theirs was not the top flight's only cage. At The Dell, Southampton's creaking if beloved old ground, some away supporters were housed in the 'Pig Pen', more a form of human aviary with bars and mesh in front, beside and above them.

Despite a scarcity of violent tumult at lower division grounds, and the lonely spaces from which supporters often watched, conditions were similarly uncongenial. In a 1986 issue of *Bolton Wanderers Worldwide*, Andy Staveley reported on a visit to Doncaster Rovers' Belle Vue ground where Trotters fans were locked into 'a steel box for two hours. I thought they might have sprayed us with freezing water at half-time just in case anyone thought that their treatment amounted merely to insult and abuse – but they were kind enough to spare us that particular degradation.' At Northampton Town's County Ground, reported *WSC*, so forbidding were the away end's high-sided mesh fences that visiting was 'like watching football in a chip pan'.

North of the border, while oppressive fences were less common, spectators watched within an atmosphere of managed, even wilful, decline. Archie MacGregor, creator of Scotland's magnificent nationwide fanzine *The Absolute Game*, summarised the situation in a late 1988 piece: 'Diminishing gates and boardroom neglect lead to lack of funds in the coffers, which in turn allows the ground to run down. Safety officers come along and lay down stringent regulations: the club can't comply with them, and so parts of the ground are closed completely, leading to further decay.'

MacGregor described the consequences for match-going, with fans forced to watch in half-abandoned, partially derelict grounds. Albion Rovers' Cliftonhill was, he wrote, 'deserted, with weed-choked terracing'; Alloa's capacity had been reduced to 300, while at Cowdenbeath, 'much of the terracing has been quite deliberately abandoned, and a small wall has been put up to discourage fans from using that area. The grandstand is also largely unusable, being partially constructed with a potentially lethal mixture of wood and tar.'

Unsurprisingly, football grounds were not easily negotiable for fans in wheelchairs. Though praising some clubs for their efforts, Rob Trent's 1987 *Terrace Talk* series on experiencing matches as a disabled fan unveiled some irritating practices. Enjoyment of Millwall was curbed by the worry of his designated position being on a steep slope. Elland Road had 'innovative measures such as six-foot fences', meaning that 'as players get further away on the near-side touchline, the view gets worse'. Burnden Park meant a spectating position at 'sub-pitch level' and at Gillingham's Priestfield, when snow began to fall and Trent moved towards cover, 'it took 10 minutes of highly intellectual debate with the stewards to persuade them that I was not a fire hazard, and that I had no intention of bursting into flames'. Notts County's Meadow Lane left him 'Drenched. . . None out of ten for a pathetic effort', a common theme for wheelchair supporters. In a 1990 issue of *Wise Men Say*, Alan Fearon recalled visiting Ewood Park during 'the Lancashire monsoon season. Fans in wheelchairs had no protection whatsoever from the elements but just sat in front of the main paddock doing their best to get a good view of the game whilst desperately trying not to catch double pneumonia at the same time.'

It was not only the physical fabric of football that could make match-going unpleasant. Amiable, nonconfrontational supporters – by far in the majority – were plagued by the actions of violent hangers-on to football. The damage suffered took two forms: physically, when the fists of unknown others flew; and reputationally, as the football savage came to represent the football fan in the eyes of the public, the press, the police and the authorities. This injustice was another motivation for the birth of the fanzine movement.

Violence witnessed and its repercussions were regularly documented and railed against. One of the worst incidents of the early fanzine era occurred at a Bradford City game during the club's enforced exile from Valley Parade. The Bantams played a number of fixtures at Odsal, the local rugby league ground (in a grim irony, a move mooted in those early days of *The City Gent*), including a local derby with Leeds United on 20 September, 1986.

That day, with City 2-0 up, tufts of away end grass were set alight. A fish and chips van was rocked menacingly as Leeds hooligans, in the words of John Dewhirst, 'tried to push it down the terraces; had they succeeded, innocent spectators would have been unable to escape onto the pitch because of perimeter fencing.' Chip fat oozed on to the terraces. The van itself was soon ablaze. Smoke mushroomed. Terrible flashbacks swarmed in the minds of home fans.

Just under a year later, violence flared in Yorkshire once more. Scarborough – new arrivals in the Football League, their first elevation to such heights – hosted Wolverhampton Wanderers and their vast, boisterous away following. Sporadic fighting broke out in the seaside sun before the game as Wolves followers rampaged through town. They then turned Scarborough's celebratory Seamer Road ground into a tetchy crucible as if performing a demonstration in Football League-level disorder. Ahead of kick-off, around 20 Wolves fans clambered on to a stand roof to watch the game. One of them – Andrew Charlesworth, aged 23 – plunged through the rickety asbestos sheeting roof, descending 30 feet on to a concrete terrace but miraculously surviving. The hole left by Charlesworth's plummet was only one speck among much damage done to Seamer Road.

Completing the hat-trick, at the conclusion of season 1987/88 Chelsea supporters set upon their triumphant Middlesbrough counterparts following a play-off defeat at Stamford Bridge that saw the Blues relegated and Boro promoted. A pitch invasion brewed into wild agitation. The FSA even claimed to have 'evidence that stewards were involved in the fighting – including information about a steward who wore two different I.D. numbers, one before he attacked a Middlesbrough fan and one afterwards.'

Whenever trouble erupted, there resulted a rare outbreak of unity between fanzines, authorities and club boards as each condemned events, albeit from opposite corners. In the summer of 1986, a *Bolton Wanderers Worldwide* editorial summarised this unlikely entente: 'The Government, police, football administrators, press and true fans will not tolerate another season marred by trouble. If it continues, we will find matches being played in empty stadia with the fans too frightened to attend. We must hope against hope that the recent trouble is merely a summer fad and the adverse publicity may have made any would-be hooligans think again.'

Demonstrating this alliance of opinion, with the fanzine's backing Wanderers were soon to launch a campaign aimed at helping fans improve their own behaviour before government and police stampeded them further. 'Don't forget,' pleaded another editorial, 'there are plenty of Bolton supporters who don't want to have a few drinks before the game and sing and dance and wave flags and throw fireworks and invade the pitch and "kill the Bill" – there are young children with their dads, old men, ladies and people who just want to watch the game in peace.' Tremendously, anyone with feedback on the provisionally titled 'out with the lout' scheme was encouraged to 'let Nat Lofthouse know'. Bolton's was a more measured approach than Scarborough's. 'I think they're a set of animals,' said their chairman, Terry Brown. 'Ken Bates [Chelsea chairman] was right. They should electrify the fences.'

Other fanzines used the power of mockery to oppose violence. *Dial M For Merthyr*'s Mark Evans – still editor of the fanzine, but also now head of the International Department at the Football Association of Wales – explains: 'One of the things that we're really proud of is that we've never been into crowd violence. In fact, we did a few articles making fun of it. We had this thing called the M5, a mock hooligan crew. I think it was good because we were the antidote to all that stuff. When we went away we were like, "I'm not interested in it." You didn't have to go along with it.' Elsewhere, the trendy plague of hooligan literature was frequently demolished in fanzine book reviews. 'Obnoxious,' said a 1989 *Fly Me To The Moon* review of Colin Ward's *Steaming In*, 'he glories in the endless tales of violence . . . this unpleasant little book would be particularly damaging to the game if it got any widespread circulation.'

Offering hope, an autumn 1988 editorial in *Brian Moore's Head Looks Uncannily Like London Planetarium* – a cult Gillingham fanzine – had suggested that following Euro '88, '. . . at long last, people are beginning to wake up to the idea that troublemakers have nothing to do with watching football'. The public had started to realise that 'Men obsessed with brawling and fighting strategies simply attach themselves to football clubs to give themselves a form of identity, and are the same people who cause trouble outside pubs and nightclubs'. Patently, fanzines were part of perception shuffling slowly in the right direction.

More common than the dark dramas of Odsal, Seamer Road and Stamford Bridge was the routine setting upon of peaceable supporters as they walked to and from matches. A March 1989 incident recalled by writer Dave Radford in Chesterfield fanzine *The Crooked Spireite* was typical. He and friends were returning to the car, having watched their team lose at Bristol Rovers' Twerton Park ground. A crew of supposed Rovers fans identified Radford's party as outsiders, 'before enquiring about the possibility of a fight. We ignored them but they continued to pester, again – and again – and again. It really was quite boring.'

The Rovers gang 'insisted it would be a fair fight, "Four on to four," the head moron continued to bleat out; the trouble was every time we turned around four increased, first to five, then six, and so on. At the last count there were nine of them. We explained that we had come to watch a football match and were not particularly interested. They stood with mouths open as we walked away. That thought had never crossed their minds.'

In the Manchester City fanzine *Electric Blue*, an article highlighted how the police practice of holding away supporters back for 20 minutes or longer at the end of matches gave local gangs the time to muster and the opportunity to easily identify outsiders. Relating a recent visit to Anfield, the piece separated these miscreants (or, 'the dickheads. Every club's got them') from genuine Liverpool supporters – 'Not for them the skills of Barnes or the agility of Grobbelaar and certainly not the merits of the opposition's play or even the comfort of home or the nearest pub. Martyrs to themselves alone, their only opposition are shadowy figures in the neon gloom, minding their own business as they make their way home.' What happened next happened everywhere, as is perhaps reflected in the writer's simple, almost weary description. '"Come on then, Mancs" they shout as they outnumber their prey four or five to one,' continued the article. 'They run past me, ignoring me and the bravest of them cracks a young lad on the back of the head before running back to the pack.'

Glancing backwards now, many fanzine editors are the very opposite of nostalgic when they think of attending football in the 1980s. In 1988, Andy Groom helped launch *The Peterborough Effect*, a Peterborough United fanzine. Now dividing his time between England and northern Italy – where he is a season ticket holder at Inter Milan – those fearsome days feel remote yet vivid. 'Over the 1980s, I was genuinely very scared at times,' he explains to me. 'There were games that you went to – not just Millwall, but Cardiff, Swansea, Tranmere in particular where you were very frightened. I remember getting chased around the back streets of Birkenhead just because we stood out – what we wore, how we talked and all the rest of it. So it was a dangerous time to be a football fan.'

Groom and three fellow Posh fans – Mark Papworth, Paul Rush and Russ Morris – had decided to create their fanzine while returning from a Division Four visit to Newport County. County were 'unusually at that time, a club that were dying. They were about to go bust.' The Peterborough quartet had grown 'quite angry about the state of Newport and the way that their fans had been treated, so we decided that a fanzine at Peterborough was what we needed, especially as we'd had no success for years. And we'd also got directors that didn't give a damn about supporters.' The four were soon joined on the editorial team by Sean Ingham and Bob Allen.

It was perhaps a surprise that Groom and friends were infused with such sympathy, because even a low-key fixture in the home of a perishing club inspired violence. 'There were only 988 people there that day,' says Groom, 'and there were arrests for fighting. In a crowd of fewer than 1000, there was still football violence going on, which is incredible. The Football League attendance is that low and people still find time to go and cause trouble. So on reflection, my memories of that time are: it was pretty dismal.'

A year earlier, Dave Thomas had launched the Queens Park Rangers fanzine *A Kick Up the R's* (*AKUTR's*). He is still to be found peddling his wares outside Rangers games today, albeit in a safer environment than the one in which he began his selling days. 'I read the eulogy at one of my oldest friend's funerals nearly two years ago,' he says in 2025, 'and in it, I started to say, "my overriding memory of Nigel will be us running everywhere." Because that's what we did when we went to Burnley or Blackburn away, or elsewhere. After the game, you'd run back to the station because you were always trying to avoid the gangs of local ne'er-do-wells who were trying to pick you out as being "Cockney bastards" and things like that.

'All I remember doing is running everywhere. The idea you'd wear colours to an away game, as many fans do nowadays, was a no-no because you would just stand out and invite trouble.'

Thomas's QPR were witnesses to one of the stranger incidences of football violence, at Nottingham Forest's City Ground on 18 January, 1989. That evening, following a 5-2 League Cup victory over the Hoops, two exuberant Forest supporters ran on to the pitch and past Brian Clough. Clough refused their celebratory overtures and cuffed both. No charges were pursued against him. 'The man should be punished, and I don't mean lightly,' said *In the Loft*, another QPR fanzine. 'If it was the fan hitting Clough, then no doubt the offender would now be serving a hefty punishment.' Later in the fanzine, a letter writer recalled arriving at the City Ground and being 'informed by the Policeman at the gate that there was to be "no swearing or V signs". Perhaps I should have thumped a few Forest fans and nothing would have happened.'

Displeasure was also voiced in other clubs' fanzines. 'Anyone else who had done the same thing,' claimed Manchester City's *Blue Print*, 'would be branded a menace to society, locked up and would be banned from watching . . . It seems that there is one law for us mere mortals and no laws for Brian Clough.' Similarly, a *Chelsea Independent* editorial implored readers to 'consider what would have happened had you or I run on the pitch and punched and grabbed a few idiots who were celebrating a big victory in a major cup competition . . . Why, then, should our Brian be any different?'

Such iniquities, however, by then seemed intrinsic to the way in which football supporters were policed.

OFF THE BALL

ISSUE 9 JUNE/JULY 1987 40p

FOOTBALL'S £3 MILLION MEN

SPOT THE CUP COMPETITION

PLUS

- HAIRCUT HIGHLIGHTS
- PETER SWALES - MAN AT CITY
- CLASSIC CLOGGERS' CLIMAX
- AND LOTS MORE BESIDES

CHAPTER 4: LAWLESS POLICING

Another worrying trend is police officers threatening to arrest players during matches for swearing.
– *THE LEYTON ORIENTEAR*, LEYTON ORIENT FANZINE

'You felt like you were a second-class citizen all the time,' says Simon Wright. 'You were fair game for police because nobody's going to worry about that – you're only football supporters. It's the horrendous thing about being tarred with the same brush.' Wright is a pioneer of the fanzine movement. Founded in 1983, his *Fingerpost* was nominally the newsletter of the Halesowen branch of the West Bromwich Albion Supporters' Club, but in content, mood and design developed into a classic, barnstorming fanzine. That the club eventually banned it from the Hawthorns is further evidence of fanzine status. Standing outside grounds across England selling *Fingerpost* and later his terrific WBA fanzine *Grorty Dick*, he witnessed the police treatment of football supporters head-on.

It was the same for Dave Thomas of *A Kick Up the R's*. 'Someone said that Saturdays are usually the day when the police are let off the leash, particularly with away fans,' he recalls. 'You were herded and you were roughhoused and all the rest.' Occasionally, Thomas's fanzine-selling courted the attention of local constabularies. 'I remember selling the fanzine at Tottenham. I was arrested for obstruction and handcuffed in the back of a police van. I had to go to court on a charge of obstructing the highway.'

Even when avoiding the ire of Chief Inspector Hartley by absconding to away matches, *Terrace Talk*'s Mike Kettlewell encountered frequent police harassment. 'It was absolutely constant,' he remembers, 'you could go to a match and the police would get away with beating you up in plain sight.' One incident, during a midweek defeat for York City at Notts County's Meadow Lane, has stayed with him. 'There was one particular Notts County-supporting policeman,' he explains, 'who was notorious around Nottingham for beating people up whether it was on a Friday night or kids with catapults. This copper decided to place himself in the middle of our away end. When we scored and were celebrating, he started lashing out. And he turned to one group of fans and said, "If you're looking for County, you're looking for me", and then punched a guy in the face. But they could get away with it. And they did.'

Terrace Talk was home to a regular series named Police & Pies, in which writer Nick Parker reviewed those twin aspects of away trips. Scores were given for both, a league table maintained and congratulatory letters sent to caterers and constabularies at the season's end.

Unsurprisingly, the Meadow Lane despot merited a scathing assessment in the October 1985 edition of the fanzine. This 'scumbag masquerading as a policeman' probed fans with a 'selective, rough searching technique', made 'threats of ginormous fines for not heeding his advice', leapt 'in the air when County got a penalty', then gave 'threatening looks when they missed it'. To top it all off, he unleashed a 'mindless attack on three York fans after the match'. However, continued this instalment of Police & Pies, 'The Wolves police will take a lot of beating this season(!). They had it sussed from the start and again lost vital points for the dirty racist remarks from one plod.'

Terrace Talk editorials set police treatment of fans firmly within the context of mid-1980s Britain. Though not always named – perhaps punching in the letters of her name endangered Women's Institute typewriters – Margaret Thatcher's influence loomed. Clubs, said the fanzine, were increasingly working with police to impose court orders banning hand-picked supporters from grounds in an effort to 'appease She-Who-Must-Be-Obeyed. We can either stand open-mouthed and watch it happen or we can join the FSA.' There was focus upon the specific case of four young fans in London and their 'alleged' hooliganism. The quartet's bail conditions had included their banning from all football until the case came to court. While *Terrace Talk* agreed that bans were a fair response to proven violence – all fanzines wished to see genuine hooligans vanquished – they argued that their imposition should come only after conviction. 'In this country you are supposed to be innocent until proved guilty,' said an editorial. 'This is not only an attack on football supporters or even on a few "morons", it is an attack on everyone's freedom.'

There was also a further incursion of wider society into football policing, according to *Terrace Talk* and others: tactics dredged from the 1984 Miners' Strike were now being used to oppress fans. At Doncaster, there had been the use of 'snatch squads to terrorise visiting supporters'. The removal of cameras from a *Terrace Talk* photographer at Rotherham United led to the Police & Pies column supposing that 'The South Yorks police seem to be putting to good effect the lessons they have been learning on the picket lines: obviously they are worried by the number of police shown in their true colours by the lenses of press photographers'.

Looking back on the decade in 1989, an article in Stoke City's *Jolly Potter* fanzine supposed a direct link between Thatcherism and the maltreatment of football supporters. Thatcher had come to power in 1979 vowing a hardline stance on law and order. Then,

> Sensationalised press and T.V. coverage of the inner-city riots and battles on picket lines during the miners' strike were reinforcing the public perception that violence and disorder were rampant in society. The demands for 'something to be done' became even more strident. The very real horror of Heysel and act of mass hooliganism involving Millwall fans at Luton

> finally catalysed the shift in attitude toward the football hooligan from someone who could be lived with . . . to someone who had to be dealt with at all costs.

Along the way, those 'costs' included subjecting normal, non-violent fans to the same clampdowns and police severity as hooligans. As Ricky Holden wrote in the Spring 1988 issue of *The City Gent*, 'The biggest change in policing at some grounds appears to be that all fans, regardless of age, appearance etc, are to be treated as potential troublemakers from the moment they arrive to the moment they leave.' Examples of their resultant ordeals were scattered across the pages of fanzines.

Travelling supporters suffered the most, their devotion rewarded with an intimate knowledge of British Transport Police (BTP) manoeuvres. 'Normally it's easier to catch a glimpse of Lord Lucan at St James' Park or Shergar at Earls Court than it is to see a transport cop – unless it's matchday,' wrote Russell Chapman in *A Kick Up The R's* about a typical Saturday night at London's Victoria station. On those occasions, BTP officers would be 'swarming the place – dogs, loud-hailers, the lot. You'd think the Krays had been spotted at the Spud-U-Like!'

Journeying on an official club coach had pitfalls of its own; most were stopped on the outskirts of the town they were visiting and treated to police lectures and bag searches hunting for weapons. 'They obviously aren't any good at maths,' wrote Dave Worton in Wolves fanzine *A Load of Bull*, 'because the last time I looked, I thought it pretty improbable that a baseball bat could fit in the average-sized carrier bag. The disappointment of finding cheese and onion cobs was obvious.' Jim Cooke of Notts County fanzine *The Pie* recalls how 'the police would make you come off the motorway and wait to be escorted to the game', then afterwards chaperone fans away from their force's jurisdiction. 'I remember going to Port Vale,' he says, 'where the Staffordshire police followed us to the county border with Derbyshire before we were allowed to stop and have a drink. You were treated like scum basically.' One standard, expensive surveillance tactic employed for long-distance travellers saw different police forces pass over the accompanying of coaches as they reached a new county's border.

Back on the rails, an exchange on an away day train, recounted in Reading's *Taking the Biscuit*, encapsulated BTP attitudes. A group of Royals fans, reported a 1990 article in the fanzine, sat as an officer approached 'and said, "You lot keep the language down" – there hadn't been any swearing when he said this – "remember there are normal human beings on this train as well." A bit of a giveaway that – the reason that football fans are mistreated by the police is because they don't think we're normal.'

Just as birdwatchers can identify a specific breed from one burst of its song, away fans could detect the distant barking of a police Alsatian from the moment they arrived in an unknown town. At railway stations there was always a welcoming committee. 'The local police were a disgrace,' wrote Darlington fan W. Dickinson of a 1987 visit to Roker Park in the Sunderland fanzine *Wise Men Say*. 'They met us off the train at Seaburn with a lot of verbal and physical abuse. They were shouting things like "Who's the hard cases?" and "Who wants a go then?"'

Dickinson and his fellow Quakers were then kettled for 15 minutes. Upon asking for the nearest Gents, the writer was told by a police officer, '*I'm* the shithouse on this station.' Walking to the ground with kick-off impending, the supporters were warned that exceeding their police-designated pace would result in arrest.

Wise Men Say also reported on the visit of another set of north-eastern fans to Roker Park the following year. As Hartlepool United devotees made their way towards a Sherpa Van Trophy tie, one of their number was arrested for allegedly refusing to move from a mounted police officer's path. The officer 'promptly showed what was described by him as restraint, i.e. a punch in the face'. The defendant was accused of attempting to strike the policeman's horse, but in court cleared of all charges. 'What escapes the media's notice,' concluded the piece, 'is that this sort of behaviour quite often sparks off violence at football matches. Why else were there 30 arrests at this match? It was not rival supporters fighting each other, but supporters and police at the away end.'

While most 1980s football fans were preceded by a poor reputation, that which beset followers of Millwall was irredeemably bleak. Their arrival in towns and cities across the nation was treated as an invasion. Via the letters pages of *The Lion Roars* fanzine's December 1988 issue, Millwall fan Alan Martin gave an illustrative account of a November trip to Anfield. At Liverpool Lime Street station, for 45 minutes Lions supporters were 'herded up like cattle', told to remove their shoes and searched by police officers, who even reached into their trouser pockets. They were then marched an hour through town – including 'walking through council estates getting abuse from five-year-olds' – before finally arriving at the ground.

Martin should have consulted a contemporary issue of *Red News*, the Manchester United fanzine. There, an anonymous writer acquainted with train station holding pens wrote of how 'the immediate aim for the seasoned traveller is to slip the awaiting police escort'. His tactic was to claim that he and those with him were in town for 'annual goose fairs, educational visits, funerals, school trips etc.' Often, amazingly, the ploy worked and his cohort were liberated to enjoy fish and chips, McDonald's and even pubs.

Three months after Millwall's Scouse sojourn, fellow south Londoners roamed north to watch their team, Crystal Palace, play Nottingham Forest in the Simod Cup. Tony Matthews, editor of *Eagle Eye*, described in his fanzine's pages how Palace fans travelling via a crawling Football Special train had arrived in Nottingham station and been squashed into a 'cage', searched and then 'herded like cattle' – that phrase again – along a circuitous route to the City Ground. Jim Cooke confirms the existence 'on the far side of the platform at the station' of 'a big cage so that when the away fans came in on the train, they were all penned in and then frogmarched down to the ground'.

In that uneasy Palace parade, wrote Matthews, many supporters were 'manhandled' and 'one was punched and sustained a cut lip. Those of us who complained at this treatment were spoken to in a provocative manner by some policemen who appeared determined to tempt people into stepping out of line.' This was no human cavalcade of male bravado – among their number were women and children, many quite clearly upset. With the game now underway, as they arrived at the City Ground the Palace supporters were once more body-searched. Some of those young fans may have been included; later in 1989, Cardiff City fanzine *Watch the Bluebirds Fly* reported that it was not unusual to 'see the police searching 10- and 11-year-old children before allowing them into the away end'. Through the 1980s, said the same article, police attitudes had shifted: 'In the past they seemed to deal with the troublemakers only, now anyone can be arrested for the slightest reason.' A top three rundown of reasons witnessed for ejections in *The Leyton Orientear* emphasised the point: '(1) Someone ejected for celebrating having backed the Grand National winner; (2) Another ejection for finishing his tea, dropping the cup and treading on it; (3) A third for throwing a small cuddly toy along the row to his mate.'

The thorough, often duplicate pre-match frisk – usually undertaken by a police officer, possibly searching for teddy bears – was a routine borne by most. Descriptions of these ordeals frequently appeared in fanzines. Travelling to watch his team Port Vale play at Ipswich Town, in *The Memoirs of Seth Bottomley* Phil Sherwin labelled Portman Road 'the only ground I know where you're searched twice. Once when you get off the bus and again at the turnstiles in case you've managed to complete a major arms deal while making the 100 yards between the two.' In late 1989, Wolves' *A Load of Bull* reported on a trip to Filbert Street. 'This must have been one of the most thorough searches I've ever had at a football ground – I'm surprised the police didn't ask us all to strip naked and collect our clothes on the way out. Through the turnstiles and smile for the camera, or scowl if you've had enough of being treated like a criminal.'

Being filmed in the late 1980s was, as is apparent above, an unwanted novelty. In the June 1987 issue of *Off the Ball*, Steve Beauchampé remarked that '. . . increasingly, our football grounds are being turned into exhibition sites for the police to stage public demonstrations of all the latest crowd control techniques at their disposal – Closed Circuit Television (CCTV) and hoolivans etc. And football fans, young and old, male and female, are the guinea pigs they so enthusiastically use.' CCTV, notably, was alien enough that its full name had to be articulated; until then, any technological surveillance was undertaken by police camcorder.

With the pre-match blend of intimidation and rigmarole over, fans pushed turnstiles in the hope of being left to sing for their teams in peace. Depressingly, police overindulgence continued on the terraces.

In 1993 *The Chelsea Independent* took us once more to Sunderland, though this time *inside* Roker Park. An unnamed writer recalled a 1985 visit that was representative of away fan experiences across the country. His court appearance had a more typical result than the Hartlepool horse botherer's. Attending a Milk Cup semi-final tie in February, the writer had been slapped square in the face by a burger hurled from the home end. 'Sit down and shut up, you cockney bastard,' responded the policeman he complained to, according to the article.

Before the match, Chelsea supporters had been told by the police that upon the final whistle they 'must' move quickly towards their supporters' buses. The writer reported that accordingly, when the game ended he had looked behind him to urge his travelling companions to hurry up. 'Before you could say

"Ha'way the lads" I was literally rugby tackled from behind by two police officers,' he claimed. 'I fell sideways between the seats ripping my sheepskin coat and was unceremoniously frog-marched away.'

The writer was then taken to a police station, charged with threatening behaviour and attempting to incite a riot (but not for wearing a sheepskin coat, surprisingly) and put in a cell with around 25 other Chelsea fans. Detained overnight, he paid for his ticket home by buying and eating a wodge of Mars Bars and utilising the free train travel offer vouchers printed inside their wrappers. Having refused to accept police charges, he was soon back in the north-east for a court hearing, travelling with his employer and another witness. Two police officers gave contradictory statements but the verdict was predictably the same: guilty, with a fine levied. At a later appeal hearing, the fine was increased. 'I've learnt one thing from this,' reflected the *Chelsea Independent* piece. 'Don't bother taking on the Old Bill because even with witnesses and overwhelming evidence in your favour you don't stand a chance in hell.'

As with the flying burger and Mars wrapper ingenuity, there was often dark humour in the minutiae of police/supporter encounters. Tales abounded of fans being ejected from games for shouting obscene words into their transistor radios or breaking wind. The season after that Sunderland versus Chelsea encounter, *Bolton Wanderers Worldwide* reported on a trip to Rotherham United. There, bored fans had decided to conga up and down the stand. Unfortunately, the rear of their snake collided with a police officer. 'Enough was enough,' recalled the article, 'the lad had to be humiliatingly dragged away suffering a few bumps and bruises on his way. Witnessed by a few hundred people, the "antics" appeared too heavy and altogether out of context. Result: a powder keg of angry fans on a very short fuse.' That short final sentence explained how such incidents so regularly frothed into something worse. Apparently arbitrary ejections felt like provocations from officers. The grabbing of a supporter by his scarf was there to remind his fellow fans who was in charge.

A number of police forces had the reputation of being particularly hardline. West Midlands Police were prime among them. They 'were notorious,' says Robert Nichols of *Fly Me To The Moon*. 'Boro playing at Coventry away in 1988 sticks in my mind. Person after person was getting chucked out and you just wondered if you were going to survive the whole match. They seemed to be getting thrown out for absolutely nothing.' It was also at Highfield Road that *Preston Pie Muncher* writer Howard Irving watched as fans were 'arrested for throwing snowballs at each other!'

West Midlands' 'Football Watch' programme intended to target the violent few who ruined spectating for the many. In reality, its measures affected all. During the 1988/89 season, their driving licences newly granted, friends from *Dial M For Merthyr* fanzine travelled over the border to watch two matches in the region. Their impressions of the West Midlands force were summarised in an expeditionary report by editor Mark Evans: 'They wear the conventional black uniform, but inside they are a breed of their own. Specially trained they can cause trouble at any time, pouncing on you at half-time as you read your programme or make your way to the toilet. The quieter the match the more lethal they are.'

The Welshmen's first game was West Bromwich Albion versus Watford, where they joined a few hundred supporters in the away end. They watched as, following Watford's opening goal, officers 'waded in, arresting fans at will for jumping up and down and throwing their arms in the air'. Evans says now of that fixture, 'I turned around and there's a policeman standing next to my brother-in-law – a quiet guy – staring at him. And he's saying, "If you move, I'm nicking you." And then my brother-in-law said, "Well, OK, I'll go. I'm not bothered. I'll go." Then, the policeman said, "Where are you from? Wales? I hate the Welsh. Fucking hate them."' The Merthyr party may well have concurred with the verdict of Blackburn Rovers fanzine *Many Miles from Home* that the Hawthorns police were 'trained by the death squads of El Salvador'.

Next, the Welsh travelled to a match between Aston Villa and Tottenham Hotspur. During the calm of half-time, as people sat on concrete terraces reading their match programmes, 30 policemen arrived and positioned themselves 'in twos and threes. The tension was obvious and it seemed the police were trying to wind the Villa fans up.'

In the second half, on-field action caused a small crowd surge. Though a common occurrence at every match with a sizeable crowd, it prompted the police to plough in and remove several fans, ejecting them from Villa Park. As was so often the case, according to fanzines, police intervening in a peaceful scene meant it quickly spiralled into chaos: 'Fighting then broke out between the police and supporters, there were more arrests and pushing and shoving resulted. And all for what? The sheer bully boy actions of the police.'

At around the same time, a writer in the Leeds United fanzine *The Hanging Sheep* observed similar tactics being employed during an away game at Walsall. Twenty or so police officers had shoved their way to the centre of the terrace following a goal for The Whites, and then apparently at random arrested anyone nearby. 'One guy around 35 with glasses on and smoking a cigar,' said the article, 'was told to move and when he proved that he wasn't as quick as Ben Johnson off the mark, he was thrown headfirst towards a crush barrier by an understandably irate constable. It was at this time that we inquired (politely and calmly) who was in charge of the police that day. The reply… was something to the effect of "Why? I don't know."'

Early in 1989, writer Ian Barnes of Bournemouth's *Out of Court* fanzine had monitored police tactics in the away end at Chelsea. He saw a superintendent at the top of the terrace directing 'snatch squads' to infiltrate groups of fans and eject them from Stamford Bridge. When Barnes complained to an officer, the response was 'you obviously don't come here often, do you?' Later, he heard fellow Cherries supporters give the reasons for their ejections. Two had been arrested for swearing – an exasperated 'Oh bloody hell' and a 'You're a load of crap, ref'. Another had shouted 'You're rubbish, Chelsea' upon arrival and been immediately detained for 'provoking the Chelsea fans'. Meanwhile, an officer had grabbed hold of a disabled fan and accused him of an attempted assault via misuse of a wheelchair.

The police appeared to be on something of a puritanical purge against cussing during those last years of the 1980s and earliest of the 1990s. In *The Crooked Spireite*, a Chesterfield supporter wrote of being dragged away for, in the words of an officer, 'sticking your fingers up at the scoreboard and flicking a wank at the Vale fans'. Baffled, he asked for clarification of 'what exactly flicking a wank involved: he obliged me with a demonstration, flicking one at me'.

The fan admitted the first offence – his team were 2-1 down, the scoreboard was flashing irritatingly – but denied knowledge of the second. The ejection stood and a 'snarling' sergeant booked him in and took mug shots. New-fangled scoreboards were, incidentally, provoking discord across the land. The unnamed writer of a March 1988 article in Swindon Town's *Bring the Noise* had been spooked by a visit to Vicarage Road and Watford fans 'who were convinced that the scoreboard was one of them . . . They kept singing "Scoreboard, Scoreboard, give us a wave", and at one stage little men with waving hands appeared . . . As to the future of scoreboards, I hope as the bulbs blow they are never replaced.' The following January in *Wise Men Say*, a Sunderland follower wrote of Roker Park's new electronic effort, 'Just because it gives you little or no information and constantly breaks down, surely that's no reason to take a jaundiced view.' Further, 'What about those bloody tanks that appear whenever we manage to put the opposition under a bit of pressure? Honestly, I half dread a Sunderland attack for fear that we're going to be treated to an action replay of the Battle of El Alamein.'

Regardless of pixel irritation, the anti-swearing clampdown continued. At Oakwell, a Leicester City supporter wrote in *For Fox Sake* of watching a 'decent' middle-aged man be violently arrested for swearing – the apprehending P.C. 'may not have liked his language, but did this give him the right to grab hold of a person by the throat knowing he couldn't defend himself and physically shake him?' Bolton Wanderers' *Normid Nomad* told of a Trotters fan arrested by the infamous West Midlands Police and charged with violent conduct for shouting 'You're fucking useless Bolton!' The fanzine, perhaps revealing a little too much about the speech patterns of Boltonian children, pondered: 'What is so wrong with swearing at football games? Foul language as it is called is now becoming the norm everywhere you go. You only have to walk past the local nursery school to hear children of 6 and 7 swearing, so why can't grown men?'

A further instance arose at The Dell. There, according to an article in Luton Town's *Depleated* fanzine, a visiting fan was ejected for 'on at least three occasions' making 'finger signs at the referee'. He was then taken to a police incident room and searched. We can only hope that he reached into his pocket and produced a V-sign, in the manner of an irritating little brother.

Although Scottish supporters generally faced less concerted police attention, the swearing shutdown filtered north. After a visit to Dundee United, an article in Celtic fanzine *Hail-Hail* deplored police behaviour 'worthy of the deposed Securitate from Rumania'. Plain-clothes officers had made countless arrests for innocuous or unclear reasons and were 'none too fussy in the manner in which they arrested Celtic supporters or who they knocked over in the process of "escorting" them down the terracing'. Apparently, it was now 'an offence to show two fingers from the stand to a referee at half-time'.

There is little wonder that another Bolton fanzine, *Here We Go Again*, caricatured this worsening situation by carrying a spoof advert for a product named 'Stop-a-Gob – the anti-swearing tape' that would prevent 'accidental swearing at the referee or linesman'. Its illustration showed a football fan's heavily strapped face, his filthy outpourings muted.

When the final whistle sounded, away supporters were rarely free to bounce gloriously into the night or trudge out in dismay. With five or so minutes of a match remaining, their exit plan would usually be announced via Tannoy speakers: 'Visiting supporters will be held back after the game to allow home fans to disperse', or words of a similar nature. Often, it would be added that this detention was for their own safety. In reaction, weary, familiar groans rumbled across the terraces – the enforced 20-minute wait was a matchday situation as familiar as bad pies or rancid toilets.

Rejoining Alan Martin at Anfield, following the game – an admirable draw – he wrote in *The Lion Roars* of how Millwall supporters were kept back and then escorted on a 3-mile traipse back to Lime Street. A group of locals 'threw bricks and rocks at us. The coppers' answer was to nick us for shouting at them.' Then, 'we got put on a shit cold train back to London.'

Such dreadful transport was known to fellow Londoner Amanda Sheahan, an Arsenal fan. Writing in *One-Nil Down Two-One Up* of a fixture at Carrow Road that same winter, she related how at Norwich station supporters had been locked out of their train's more palatable carriages and forced to sit 'amongst grime, vandalism and graffiti for two hours'. Sheahan deplored this 'carte blanche' treatment of all fans as hooligans. Such 'precautionary measures', she continued, contributed to a 'vicious circle', feeding 'the image of soccer fans that has been created by the tabloid press as a monster of uncontrollable proportions. When fans are marched through the streets and forced onto vandalised special trains it breeds a feeling of resentment that sadly manifests itself in more unsocial behaviour.' With their 'Military Operations', the authorities were fomenting hostility and 'doing nothing to face up to the real problems the vast majority of fans have'.

A season earlier, Chris Jones had written in *A Kick Up The R's* of leaving Anfield following a 4-0 defeat for QPR, 'We had to endure the second-class citizenship habitually granted to travelling football supporters – kept in for twenty minutes, herded like cattle onto buses and unceremoniously dumped back at Lime Street.' Notably, despite arriving home late having watched his side suffer an Anfield pasting – and with '£25, half my giro' spent – Jones's 'enthusiasm was not dampened, my love not in decline'. Affection, once again, conquered rationalism.

Among the deluge of grievous police conduct were glimmers of fair treatment and hope for the future of match-going. Following a November 1986 Trotters visit to Middlesbrough, *Bolton Wanderers Worldwide* applauded Cleveland constabulary for 'allowing everyone to enjoy a superb night's football without having to fear either the police or the home supporters'.

Such was Humberside Police's benevolent leniency, in *Off the Ball* even Steve Beauchampé felt moved to salute their willingness to admit into Boothferry Park 'a whole coach load of fans, each of whom had drunk enough to soak a dartboard' and noted that 'The coppers actually watched the match – not us'. He and other fanzine writers also offered simple remedies that might nurture better supporter/police relations – greater use of stewards, meetings between local police and FSA branches, more visible police liaison officers and instruction in fan culture for officers.

Further examples of positive policing followed. In February 1987's *Dons Outlook*, the editorial recalled a recent visit to Goodison Park when standard dreads were pleasantly contradicted: 'As I prepared to enter the turnstile, a policeman came over to me. Visions of Alcometers, handcuffs, police cells etc flashed before my eyes. But no, he gave me a complimentary ticket for one of the best seats in the stand, wishing me an enjoyable game! I was stunned, lost for words!'

Recovering from his West Midlands experiences, Mark Evans of *Dial M For Merthyr*'s gang had travelled to see Aston Villa at Old Trafford. 'The Greater Manchester Police were very courteous and helpful,' he reported, 'we were shown where to park, where to stand and even where the best food was. Inside the ground the Villa fans were packed into the small away end but the police coped admirably with the crush (even helping throw up balloons!) No pointless ejections or arrests, just a quiet word when necessary.' Another fanzine accustomed to printing negative stories about the police, *Wise Men Say*, reported on the 'courteous' Devon & Cornwall Police. During a December 1988 Sunderland visit to Plymouth Argyle's Home Park, they had been 'helpful and (something of a rarity, this) even treated football fans like human beings'. Their actions following the final whistle were 'astonishing', as fans rushing for the 1710 train to London were hastened to the station in a police van.

On a visit to watch his side play at Cardiff City in the winter of 1990, Fulham fan Richard Newsom reported an unusually jolly encounter with police officers at the away end turnstiles. 'Bugger me, he's smiling!' he wrote in *There's Only One F in Fulham*. 'They all are, and not in that familiar get-inside-and-shut-up way either. These coppers are being friendly!'

Such glowing accounts, however, remained rare exceptions – that the very notion of a policeman smiling genuinely or offering help had to be mentioned spoke loudly. Steve Beauchampé of *Off the Ball* perhaps best summarised how fans more typically experienced relations with the police. Whether they were en route to a game, inside the ground or retreating home, 'Much of the time,' he wrote in issue 9, 'the police unreasonably view football fans, especially young or visiting ones, with acute suspicion. We are seen as lowlife, hell bent on trouble . . . And in a way that the rest of society would not tolerate . . . supporters are lied to, abused, insulted, and even physically assaulted – not by all coppers – but sometimes it seems that way.'

STOP-A-GOB

THE ANTI-SWEARING TAPE

revents accidental
wearing at the ref
or the linesman!

hy spend sleepless
nights worrying
about what remarks
you might come out
with, when you can
ear this effective
adhesive tape?

lan Smith and Gary
ineker swear by it

Available in
various tones of
flesh colour to
suit your nationality.

Tried and tested on
Mick Brown - If it
works on him it'll
work on anyone!

Tony Kelly says:

I'm buggered if I'm
gonna' use it, just
sod off, will you?"

AVAILABLE ONLY BY MAIL FROM:
STOP-A-GOB LTD, FUKHAM HALL, BUGGARY-ON-SEA, SODDEM, BN4 8SL.

THE
OCCASIONAL
TERRORIST
ISSUE NO. 2
A RIP OFF AT 50p

CHAPTER 5: DEMONISATION AND CONTROL

If Luton Town's piss pot Kenilworth Road premises were obliterated from the face of the earth tomorrow then all true football supporters would breathe a hearty sigh of relief.

— *THE FOX*, LEICESTER CITY FANZINE

No one wept for football supporters, nor pleaded their case. In the eighties, fans were vilified across society, an underclass of scoundrels partaking in a diabolical, violent hobby. This demonisation enabled police pestering from train station to terrace. Public opinion was reinforced by half-blind media coverage; the only time a follower of football was shown on television, it was in the form of a hooligan hurling a brick. That hooligan and his crew became the nation's idea of a fan.

As writer Gerry Lynch lamented in a 1989 issue of Newcastle United fanzine *The Mag*: 'If you are a football fan, you are regarded as almost a second-class citizen by most of the people who have no interest in the game. Our image has been tarnished by what virtually amounts to a hate campaign by sections of the government, media and police, which has seen some appalling double standards applied to us in comparison to followers of other sports.' Following football was not something to boast about. 'If you went for a job interview,' says former *King of the Kippax* editor Dave Wallace, 'you couldn't admit to being a football fan.'

No regular supporter – and ergo fanzine contributor – would deny football's ailments and what Andy Lyons of *When Saturday Comes* calls 'a general sense of pervasive decline', from falling crowds to the crumbling hovels in which they watched games. It was supporters who suffered repulsive toilets and stretched on tiptoes to see over fences, after all, and they who most often heard racism and witnessed violence. 'We acknowledged the reality of hooliganism,' says Adrian Goldberg now. 'You couldn't attend football in that era and not acknowledge that matchday violence was a real thing. We knew that there were games where there would be trouble and we didn't welcome it, we didn't like it, but equally we kind of knew the craic at football.'

'You were made to feel the stigma of everything that was going on,' adds broadcaster Paul Hawksbee, then an avid fanzine reader and later the co-creator of *90 Minutes* magazine, 'whether it was involving your club or not, and whether you were someone who got mixed up in that sort of thing or not. And it was sometimes difficult not to. If you went to an away game, you'd find yourself caught up in some of that stuff, even though you weren't the people looking for trouble.'

Mike Ticher, Lyons' *WSC* co-founder, feels that supporters were treated with 'contempt' and seen as 'an alien force within the game. It was hard for people who just loved watching football to feel a lot of joy about the fan experience. A lot of the time it's a communal experience that waxes and wanes depending on the circumstances, but the surroundings and often the people that you shared it with and the way they behaved and the way the authorities reacted to that behaviour was pretty unpleasant.'

When violent incidents occurred, what happened next worked to a standard formula. News outlets would often embellish and hyperbolise events. Politicians would then scramble to be the most hardline in their responses – 'the government of the day saw football as a "law and order issue", that was the expression used at the time,' adds Lyons. Columnists fanned the flames and the police felt emboldened in their draconian attitudes to matchdays. Meanwhile, the watching public shook their heads and tutted at the soccer rabble with renewed vigour. Where fans were not tarred they were ignored, their game ostracised. For a while, ITN ceased giving football results on *News At Ten*. 'Perhaps they assumed there wouldn't be enough interest. They just stopped acknowledging them. It's a curious thing,' says Lyons. Further emphasising the game's pariah status in the media, due to a contract dispute that no network was desperate to solve, live football disappeared entirely from screens for the first four months of the 1985/86 season. Expressing sentiments unimaginable now, BBC Head of Sport Jonathan Martin opined that 'Football rates itself too highly. . . It does not have a God-given right to appear on the BBC.'

Goldberg saw this cycle in wider societal terms. 'It was wrapped up in the whole moral panic of the time,' he explains, 'against young working-class men, and it fed into other narratives around the miners' strike and how if you were a working-class young man, you were very easily demonised by the tabloids. So we saw football hooliganism through that prism, really, that it was a real thing, but equally it could often be exaggerated and sensationalised. We were aware of England matches where journalists or photographers would offer fans money to throw bricks through windows.'

The stereotyping of all fans as the same sinning creed chiselled away at the joy of match-going and provoked exasperation. In *A Kick Up The R's*, Lara Kelleher related how she had travelled home from the USA and gone straight to a QPR fixture. At the turnstiles, police had examined her two combs. 'What are these for?' asked an officer. 'I plumped for the obvious and told her that I was planning on combing my hair with them. She wasn't impressed and suggested that I was going to use them to hurt someone. They were duly confiscated.'

Kelleher expressed her resentment at being 'branded a football hooligan' and wondered, 'Why is it that when I tell people that I'm a football supporter they usually say that I would never catch them going to a football match – too violent! Where do they get all their ideas from? The Prime Minister claims that football fans are a disgrace to the country because of all this violence – violence that none of us ever sees. I have been going to football since I was able to see the pitch and because of this am labelled a thug along with everyone else who calls themselves a football supporter.'

Author Harry Pearson, a key *WSC* writer since 1988, recalls a specific and typically amusing example of this cynical labelling. One mid-1980s Saturday, he had travelled to watch his beloved Middlesbrough playing Portsmouth at Fratton Park. Four decades on, he can still picture the away end Gents, which were 'prison-style. There was a toilet but it didn't have any kind of enclosure around it. It was just sitting there in the corner.' That evening, as a plus-one guest at a grand dinner held in London's Dorchester Hotel, he was asked by the woman next to him where he had been that day. 'I said, "I've just been to watch Middlesbrough play at Portsmouth",' he remembers. 'And she looked at me as if I'd come back from a war zone. She said, "But that must have been terrifying." I replied, "Oh, well, yeah, the toilets were terrifying, so it was pretty terrifying," and she was just aghast. You would encounter people all the time who were absolutely appalled at the thought you would go to football. They were hostile to the whole concept of the game. To say you were a football fan was like saying you were engaged in some dirty cult.'

Pearson recalls the wider context to these commonplace encounters. 'Football felt like a real minority interest,' he adds, 'and people talked about the game completely dying. I remember Brian Glanville writing that all of football could die out. There was a real feeling that the game wasn't worth it anymore for all the trouble it was causing, and it would die of natural causes.' Jonny Owen, an actor, writer, producer and long-time *Dial M For Merthyr* contributor remembers how 'People weren't watching football, it was seen as dangerous. Football fans were folk devils. We were all dismissed as hooligans. Football was seen as some kind of dangerous activity for unhinged young men to go rampaging up and down the country on a Saturday afternoon.'

Kelleher, Pearson and Owen's ponderings chime with Tom Davies' recollection of the same period. However, the long-time *Leyton Orientear* writer and former editor, now a *Guardian* journalist, took comfort in the way that vilification resulted in downtrodden unity. 'The dividing line then was football against non-football,' he tells me in 2025, 'football against society. So basically, anyone who was a football fan, you felt there's already a certain kindred spirit because you were part of this sort of slightly besieged, demonised group.' Fanzines, then, would come to enable a certain brand of supporter to find his or her tribe.

Meanwhile, those negative media depictions of supporters repeatedly reinforced the besiegement. 'The only way fans were seen in the mainstream media lens was through hooliganism,' says Mike Ticher, 'They weren't really represented at all in the coverage of football matches or on televised football, or anywhere except when there was violence at matches, which was often. I mean, that's not to say that shouldn't have been reported. It absolutely should, because it was a real and terrible problem. But there was no other kind of representation of football fans.' A May 1989 article in establishment magazine *The Field* stretched this representation to the extreme, praising matchday's gift of 'temporarily purging the general community' of supporters and concentrating 'the dregs of the nation in relatively few places on Saturday afternoons'.

Neither could supporters look to the fictional world for accurate portrayal. Cinema offered only *The Firm*; in television dramas, football storylines usually involved hooligan crews with ropey accents. Perhaps the exemplar, a March 1989 episode of ITV mainstay *The Bill* both riled and amused a number of fanzine writers.

Filmed at Loftus Road – forever the London television producer's go-to stadium – the scatty plot of 'A Good Result' centred upon an undercover police officer's infiltration of a hooligan gang. Sitting around a pub table in that year's finest beige C&A dad wear, in drama school interpretations of cockney accents the group boasted of battles gone by. 'It was brilliant last time at Old Trafford,' the viewer learned. 'We got in amongst them at the Stretford End – beautiful . . . we done about 20 of 'em before they realised what was happening, then out and away. Poor old Plod was nowhere to be seen – it was so clinical, so clean – the SAS couldn't have done any better.'

The exploits of this smart/casual crew – none of whom would have looked out of place on the committee of their local CAMRA branch – brought amusement to fanzine writers. What inflamed their ire was the way their visiting counterparts were presented as normal, team colour-wearing fans. First, a lone man in a red scarf and hat was searched at the turnstile and found to have a Stanley knife on a string around his neck. 'Thinking of doing some DIY before kick-off, were you?' asked a *Bill* back-room copper, RADA dreams of what might have been tangible in his sad pale eyes. Then, a group of 20 or more similarly dressed red hoodlums rampaged through the streets, leaping on to cars while singing that football standard heard everywhere apart from football, 'Here we go/Here we go. . .'

Fittingly, given that these 27 minutes of televisual gold were filmed on their manor, *A Kick Up The R's* had their say. 'The laughable image of a typical football fan complete with hat, scarf and shirt (where was the rattle?) was presented as the norm,' said an article in issue 6. 'Presumably, the image that knives are equally as normal would be created by the non-football going public. Thus the game takes another knock.' Sunderland's *Wise Men Say* echoed those sentiments: 'This constant drip-feed to the public at large of football matches as battlegrounds inhabited solely by mobs of murderous thugs bent on violence is pernicious. We may all agree that this is palpable nonsense, but how many people do you know who don't go to football matches but have this perception?'

The violent reputation of supporters created a thirst to control them. Demonisation paved smooth ground for stringent actions, whether by the police or politicians. Freedom of movement could easily be denied and rights suspended in the name of law and order. It is unsurprising that comparisons between striking miners and football fans appeared frequently in fanzines. Supporters were another 'enemy within'.

Government measures were mooted and fed to the ravenous press. In the autumn of 1987, it was reported that sports minister Colin Moynihan – for a while the loathed enemy of fanzines everywhere, who delighted in mocking his miniscule stature and regularly adopted Dennis Skinner MP's nickname for him of 'the Miniature for Sport' – was planning the forced breathalysing of travelling fans as they queued outside grounds. 'The very air breathed by the poor down-trodden football supporter is to be tested for delinquency,' said *Balls* fanzine. Meanwhile, tabloid stories claimed Moynihan was to begin making incognito missions to Britain's football terraces with the aim of spying on supporters' behaviour. As he stood inconspicuously at just over 5 feet tall, this was not such an outlandish claim. 'Whether it's sunglasses at Sunderland or false beards at Birmingham, we will stop at nothing to track him down,' proposed the cover of *WSC*'s September/October '87 edition.

With the aim of controlling who could watch football, Moynihan's Conservative Party announced a scheme that would, in theory at least, compel all English Football League clubs to designate a minimum 50 per cent of their stadium capacity for the sole use of members. To ensure attendance, supporters were expected to buy club memberships. Some clubs levied a nominal charge of £1 or £2. Others went higher – Manchester United membership cost £5, although that fee did include the luxurious bonus of a Christmas card. *Off the Ball* saw an opportunity for clubs to include supporters in decision-making, even if they knew it would never be taken: 'It would be some consolation if the clubs took advantage of this enforced scheme by making supporters proper members of their clubs, with voting rights and consultation about important decisions. It can't be that radical an idea; it's exactly how County cricket is run.' An article in October 1987's *Orientear* concurred. 'I wouldn't mind so much if this "membership" really meant something,' supposed Tom Davies. 'It doesn't, we'll get no democratic influence or representation on the board.'

A number of clubs interpreted the membership directive as an opportunity to curtail fan freedoms. Bournemouth's scheme created members' only terraces and coincided with the installation of new steel fences and CCTV cameras. Torquay United barred away fans and before matchdays local police threatened to arrest anyone in possession of a visiting club's local accent. Colchester United made Layer Road 100 per cent members-only and also banned away fans. Attendances halved and visiting supporters swerved the ban by obtaining 'guest' cards. 'At first the locals were wary of us as we proudly proclaimed our presence with chants of "You'll never ban the Orient",' said another article in the October 1987 issue of *Orientear*, 'but they soon realised there would be no trouble.' The scheme was abandoned early in 1988. The most infamous club scheme, however, arose before that trio of experiments, and was – for once – rooted in actual hooliganism.

Two months before Bradford and Brussels, followers of Millwall and marauders from other London clubs had unleashed cataclysmic and terrifying violence at Luton Town's Kenilworth Road on the occasion of an FA Cup quarter-final tie, and in the streets surrounding the ground. Images of that night's chaos and destruction helped sketch the public's outline of what a football fan was. The fact that duty officers were brutally injured perhaps influenced future police treatment of supporters. Margaret Thatcher demanded hardline reprisals. Before the start of the 1986/87 season, Luton's chairman, David Evans, responded with a membership scheme that brought flutters of approval from the Prime Minister. At the 1987 general election, he became a safely seated Conservative MP.

Evans' club spent £250,000 on a system of automated gates that would admit only pre-vetted supporters possessing electronic identification cards. Away fans were forbidden. Bobbers Stand terraces gave way to sheeny executive boxes and pitchside fences were removed. Writing in *WSC* under the pseudonym 'Joe Payne', however, a Kenilworth Road regular argued that: 'The carnage that followed the Luton v Millwall game in 1985 did not make a case for banning away fans. With more competent ticketing arrangements and, according to observers, better policing, it might never have happened. However, the board were determined to up the stakes and set a challenge to the hooligan.' A similar line of thought appeared in an *Off the Ball* piece by Steve Beauchampé: '96 arrests out of 250,000 paying customers last season is not riotous mayhem. As the first club to make supporting their team a condition of entry, Luton's gross infringement of personal liberty and free speech so enthusiastically supported by the police has nothing whatsoever to do with the ideals and principles of football spectatorship.'

In the government's eyes, though, the Luton scheme was a model for football's future – here would queue orderly, documented customers who had no opportunity to clash with lowlifes visiting from out of town. Money lost at the turnstiles would be bounteously replenished by corporate guests' spend. Thatcherite football had arrived. Leicester City fanzine *The Fox* was less than complimentary about the new executive boxes, which resembled '. . . a row of bloody holiday chalets . . . visiting players are treated to the sight of spoilt brat kids of the match sponsors watching Tom and Jerry videos while they get cheated out of the game in an atmosphere half-way between a wake and a Ronald McDonald birthday party.'

For the new system's first game, a friendly against Monterrey of Mexico, the automated gates' identification card reader screens glared invisibly in the sunshine. The gates were switched off, a fate repeated when dense summer rain fell before The Hatters' first league game of the season, against Southampton. Authorities and news outlets, nonetheless, lauded Luton's approach. Here was a cure for this ailing sport. It did not matter if normal fans were collateral damage in the name of pursuing the minority.

Many away supporters, meanwhile, plotted how best to beat the Hatters' ban in order to watch their teams. *Off the Ball* ran a Membership Exchange Scheme to help them; club fanzines such as *A Kick Up The R's* co-ordinated similar efforts. Easily transferable, Luton membership cards were shared freely by post. Guest passes were easier still to come by; one neighbouring newsagent sold them over the counter. Accounts of sneaky attempts successful and otherwise appeared across fanzines.

In *Off the Ball* itself, the tale of a small band of Everton fans attending their fixture at Luton in September 1987 appeared. They had bought their tickets from a tout outside Kenilworth Road 'where they were approached by an "ordinary-looking" bloke who asked where they came from. He didn't seem to be after trouble, but neither did he have any obvious reason for talking to them, so the Everton fans ignored him. Until, that is, he produced his ID card, and revealed himself to be a plain-clothes policeman.' Luckily, one of the gang had a sister living in Bedfordshire and had already secured a Luton membership card by using her address. Somehow, it was enough to deter the police officer from taking further action.

Perhaps boldest were the Millwall interlopers who went undercover for a Division One game in March 1989. Lions fans and the club had of late done much to improve their reputation, the latter even appointing a Hooliganism Consultant, John Stalker, whose previous job involved enforcing justice on rogue Northern Irish policemen. Now sponsored by their local council – Lewisham – a concerted effort was made to grow a community club, with funding even allocated to Millwall's women's team, a rarity in the late 1980s. Yet still the vaguest hint of a South London accent that day in Bedfordshire summoned scowls. When Millwall scored, reported *The Lion Roars*, 'the police and stewards down the front would stand up, spin around, their eyes scouring for the flicker of a smile. It was like something out of an old war film, with us cast in the role of escaped P.O.W.s trying to dodge the Nazis.' Suspects were interrogated on the spot and then marched from the ground, 'doubtless to have their membership cards pulled out with pliers without anaesthetic'.

Some Luton fans turned on them, with 'yelps of "there's another one!" from finger-pointing collaborators'. However, 'most of the Luton fans didn't seem to mind the handful of Millwall supporters being present; I heard one complaining, "Why don't they leave 'em alone? They're not causing trouble."' Luton versus Millwall in 1985 had been 'one unacceptable side of football, but Luton versus Millwall 1989 was another, both equally repugnant'.

Newcastle United followers who skulked into Kenilworth Road in November 1987 had perhaps been encouraged by the Magpies' most recent matchday programme. Its pages contained both a story headlined 'Luton Ban' that forbade them from travelling to Bedfordshire and a feature giving detailed AA road instructions of how they shouldn't get there. One Geordie who travelled, Steve Brennan, reported in *The Mag* on what he had witnessed inside 'Colditz', which was 'contrary to David Evans' opinion, English football at its worst'. From the absent atmosphere to Luton's plastic pitch, Brennan concluded that 'If many more follow Luton's example then football will be dead in 10 years' time. Football is a spectator sport and your average spectator is not permitted within Kenilworth Road unless he bends the rules and spends a fortune.'

As Brennan's tone suggested, Evans' Kenilworth project had cultivated shared contempt for Luton Town from followers of other clubs. 'They disappointed everyone by staying up last season and are undoubtedly the most disliked team in the country,' said *King of the Kippax* in the summer of 1989. Leicester City's *The Fox* went further: 'If Luton Town's piss pot Kenilworth Road premises were obliterated from the face of the earth tomorrow then all true football supporters would breathe a hearty sigh of relief.'

Understandably, some Luton supporters responded by creating fanzines of their own. An early 1990 editorial in the maiden issue of *Town* sighed how it had become 'pretty boring seeing every other fanzine having a go at Luton all the bleeding time, so we're here to present a view from where it matters most'. Despite being made to feel like 'social lepers', 'there is a spirit amongst the fans at Luton that many had thought was lost'. By issue 3, one particular national fanzine was in contributors' thoughts. 'Hardly an issue of *When Saturday Comes* goes by without a dig at Luton, and why?' said one, before highlighting that the Hatters were not the only club in football to have unpopular figures in the boardroom.

'Anyone who reads *When Saturday Comes*,' stated a second article articulating the same viewpoint, 'knows how unpopular the Town are with the self-respecting football fan – but while agreeing with their arguments (which are by and large justified), lying back and crying "Yeah, you're right, we're wrong and we're scum" can get boring . . . we agree the membership card scheme is crap but we're not the ones who should be dealing out apologies.'

Not all Luton fanzine contributors concurred that the membership scheme had been a negative development. A February 1991 article in *Depleated* – submitted, perhaps tellingly, anonymously – argued for the away supporter ban to be maintained. The writer had attended the infamous 1985 fixture with Millwall alongside his terrified young sons, whereas now, 'I can take my lads to games with no worries . . . There is absolutely no hint of menace or violence. The town centre and areas near the ground are safe again.' It was then noted that Kenilworth Road now attracted a higher-than-average number of female and child attendees. 'Luton's ground is said to lack atmosphere since the away fans ban,' he concluded. 'This is clearly true. Oh how we long for the return of obscene chants and threats being merrily passed between the two sets of supporters.'

When David Evans announced that he would be leaving Luton Town at the end of season 1989/90 to dedicate more time to politics, *Town* fanzine summarised the calamities of his reign. The membership scheme had been unjustified at the beginning and maintained through a period when 'football hooliganism is on the way out'. His eyesore plastic pitch was 'no good for football', he had attempted to move the club to Milton Keynes and Luton's reputation across the game had taken 'a right nosedive'. His actions had validated – and perhaps inspired – a phrase coined by Adrian Goldberg: 'the hooligans in the boardroom . . . the people who didn't care about football or its tradition or its culture and its clubs, and who were only too willing to see football shrink. They wanted to destroy clubs and didn't care about the football world that we cared about.'

Over the three years it ran, the Luton scheme unified fans in disgust. They abhorred this restrictive, dismal version of attending football and wished to shape a different future for their game. The Kenilworth Road vision of the sport was based on the demonised version of supporters propounded by politicians, police and media. It gave normal football fans the experience that hooligans deserved.

There was solidarity in fans' rejection of the Evans way and in their battling against demonisation. It showed that supporters could shed the tribalism of following a club to champion their shared interests. This was something that Frank Ormston of *Terrace Talk* found to be integral to the early fanzine movement. 'It's very easy to get sucked into the tribal thing and think, "oh, it's, you know, whatever club, they're pillocks",' he says. 'But it was important for football fans to come together because they were so demonised. That was the case in the mid-80s because there was a moral panic over hooliganism and "football fans" was almost a byword for hooliganism, violence and anti-social behaviour. So to us it was always important to counter that and stand in solidarity when people were attacking football fans.'

Those fans had a lot to say. Across the land, typewriters were being dusted down and the basics of Letraset rapidly learned.

WHEN SATURDAY COMES

20p

No. 1

MARCH 1986

As I write this I'm looking at two pictures which just about sum up everything that's right and everything that's wrong with British football today. One is of Pat Nevin and the other is of Ken Bates. They're both smiling, but Pat's smile says: "I'm doing something I love", and Bates's says: "I've fooled you all". I could go into detail, but I'm sure you know what I mean. Some people are in football because it's what they do best and what they enjoy doing, others are in it to squeeze every last drop of prestige, power and money out of it - and at the moment The Squeezers are having a fine old time of it.

Right, hopefully that'll be just about the last bit of moralizing and pontificating in this issue. This paper isn't going to be any sort of crusade,* which is just as well, considering how many people are likely to read it, but I thought I ought to sketch in a bit of background first, in case you thought I was coming to laugh at football's funeral. Of <u>course</u> the game's in a bad way, but if everyone's just going to be miserable about it and go around wringing their hands all day, then there's not much point trying to save it at all. It's meant to be <u>fun</u> for Chrissake!

OK, <u>definitely</u> no more preaching. Maybe I should try to say what I want 'When Saturday Comes' to be, or at least what I <u>don't</u> want it to be. It's not going to be cliched, hackneyed, lazy journalism, it's not going to be banal ghostwritten platitudes, it's not going to be tedious, whitewashing interviws, it's not going to be full of statistics or match reports, and it's certainly not going to indulge in petty rivalries, though it must be fairly obvious already where my sympathies lie! All that sort of stuff is available in abundance elsewhere.

* Some bits of it might be!

What it might be a bit more like is the sort of thing you talk about in the pub. Gossip, stories, arguments, some serious things that never get discussed anywhere else, like racism at football, but mostly not. It depends a lot on what other people contribute - obviously I really only know about things that go on in London, so I really want to hear from other places. Why <u>do</u> Forest (and Mansfield) supporters chant "One, One, One" when they get a corner? What exactly is a Perrie? What is it about certain clubs (e.g. Liverpool, Ipswich, Arsenal) that attracts so many players with big noses? Does anyone in football actually <u>like</u> Ron Saunders? What sort of crowds do Stenhousemuir get? These are the sort of questions I've always wanted the answers to, but no publication ever tells me. Maybe 'When Saturday Comes' will, it's up to you.

Write to:

MIKE TICHER
157 ROBINSON ROAD
LONDON
SW17 9NS

Well, go on then...

'When Saturday Comes' is an offshoot of 'Snipe!' fanzine, available from the same address. Although 'WSC 1' is coming out at the same time as 'Snipe!' no. 3, I don't know if they'll always appear simultaneously, it depends on the demand really. For the moment we'll just take every issue as it comes. At the end of the day I'll always give 110% and you can't ask for more than that really, can you?

Seeing as I don't fancy taking my chances selling 'WSC' alongside 'Bulldog' on the Fulham Road on a Saturday afternoon, it's going to rely completely on mail order sales. So if you think you could get rid of a few for me, it would be more than welcome. I don't know why I bother to say this really, just tradition, I suppose.

Please don't bother to turn the page if your name is: Jimmy Hill, Brian Moore, Bert Millichip, Ted Croker, Robert Maxwell, Kevin Keegan, Clive Thomas, Don Revie, Ron Saunders, Ken Bailey, Irving Scholar, Don Howe, Bobby Robson, Jack Charlton, John Bond, Bob Wilson, Graeme Souness, Ron Noades, Howard Wilkinson, Ron Atkinson, or anyone else who thinks they know what's good for us. You wouldn't enjoy it, anyway, at least I sincerely hope not.

PART TWO
MAKE DO AND MEND

CHAPTER SIX: FINDING A VOICE

People related to it and it didn't matter that it looked like shit.

— MIKE TICHER, CO-FOUNDER OF *WHEN SATURDAY COMES*

Over one blazing London week in the summer of 1976, two dozen people lodged themselves in a vacant Blackheath house and cut the same page from 15,000 copies of one book. Each was replaced with a chit, apologising for the words those single folios had once carried. When their task was complete, the books were returned to shops and warehouses for onward sale. *The Foul Book of Football* was back on the streets.

Their scissors saw action due to the threats of one man. Mike Langley, a football journalist with the *Sunday People*, had been riled upon seeing an article in the book that lampooned Fleet Street scribes as feckless boozers and shoddy writers. A libel case beckoned. To save their publication and avoid financial desolation via court trial, the book's producers could only say sorry with their snipping and hope for the best.

The book's compilers had in 1972 become the first football followers to print an alternative, fans' eye view national publication. *Foul* magazine was created by Steve Tongue and Alan Stewart, two Cambridge University undergraduates. Founded upon what they termed a 'mountain of disgust' at early 1970s football, *Foul* was a heady brew of satire ridiculing those who ran the game and taking a great sword to their egos, and deep-trawling investigations of all that had gone wrong since the heights of 1966. All the while, sarcasm and parody were pursued just as studiously. With a strapline of 'The Alternative Football Paper', *Foul* was written for the lesser-publicised intelligent football fan, sceptical of the game's governance and displeased by the dull, industrial playing style lately in vogue. Naturally, it provoked detestation from figures inside football and the mainstream press. It possessed, said the *Times Literary Supplement*, '. . . a strong vein of sanctimoniousness which sits oddly' with its 'effortfully iconoclastic posture'.

The Foul Book of Football was a compilation of articles from the magazine's first 30 issues, mixed with a smattering of new material. It was hoped that it would raise funds for a business forever relying on the kindness of subscribers and the generosity of donors, one of whom, the songwriter Tim Rice, paid off many *Foul* debts. Prior to its removal from shop shelves and hasty surgery in Blackheath, 5,500 editions of the book were sold. Upon its return, however, sales slowed. Most copies were eventually destroyed by bonfire. *Foul* itself stumbled on until a final issue in October 1976. For the many thousands who revelled in its disrespectful ways, it became a fond memory. For others, it was an inspiration.

As *Foul* faded away, punk fanzines flowered indignantly. Their design and ethos would later influence many of their football counterparts. *Sniffin' Glue*, the most well-known, led the way. Martin Lacey – an editor of several music and football fanzines, and the printer of many more – recognises its significance. '*Sniffin' Glue* was badly laid out and the writing wasn't always great,' he says, 'but it was important because it was the first punk fanzine and they were writing about things no-one else was.' As a schoolboy, James Brown, a Leeds United supporter and influential figure in the magazine industry, founded his own music fanzine, *Attack on Bzag*. 'Every town and city had a record shop then,' he recalls, 'and all of them had a little stand or just a pile of fanzines on the countertop. It changed everything.'

Music mattered considerably to innumerable people who would go on to establish or write for football fanzines. They were gig-goers and bass players in bands, record-buyers and vinyl collectors. The principles of punk in particular appealed. As *Dial M For Merthyr*'s Mark Evans says, 'The football fanzine movement repeated the punk movement and that idea of: If you want to do it, go and do it.' Post-punk but prior to editing *Fly Me To The Moon*, Robert Nichols sang in a band named Shrug and helped produce a music fanzine, *A Mile of Bad Road*. 'But,' he remembers, 'it was really hard to sell fanzines at gigs because people would say, "No, I want to save my quid for a pint." So there was no contest between 60 people at a gig who wanted a pint and a big football crowd who were interested in anything about their team.'

One gig-goer skipping a pint for print, though, was *Off the Ball* co-founder Adrian Goldberg. A young punk in Birmingham, he 'avidly bought' music fanzines including *The Sound of Spaghetti* and 'just loved the idea of getting this stuff that you could only buy if you were at a gig, this alternative media and the whole DIY culture'. Goldberg also procured legendary Liverpudlian fanzine *The End* – 'a music and lifestyle fanzine that had some football in it, rather than a football fanzine', he reflects, but nonetheless influential on he and Steve Beauchampé's pioneering *Off the Ball*, launched in January 1986. They would not be the last fanzine creators inspired by *The End*, co-founded in 1981 by Peter Hooton, later lead singer of The Farm. It was, wrote John Peel, 'an impudent farrago of music, football and social irresponsibility.'

As punk frazzled and its fanzines vanished, Goldberg and Beauchampé turned to football and found a dire West Midlands scene. The 1985/86 season would conclude with the former's West Bromwich Albion relegated from Division One and the latter's Birmingham City departing Division Two. Blues were owned by secretive scrap merchant Ken Wheldon, whose main objective was to cut debts by fanatical penny-pinching; in turn, the regime at Walsall – the club Wheldon left for Birmingham – seemed fixated on selling off their Fellows Park ground and squatting at St Andrew's. Meanwhile, Division Four club Wolves were playing at a two-sided Molineux and flirting with extinction under owners Mahmud and Mohammad Bhatti – 'brothers who were supposedly related to the Saudi Arabian royal family, but in fact were two property developers from Manchester,' says Goldberg.

The degeneration of West Midlands football was neither a freak show nor an aberration. Across the land, multiple clubs were subject to the wonky stewardship of incompetent owners. Above them, custodians of the game and those in authority were drawn from a melange of the useless and the hostile. It made football fanzines a required development, both in order to hold the powerful to account and to ridicule them. 'Football then was run by these old men who were completely out of touch with reality,' says Harry Pearson. 'It's like when the Beatles appeared in the 60s, or punk in the 70s. You've got all these crusty old people. And then you've got Thatcher as well, who really hated football completely. So, you had all that to kick against.'

Both local and national football scenes greatly worried Goldberg. Music, his other great cause, had enough print vehicles and champions. Leaning on the punk fanzines he had loved, the sport would get the alternative press it deserved and needed. He called Beauchampé – 'my kindred spirit in these things' – and the two met 'by the canal at Gas Street Basin, a place where shopping trolleys would be dumped and you might see dead dogs floating past'. Knowing, 'with him that I had to say I was doing it, as opposed to vaguely having an idea, I said: "Steve, I'm going to start a football fanzine. Are you in or are you out?" I had to plant my flag in the idea. I wanted to write. I cared.' The next day, Beauchampé telephoned to give his yes. Britain's first national football fanzine since *Foul* was alive and would be 'informed by the ideals of punk rock: get in there, tell the story, get out again'.

Goldberg liberated his father's old-fashioned typewriter ('One of the keys didn't work properly'). His girlfriend, Sally, typed up most early handwritten articles and for headlines they employed 'a mixture of Letraset, which was a system of transferable letters, and hand-drawn letters and using a ruler to keep stuff vaguely on line'. Sheets were organised into a vague magazine formation and printed stealthily at Beauchampé's workplace, the local council. Vital assistance was also provided by another friend, Sid Collins. 'We just felt our way through it,' reflects Goldberg, 'the production, the layout. Everything was made-up and driven by our collective arrogance and ignorance walking hand in hand.'

In the 10-month space between Heysel and the birth of *When Saturday Comes* (*WSC*), torrents of negative publicity had been bestowed upon football fans. English clubs were now banned from European competitions, adding to the popular notion of a decaying sport. Andy Lyons and Mike Ticher no longer worked in the same Our Price shop but did share a house and many discussions about the game and the way others saw it. 'We felt we didn't recognise the picture,' says Lyons. 'People who weren't fans had this negative archetype in mind. I suppose we felt a bit defensive about being interested in football. We wanted to show that ordinary people followed football, which had obviously been a big part of popular culture in the UK for 100 years.'

'It just felt so grim that these things had happened,' adds Ticher, 'and yet no one watched football because they were made to or they hated it. They loved it. These dreadful things had happened to something that people really loved, including us. It was no good waiting for the people who ran football to do it better, because that wasn't going to happen. We had to do something about it, or at least say something about it.'

That 'something' would be said in *WSC*, although there was no grand scheme or manifesto; 'We had no expectations of doing more than one issue, really,' says Ticher. Their first issue was an offshoot of Ticher's music fanzine, *Snipe* ('I had no idea about design or production, that was all terrible. But I'm not sorry I did it.') There was no headline, just the bold, underlined declaration of WHEN SATURDAY COMES, a title borrowed from an Undertones song. Next to it appeared a Victorian ink illustration of a strapping footballer, ball under arm, perhaps running on to the pitch. Across his chest ran two capitalised words: The People. Although a handy declaration of who the publication stood on the side of, it was actually taken from a 19th-century advert for a newspaper of the same name.

There would be no editorial strategy, just an intention, says Lyons, 'to write about the sort of things that football fans would be likely to talk about. The conversations you might have before or after a game, some funny stuff, some serious.' *WSC* would demonstrate that many different types of people followed football, and that 'You could be a fan and also be interested in other things – music, politics, books'. Beyond the nascent *Off the Ball*, nothing else available talked to adult football supporters in the way that *WSC* did, its tone influenced by *Melody Maker*, *NME* and *Viz*.

In five opening front-cover paragraphs, issue 1 declared intentions that chimed with earlier publications such as *Terrace Talk* and influenced the fanzine flurry soon to begin. It was time to question 'The Squeezers' – owners, administrators, authorities – who took from the game and gave nothing back, while simultaneously laughing at them. 'Of *course* the game is in a bad way,' declared one telling line, 'but if everyone's just going to be miserable about it and go around wringing their hands all day, then there's not much point trying to save it at all.'

Almost as essential to what *WSC* would be was what it wouldn't, namely 'cliched, hackneyed, lazy journalism . . . banal ghostwritten platitudes, tedious whitewashing interviews . . . it's not going to be full of statistics and match reports, and it's certainly not going to indulge in petty rivalries.' In the bottom corner, a further paragraph listed 20 football figures after the instruction 'Please don't bother to turn the page if your name is . . .', from Jimmy Hill to Ron Atkinson via Bert Millichip, Ted Croker and Robert Maxwell, 'or anyone else who thinks they know what's good for us'.

Its 12 pages of articles were completed on one typewriter, pasted on to sheets alongside pictures cut from old football annuals, and 100 photocopies made. 'The production standards were absolutely terrible,' reflects Ticher, amused. 'It was experimenting with something and gradually you worked out that maybe it's better if the columns are all the same width and you kind of use the same typefaces on some of the articles. But it was the first time I'd ever thought about anything like that, or not thought about it and done it – just sort of typed stuff and then stuck it on the page and flagrantly stolen photographs.'

The pair sent a copy to the *Guardian*'s Phil Shaw, a rare fanzine advocate inside the mainstream press. Shaw mentioned *WSC* in his sports section 'Diary' and over 100 orders quickly followed, 'so we had to do a reprint – or re-photocopy – and put up the cover price, from 15p to 20p, capitalists from the start,' recalls Lyons. Over the following week, 200 letters arrived at 157 Robinson Road, their houseshare address as printed on the issue 1 cover and by the *Guardian*. 'We suddenly thought, "Blimey, this is something",' he adds. 'So that was the moment, really; a very sudden response to it that made us think: "Shit, there might be something here in this", in a small way.'

Sustained interest came as a genuine surprise. 'We had no expectation this would amount to something,' continues Lyons. 'I remember with the first few issues each time I thought, "God, we've done another one, that's five now", or "that's seven". I recall doing an interview early on with somebody from *Time Out* and they asked, "Where do you see yourself in five years?" I honestly thought, "Probably back in the shop or an office."'

Orders and enthusiasm, though, flowed. Despite their applaudable lack of ambition ('We *were* in our mid-twenties, remember,' says Ticher), a professional printer – in Martin Lacey – and a publishing partner – Brass Tacks, whose only other publication was *The Mortgage Magazine* – were engaged. From knockabout conversations at the kitchen table, something that very rapidly meant so much to so many, and galvanised the fanzine movement, had sprung. 'People recognised something in *WSC* that struck a chord with them,' reflects Ticher, 'It was the feeling behind it. The point was that football fans deserved better.'

Unlike other doom-drowned national media, beyond the constructive swipes at how the game was run and suggestions as to how it might be fixed, *WSC* content demonstrated affection for football and its history, and reflected the minutiae of being a fan. Further, says Ticher, across its pages were 'just good writing about football, about much-loved players or incidents that had happened or the amazing emotions running through it. And that's what people were missing in other coverage that was available at the time, whether newspapers or magazines or TV. People related to it and it didn't matter that it looked like shit.'

'*WSC* was unique. There was nothing out there like it,' says Paul Hawksbee in deep admiration. 'There'd been music fanzines and they had the spirit of that. They had the spirit of *Viz*. It was football finally getting that treatment of the people who'd written for music fanzines. And it's all the more amazing that they did it at a time when football was seen as an absolute pariah.' Those sentiments are echoed by Harry Pearson, who quickly turned from *WSC* reader to writer: 'You didn't realise that you were waiting for it, but that's what you were waiting for. Something happens and you realise that's your place – that was *When Saturday Comes*.'

For the remainder of 1986 and through the years that followed, much more post would arrive for *WSC*. A majority consisted of A5 envelopes, their contents often wildly different yet united in spirit: club fanzines dispatched from across the land, some titles that would breathe for decades, others that never reached sequel status. At first, *WSC* printed reviews of them, which in turn would become a staple feature in most fanzines themselves. When the trickle became a stream, space meant they could only be simply listed – team, title, price and mail order address. Soon, lists had to be run over two issues, one half of the alphabet in each. Organically, these inventories created an audience unknown to each other, but gladly sending off their 50 pence pieces for fanzines about teams they felt nothing for, from towns they could seldom point at on a map. 'It was a genuine subculture,' says Lyons. 'It was something that was going on, on the quiet around the country. Lots of like-minded people, buying fanzines without knowing each other.'

An article entitled Unholy Alliance appeared on the inside cover of that first *WSC*. It detailed 'a nasty sort of comradeship' that had formed between some Chelsea and Rangers supporters following a May 1985 friendly between the two sides, hastily organised to raise money for the Bradford Disaster Appeal Fund. Together at Stamford Bridge, they exchanged racist, antisemitic and anti-Catholic songs. Then in November, Rangers followers travelled south to Anfield to back their new English team in an away fixture against Liverpool, singing 'such timeless football classics as There's Only One Ian Paisley and The Sash My Father Wore'. This had resulted only in English confusion, yet a long-lasting friendship was fostered, and, with it, eyes previously closed to Old Firm sectarianism had been prised open.

Just as hooliganism, policing and other social ills littered the pages of early English and Welsh fanzines, it would perhaps be natural to assume that the blight of sectarianism featured heavily in their Scottish counterparts. Yet beyond occasional early lapses into sectarian language in some Old Firm fanzines, and perhaps in reaction *to* bigotry, a fanzine movement of a very different, very droll nature dominated. *The Absolute Game* – Scotland's national fanzine equivalent to England's *Off the Ball* and *WSC* – typified this spirit.

There had been other club fanzines – or publications that were arguably fanzines – in Scotland prior to *The Absolute Game*'s launch in 1987. Two pre-dated York City's *Terrace Talk* and were infused with this Caledonian spirit in which irreverence overcame hand-wringing. Founded in 1979, for a while Meadowbank Thistle's *Cheers* straddled a place somewhere between matchday programme and fanzine. Photographer Colin McPherson, a Thistle fan until their franchise move to Livingston in 1995, describes *Cheers* as 'a bit of an of outlier but still infused with an independent anarchic spirit. It would say what it liked, but it also on occasion doubled as the match programme. It was something you really looked forward to. And you knew that your club was producing something that nobody else was.'

After a dozen or so issues, editor Alastair Petrie-Hay defined *Cheers* as distinctly a fanzine. Supporting his viewpoint, McPherson recalls the way it 'functioned as a protest portal and the only way you could actually articulate and ventilate' about the club. Such articulation went too far for Thistle chairman J.P. Blacklaw, who early in 1980 banned sales of *Cheers* from Meadowbank, the municipal stadium where Thistle played. The official reason was that supporters were being conned into buying the fanzine when they intended to purchase the official programme. 'Such misgivings, however,' responded Petrie-Hay, 'should not warrant censorship. This is a Sports Centre, not Moscow Centre.'

In that banning year of 1980, across in Glasgow the Queen's Park Supporters' Association launched *The Web*, a distinctly fanzine-like production. Three years later, editorship passed to the 19-year-old Iain Campbell. 'I was very shy in those days,' says Campbell of being asked to take on the role. 'And then I thought, "Well, why don't I just have a go at it?" And it was great. It was a hassle, it was annoying, but I loved it.'

To start the young Campbell off, more senior supporters' club members 'came to my house and showed me how to do all the straight lines and all the cow gum and things. But I thought "Straight lines? I'm not doing that,"' he laughs. 'I did a 48-pager for Christmas one year. I couldn't sleep in my own bedroom that night. There was stuff everywhere. Do you think I was seriously going to be doing straight lines?' For typing articles, Campbell borrowed a 'spare' typewriter from his day job with the local council and took it home. The mother of Keith, a fellow Queen's Park fan and *Web* volunteer, 'basically did most of the typing. Then you had to cut it out, stick it down with cow gum and let it dry.'

Aside from its status as the organ of the supporters' club – something most fanzines actively, and occasionally militantly, avoided – *The Web* differed from other publications in its knowingly narrow outlook. 'I used to produce it for the people on the supporters' bus,' adds Campbell. 'Against the norm, I thought it was better to bring it out for away games because people would have to buy it as we were stuck on the bus. And I wasn't writing it for people across the rest of the UK. It was for the people on the bus. It was very, very parochial. We just wanted to keep it to our supporters.'

Regardless, many articles had universal appeal and struck familiar themes. There were gripes about the running of the game, reviews of other fanzines and rich accounts of away days ('The train journey was memorable as Davey borrowed the conductor's clipper to get some chewing gum out of his hair'). As early as issue 5, printed in late 1980, writer Simon Lewry's Food and Facilities review was setting a precedent for what followed in later fanzines. Instead of a terrace, Albion Rovers' Cliftonhill had 'a slope which seemed to be made partially from pieces of the brick wall at the back'. At Queen of the South, Lewry encountered 'the worst bog of the year . . . Fortunately I can't use it because the barbed wire overhead sags down so low that it would scratch my head.' East Fife was 'a death trap. The wooden parts of the terracing are very slippery . . . I know of at least three cases of people actually falling over. The wall that was called a toilet was falling down at one end.'

St Johnstone supporter Archie MacGregor had already been impressed by the irreverence of an early Scottish fanzine whose name now escapes him, and *Off the Ball*. Then *WSC* arrived. He was 'besotted, and delighted every time a new issue dropped through the letterbox', and instinctively felt that 'there was more than enough going on in Scotland for it to have a *WSC*-style fanzine in its own right'. His creation would be called *The Absolute Game*, a name taken from the title of a Skids album, and MacGregor was assisted at first by Stuart Bathgate, later a distinguished sports journalist. Dispensing with any hopes of comfortable profit before *The Absolute Game* even launched, MacGregor decided it would 'shun all things Celtic and Rangers, except for poking a bit of ridicule and ire. If it was about anything it was about exploring and enjoying Scottish football outwith the mind-numbing Old Firm prism.'

Treading the *WSC* path, MacGregor and Bathgate used a battered old typewriter for issue 1 and photocopied the final product. However, 'We kept on running out of copies,' remembers MacGregor, 'so I was sneakily using the work photocopier to produce more. There I am, running off 25 copies of each page, and just praying that nobody comes in. And of all the people that walked in the room, it was the boss. A real tumbleweed moment. We found ourselves a friendly printer for the second issue.' *The Absolute Game* would remain in print until 2002, becoming a beacon of unity for fans who wished for something beyond gluttonous Old Firm coverage, and frothing with sarcasm and satire.

Looking back now, MacGregor sums up the differences between attending games in Scotland and the rest of the mainland. 'I don't think the air of crisis and impending doom was quite as acute up here. There wasn't much crowd trouble. The Casuals were quite a thing at that time, although it tended to be that they fought amongst themselves. You didn't have the likes of the Luton v Millwall FA Cup violence and similar really scary incidents like that.' A 1988 article in *AWOL*, the successor fanzine to *Cheers* co-edited by Colin McPherson, sardonically summed up the scene. 'In the lower divisions of Scotland,' wrote PC Kostas Mavridis, 'where paltry crowds are scattered around vast crumbling grounds, a mood of serene indifference usually reigns.' Trouble was a rarity and arose among Casuals and 'extreme sectarian groups' whose fights began with 'ideological disagreements fuelled by 140 pints each of some Dryburgh's filth'.

That things were calmer – and admittedly, much of this relative serenity sprouted from law changes after Old Firm rioting at the 1980 Scottish Cup Final – adds MacGregor 'was a differentiator between Scottish and English fanzines. And I do think Scottish ones were funnier, but maybe that's just because I'm Scottish and I know more about Scottish football and the characters up here. That worked particularly with us, because we took the conscientious decision that we wanted to focus on the smaller clubs. There's such a rich culture of storytelling and all sorts of weird and wonderful goings on at small clubs. Our fanzines reflected the self-deprecating humour of those clubs.'

Neil Forsyth, now the screenwriter behind the BBC dramas *Guilt* and *The Gold*, as well as *Legends* on Netflix, tells a story that perhaps best sums up this prevalence among Scottish fanzines of self-deprecation, whimsy and even surrealism. A teenager writing for and selling *When the Hoodoo Comes*, the Falkirk-based fanzine dedicated to his treasured Dundee United, Forsyth recalls one Saturday afternoon arriving outside Tannadice to see co-editors Scott and Norrie 'with big boxes of our new issue as usual'. However, 'arranged around their feet were about 200 Dundee United-themed garden gnomes, quite sizeable orange things. I said to them, "What's going on with the gnomes, lads?"'

Sales had been going well, it transpired. The fanzine was in profit. A kitty had grown and now in a lunge at business expansion, the *When the Hoodoo Comes* trio would be selling garden gnomes alongside fanzines. 'This was maybe about one o'clock,' continues Forsyth. 'Me, Scott, Norrie and 200 garden gnomes. Cut to three o'clock as the game kicks off. Me, Scott, Norrie and 200 garden gnomes. I think they made a few miscalculations, one of which was how many Dundonian men they thought were going to not only buy a garden gnome, but then take it to the game.' After the match, the young apprentice helped his masters load their car. 'I often think about them on the drive home that night to Falkirk,' he adds. 'A vehicle full of slight regret. And every time they looked in the rearview mirror, they'd have 200 gnomes looking back at them.'

4000 HOLES

SEPTEMBER, 1989

"A Northern Horde of uncouth Garb and Strange Oaths"

Issue no. 1

50p

CHAPTER 7: IN THE BEGINNING

The fanzine is an outlet where slaggings and wicked lies can be heard without bald men in suits slapping down fines.

– *THERE'S A STORE WHERE THE CREATURES MEET*,
ST MIRREN FANZINE

Early fanzines had demonstrated to countless football supporters that they could speak up for themselves. Previously ignored and muted, in typewriters they had found megaphones. The spread of *Off the Ball*, *When Saturday Comes* and *The Absolute Game* emboldened and stimulated fans to express themselves. From Cornwall to Caithness, hundreds of editors were unleashed, self-appointed Generals of the Pritt Stick.

Absolute power of the pages soon gave way to democracy. Once they had picked glue from fingernails and completed their debut issues, a clarion call would be made for more contributors, more voices. 'The aim,' said the opening editorial in Manchester City fanzine *Electric Blue*, 'is to give to anyone who wishes the chance to get up, stand up and say their piece, a soapbox if you like.' In its own starter message, Brighton & Hove Albion's *Gull's Eye* asserted that 'Views can and will be expressed without fear of censorship'. Swindon Town's *Bring the Noise* went somewhat further. Their fanzine would be 'A chance for the voice of the real supporters to be heard around here for a change. And that means we aren't toeing anybody's party line. We're sick of being messed around over big match tickets (take a bow, club officials) or portrayed as mindless hooligans (stand up, *Evening Advertiser*) or constantly treated like criminals (that's you, Wiltshire Constabulary) or forced to look at awful hairstyles (come in, Bobby Barnes).'

Despite their differing context, Scottish fanzine pioneers began with similarly terrific bolshiness. Airdrie's *Only the Lonely* wished to be 'a voice for fans of a club who are usually seen as criminally apathetic and fickle'. As official club communications offered 'little scope for free speech', their pages would be a repository for criticism, and 'Hopefully this little mag will not be frowned upon, but we won't kowtow to avoid this. If the board don't like it then we must be too near the truth for comfort, or they're little Dictators.' For its own opening rebel yell, *The Falkirk Unofficial Fanzine* chose as a subject the mainstream football journalists it sought to displace. They were on the whole 'name dropping, drunken old hacks, over-inflated by the obnoxious gasses of their own egotism tirelessly grovelling at the feet of the fabulous Old Firm'. Hardly auditioning for membership of the Scottish Football Writers' Association, the editorial continued, 'They are so far removed from the ordinary punter that they don't have a clue about the supporters' views, let alone what it's actually like to stand on a terracing surrounded by opposing supporters spitting on and insulting you (i.e. home games versus Rangers and Celtic).'

The founders of St Mirren's *There's a Store Where the Creatures Meet*, however, were a little more sanguine. Their fanzine was 'not born from being fed up with the very little media interest in our club . . . The truth is we just thought about doing it after a few pints down the pub. Alright the fanzine was Dry Blackthorn inspired, this does not mean however that it will be free from passionate scribble.'

Graham Ennis of Everton fanzine *When Skies Are Grey* recalls the context of this sharp shift. 'Before, the fan's voice was completely unheard and there was no outlet for it whatsoever. It seems really odd in today's game where fans' voices are absolutely everywhere. There was none of that.' Ennis continues, 'Suddenly there was this groundswell of people who not only were finding a voice but were finding that they had similar things to say and similar experiences, and that grew to become a movement.'

Official matchday programmes were another, related motivation for starting a fanzine. A club may well communicate with its supporters through the programme, but here was a one-way conversation. That supporter – save for the odd, highly censored and sanitised letters page – could not reply, never mind initiate questioning of club affairs. Dissent was impossible, discussion of the ills afflicting football unthinkable. Further, programme content itself was frequently insipid, its prose a form of procedural, template writing. Fanzine creators wanted to provide something different, something well written, something *interesting*.

Off the Ball exhaled some biting descriptions in a December 1986 article. These 'sham sheets' remained marooned in the game's glory days of ten or more years previous and were 'a cheerful insult to all who fund this financially decrepit and spectatorshod game'. With their glossy pictures of board members and match action, programmes entirely ignored the supporters who bought them. Nowhere did they 'reflect, or even acknowledge, the pleasure of the pre-match pint or the perverse enjoyment of a cardboard-crusted sawdust pie'. *Tired and Weary*, the Birmingham City fanzine, meanwhile, called programmes 'miserably uninformed… riddled with adverts, uninteresting quizzes and worthless sparse articles'.

One common frustration with programmes – and indeed the wider media – was the way in which matchdays were covered. 'The game was divided by a huge reality gap,' said an article in *The Fox*, a long-running Leicester City fanzine. 'Things happened that you could never read about. If the police launched a horseback charge at you as you were leaving a ground in an orderly fashion you could tell everyone when you got back to Leicester but where could you read about it? It wouldn't be in the papers, it wouldn't appear in the programme the next week, or in *Shoot!* There was nothing more galling than hearing John Motson tell you all about how great Anfield's Kop was after you had been chased across Stanley Park the week before.'

Had programme editors wished to report such details, of course, they would have been stymied by protocol and having to uphold a club's imagined reputation. 'The match programme which we love dearly,' continued that first editorial in *There's a Store Where the Creatures Meet*, 'sadly cannot print anything that may offend the S.F.A... Therefore the fanzine is an outlet where slaggings and wicked lies can be heard without bald men in suits slapping down fines... We will be slagging any subject brought to our attention from Bros to Kate Bush.'

As supporters cleared their groggy throats and spoke through fanzines, the voice they found was often angry. Another motivation for striking keys – and usually, many of these inspirations overlapped – was boundless disgust at those who ran the game, and despair at the owners and chairmen apparently butchering their clubs.

Balls – a short-lived national fanzine co-founded by Julie Pritchard, Pogues bassist Darryl Hunt and journalist Myles Palmer in 1987 – was dedicated to 'everyone whose heart goes funny upon sighting from a train the floodlights of Wigan' and 'the sheer communal joy at the talents of individuals that transcends all discomfort'. Yet within that romantic core gurgled outrage at the game's administrators. 'These men are destroying football – Burn Down the Boardrooms!!??' declared its maiden editorial. 'Instead of this crap about Superleagues and executive club member schemes and play-offs, perhaps they should consider making things more comfortable for us masochists . . . and feeding us something that doesn't taste like polystyrene and basically not ripping us off.' Two years later, Preston North End fanzine *Tales From the Potting Shed* was even blunter in its own opening salvo. Their board had 'always been a pack of complete bastards' who now 'must go'.

In April 1987, a *Bolton Wanderers Worldwide* headline demanded that football 'kick out' four influential figures – Bulstrode, Ramsden, Clay and Noades. Each was a club chairman with real estate links driving an agenda to merge their club with another and/or evict them from their home grounds and sell those sacred lands for commercial gain. Through his Marler Estates company, Fulham chairman David Bulstrode had purchased Craven Cottage and intended to merge the club with Queens Park Rangers, whose Loftus Road stadium Marler also bought, for £5.8m. 'Fulham Park Rangers' would play there, with luxury flats built on the site of the Cottage. Ernie Clay was the Cottagers' owner who sold Fulham's home to Bulstrode, profiting a reported £6m in the process. Terry Ramsden held a 29.9% stake in Marler and his ownership of Walsall saw them almost fold. He would later serve a prison sentence for failing to disclose assets after being declared bankrupt. Crystal Palace chairman Ron Noades floated unions with Wimbledon and Charlton Athletic, among other harebrained proclamations. Such nefarious plotting fired the furies of existing fanzines, helping foster solidarity with other clubs. In addition, the grotty shenanigans of Bulstrode et al were midwife to new fanzines aimed at co-ordinating protest against their schemes.

'Rich property speculators treat football clubs as dispensable pawns in their efforts to make themselves even richer,' thundered the April 1987 *Wanderers Worldwide* piece. 'They don't give a toss for the communities in which the clubs are rooted, or for the people who have supported them all their lives . . . It's our bloody game – we may not own the bits of paper saying the club is our property, but they're our clubs far more than the fly-by-night property barons, because it's us and our communities who've supported them through thick and thin.'

Having left Fulham, in May 1987 Bulstrode had become chairman of QPR. Four months after the *Wanderers Worldwide* article, his plotting – and the matchday programme's support of the merger – incited the launch of the QPR fanzine *A Kick Up The R's*. 'We will be monitoring the intentions of David

Bulstrode so that we may help safeguard a secure future for our club,' declared early words in issue 1.

Typing that line of measured rancour in August 1987 was Dave Thomas. 'I'd been roused from my lifelong slumbers of never protesting anything,' he says, 'and the only thing I'd ever written up to that point was a betting slip. The merger plans galvanised me.' Appalled by the idea of his beloved club being melded with another and the loss of identity that would entail, Thomas sought the advice of Adrian Goldberg and Steve Beauchampé. Quickly, and with the help of fellow protesting West Londoners, *AKUTR's* was on sale outside Loftus Road. It provoked an immediate club request that Thomas cease publishing. Refusing such demands the fanzine continued, an important part of a wider victorious campaign that involved great unity with Fulham fans and the similarly diligent *There's Only One F in Fulham* fanzine.

There was no chance of *AKUTR's* ceasing, either, once the merger had been halted. 'I still felt that I wanted to have some way of continuing to protect the club,' adds Thomas. 'I had very grandiose ideas in those days! But the idea was not just to go, "yeah, QPR and Fulham are saved, there's no merger, we go back to normal" and then just disappear into the ether. I wanted to do something that enabled me to maintain a vigilant watch on the club. And that was the fanzine.'

Two earlier fanzines also had their origins in their clubs' existential crises, *The Leyton Orientear* and *The Pie*. In the summer of 1986, local press reported that Division Four Orient were close to financial collapse. Dave Knight, a lifelong supporter, had been enthused by *Off the Ball* and *When Saturday Comes* and in a pub conversation suggested a similar publication might be the place to register vexation and ask vital questions. 'There was a lack of information coming out of the club,' remembers Tom Davies, 16 years old at the time. 'Starting the fanzine wasn't a protest against a specific thing that the club was doing, but more like a statement that we as fans felt in the dark. So we managed to get some thoughts down on a scruffy bit of A5 and then take it from there.'

Meanwhile, in Nottingham, Jim Cooke attended a September 1986 crisis meeting aimed at finding a route to salvation for troubled Notts County. Cooke was manager of the city's Selectadisc record store and had seen the possibilities of joint action while co-organising benefit gigs during the miners' strike. At the meeting, he began to feel that a printed fanzine could play a similar role for uniting Magpies fans. 'Adrian Goldberg was there selling *Off the Ball*. I got hold of that, and I thought, "This is just right, this is what needs to be going on" and got talking to him and he said, "Why don't you do your own fanzine?" He encouraged me no end.' En route to Carlisle for an away match later in the year, Cooke and some friends made their pledges to embark upon *The Pie*. It would rally fans to help save Notts County. Any profits would be donated to the club. Further, says Cooke, 'We wanted supporters to be activated to fight against the way we were being treated at games.'

Not all motivating concerns were as grave as those at QPR, Orient and Notts County. Perhaps in keeping with the lighter tone of Scottish fanzines, in 1989 Greenock Morton's *Cappielow Bugle* stated its intention to be a conduit for addressing club issues. 'It is felt that the Cow Shed is in desperate need of a new covering,' sighed the *Bugle's* introductory issue. 'It's only a matter of time before one of the swinging lamps attached underneath the roof is blown down in a gust of wind and skelps someone on the head.'

Further reasons for starting up vaulted from fanzine pages. Beyond promoting the good name of their team to the world, *Dial M For Merthyr* hoped to forge solidarity with other fans, 'pushing down the barriers that lie between supporters of different clubs'. Boston United's *From Behind Your Fences* would show fans as they truly were – not hooligans, but normal people 'out there on the terraces representing the frontline of decent soccer support, believing in football as the unification of men and women for a shared experience'. If that sounded too radical, then a disclaimer was offered: 'Dismounting from our soapbox, we are not a burn-down-the-boardrooms revolutionary force – our idea of anarchy is crossing the road while the little man is still red.'

It would be particularly strenuous for any Millwall fanzine to similarly combat stereotypes, but nonetheless *No One Likes Us* pledged to engage with a world where 'Bad news sells newspapers, so the media created the monster of the football hooligan with sensational headlines. The publicity encouraged a lunatic fringe, so the bandwagon rolled on – more idiots and more stories about minor skirmishes.'

For all the principled grounds behind starting a fanzine, it should not be ignored that curiosity and joy played their parts too. Many founders admired other titles and thought their club should be written about in a similar fashion. The growing fanzine movement seemed an attractive, intriguing one to join. 'I often wish I could honestly claim that the magazine sprung out of discontent for something or, more excitingly, someone at Arsenal,' wrote *The Arsenal Echo Echo* editor Guy Havord, now a football commentator, 'but unfortunately it wasn't. It just seemed a good thing to do.' For others, there was also artistic lust. Often, editors and their supporting cast were talented creators who had thus far been given little opportunity to express themselves. Now, the blank page belonged to them.

Some like Martyn McFadden, co-founder of Sunderland's *A Love Supreme*, were cajoled into starting fanzines, reluctant pioneers. 'In fact,' says McFadden, 'I was dead against it. I was a train driver at the time and I wasn't even that into fanzines. But the mates who I went to the match with, in particular Jez Robinson, were into them and buying random ones.' Robinson felt Sunderland merited the same treatment. The birth of *Wise Men Say* left McFadden relieved: 'All right, good, that means we don't have to do one now, we can just go to the pub.' Yet he was persuaded to continue and 250 copies of the first *A Love Supreme* went on sale before an evening fixture against Chelsea. 'Is anyone going to buy this?', we thought. 'Will we get our heads kicked in? We sold out in 20 minutes.' Almost 40 years later, McFadden is still editor.

In order to clarify their motivations, some fanzines dispensed with considered prose and listed their credentials manifesto-style. *King of the Kippax* pledged:

> 'To bare the soul!
> Show the way it is.
> Show the way it was.
> Chart our progress in Div 1 and the cup competitions.
> Encourage support and acknowledge our fans.
> Provide a stance against injustice and I.D. cards.
> Champion the cause of the "henpecked fan".
> Provide info not easily found elsewhere.
> But really to provide an alternative and humorous look at our club and football by the fans on the terrace, in the seats and in the pub – so there!'

Fifteen miles north, in Rochdale, *Exceedingly Good Pies* offered a list of what it was 'Committed To' and 'Committed Against'. The positive column included 'Winning promotion. . . Getting behind the team. . . Walking round at half-time. . . Keeping prices down. . . Less policing. . . Independence from the club.' In the negative were, 'Rochdale's membership scheme. . . Most other North-West clubs. . . The ratio of police to stewards. . . Lack of communication from Board to fans over important decisions. . . Appalling Catering: Please note that good pies are now bought from Wilbutts Lane Chippy at considerably less cost than in the ground.'

Whether lamenting pies or police, voices were rising and sales in Tipp-Ex, Pritt Sticks and typewriter ink boomed.

MEADOWBANK THISTLE BRAKE CLUB

AWOL #3

36 pages CLIMAX EDITION 50p

JOHN M'GACHIE INTERVIEW
LYDIA LUNCH
VIC KASULE
INDIEPOP '87
FOOTBALL PUBS
SAD SOCIETY + MORE

inside:

Warning The foul and degenerate language contained in this fanzine may cause your little Giles and Camillas to grow up into wild-eyed psychotic stockbrokers or prospective Tory candidates for Spanking-on-the-Vold. Nothing to do with the football club proper. We assume it wouldn't comply with Scottish League regulations. Registered at the post-office as a firelighter.

CHAPTER 8: INK, GLUE AND NIGHTCLUBS

> *Several months, two typewriters, fifteen bottles of Tipp-Ex and half an index finger left later, I've finally got a product together.*
>
> – *ELECTRIC BLUE*, MANCHESTER CITY FANZINE

'Even if you're on the dole,' declared an encouraging *Off the Ball* article in the tone of a *Blue Peter* crafting segment gone rogue, 'you can get a typewriter for a couple of quid a week through a Mail Order catalogue.' Other requirements for starting a fanzine included a stapler, glue and a 'stencil (less than a quid) for headlines' although 'about £10 worth of Letraset gives you the opportunity to make far more striking and varied' versions. It should be remembered, though, continued the piece, that 'what the mag says is more important than how it looks'.

It was a have-a-go, DIY message that resonated. In 1991, *The Leyton Orientear* glanced backwards at its first five years of existence. Editor Dave Knight recalled, 'Three of us gathered in my kitchen with a typewriter, a tube of Pritt stick, some paper and a pair of scissors.' Their discontent with how Orient were being run 'poured itself over 16 pages of vitriol. The next day I took this wad of papers up the West End, found a photo-copy firm and got 100 copies knocked out.' Spurs' *My Eyes Have Seen the Glory* set a similar scene. 'We make no apologies,' ran its opening editorial, 'for struggling to compile this badly photocopied and appallingly stapled cornucopia of footballing fun… under the half-light of a 40-Watt bulb and with only a blunt pencil to transcribe our thoughts and memorable glories to paper.'

Andy Groom of *The Peterborough Effect* remembers 'Three or four of us sitting around the house a week before the fanzine was due out, panicking for articles, writing all sorts of nonsense at the last minute to try and fill it up'. Present too were 'A lot of scissors, a lot of Pritt Sticks. We were cutting – *stealing* really – images straight from magazines and pasting them on to the page.' As his partner owned an electronic typewriter, Groom was nominated to type articles, 'one-fingered, longhand, and then we'd all sit down, check them, cut them out, paste them on, take them to the printer'.

All early editors knew the pain of trying to decode a handwritten article sent in or passed to them in a pub. Simon Wright of *Fingerpost* and *Grorty Dick* estimates spending 60 hours on each pre-computer issue, much of that time being lost in transcription, not least because of his lifelong one-finger typing method. *Fly Me To The Moon*'s Robert Nichols still has nightmares about articles 'written on foolscap with Biro'.

Once the pages were complete and printed, the task of collating and stapling issues together would often fall to editors and anyone who could be coerced. Racing against the clock on a Friday night to have *FMTTM* prepared for sale the following day, Nichols and colleagues had 'the idea of going to a nightclub in town and asking people to come back and staple with us'. However, 'funnily enough, it never, ever worked. We got close a couple of times but no one would come back at three o'clock in the morning to staple paper. I can't think why.'

It was a similar tale 30 miles north. Following their first issue in March 1989, *A Love Supreme* established a PO Box address. 'It was what you did then, in case people firebombed yer mam's house or something,' says editor Martyn McFadden. 'After a couple of weeks there was a sack full of mail with contributions and subscriptions and ideas,' continues McFadden, 'enough to print the second issue. We printed 1000 of that one, and they sold out in two games.' The friend's photocopier they were using had 'actually died' before completion of issue 2. In need of assistance to collate its pages, the night before launch day McFadden and co-founder Jez Robinson 'got a group of friends and some girls who we met in the pub that night to come back to a party at my house. But it was a folding and stapling party. We stayed up all night finishing the magazines off. I don't know what the girls expected, but they were very helpful in terms of putting the mags together.' The following season, *A Love Supreme* was selling 3,000 copies per issue. At its peak during the late 1990s, that number reached 10,000.

Rather than recruiting at the bar, Jim Cooke and *The Pie* team took work on nights out with them, collating and stapling fanzines in their local pub, The Loggerheads. At closing time, they would be left alone by the landlord and asked to leave cash for any drinks enjoyed and then lock up after themselves. Necessity – and day jobs – made constructing issues a moonlight job. Start one, wrote Mike Kelly of Manchester City's *Blue Print*, and soon you would 'find yourself at some unruly hour frantically rubbing Letraset while watching *Prisoner: Cell Block H*'.

In Edinburgh, nominative determinism struck *AWOL* when stapling volunteers regularly went missing in action. 'Angry Al [former *Cheers* editor, Alastair Petrie-Hay], one of the gang of four behind the fanzine, had this flat with a very long corridor,' says Colin McPherson. 'The pages were all laid out along it and there was a long-arm stapler. It was a treadmill and it went on and on and on. We'd rope in other Thistle fans and they would come along, do an hour and then disappear to the pub. It was back-breaking.' More helpful were McPherson's printing contacts. Each completed issue would be secretively delivered to the back doors of Edinburgh District Council's main offices. There, a printer would produce copies out of hours for a cash payment. When this arrangement became 'unsustainable and borderline criminal', another rascal printer, at the Edinburgh College of Art, fulfilled the same clandestine role.

Mark Evans confesses that the first *Dial M For Merthyr* was 'side-stapled because I didn't have a clue about anything else'.

Mercifully, like McPherson, Evans had a willing insider to assist with future production. Neil 'The Gate' Morris was a turnstile operator at Penydarren Park who worked as a caretaker in the local law courts. 'He said "Come after 6pm, we'll let you in with the cleaners, and you can use the photocopiers in the office",' says Evans. 'We were there to the early hours just photocopying, and then he got us these long-arm staplers. So we sat on the floor in the law courts, producing the fanzine.'

Evans would soon find a professional printer based in Cardiff, Blueprint, in time the producers of many other titles. Meanwhile, in Sheffield Martin Lacey's young company, Juma, was by 1988 printing 30 different fanzines. 'They did all the typesetting and things but when the first one came back,' says early customer Dave Thomas of *A Kick Up The R's*, 'I thought I'd just painted the *Mona Lisa*. It was amazing to turn all these thoughts and ideas into something.'

Further support in fanzine production came from family members. Editor Dave Wallace's wife, Sue, was the talented artist who made *King of the Kippax* elegant, while five other family members helped type or sell. For Everton's *When Skies Are Grey*, the mother of an editorial team member designed article headings at work. 'She was obviously very broad-minded,' says Graham Ennis, 'because some of the titles we used were a bit sweary, shall we say, and she never asked many questions.' Ennis's parents and sister ran the fanzine's subscription service, stuffing 500 copies of each issue into envelopes and sending them out into the world, filling pillar boxes and waiting in lengthy post office queues.

As the fanzine movement gathered momentum, some production migrated from back bedrooms to dingy offices. *AWOL* shared with McPherson's 'underground graphics design company, which specialised in not doing a lot of work and being famous for having the world's first fax machine'. To this 'den of utter iniquity and creativity', in 1989 a primitive computer was introduced to the page-manufacturing process. It was provided by a contributor, David Hunter, who worked for the Department of Social Security and would regularly 'borrow' an early Apple laptop, 'this massive block with a tiny screen'. With blinds down and lager cans hissing open, issues would be produced overnight. McPherson's printer spat out pages 'while we watched in total wonderment'. Then, 'at about 5 a.m. we would all go home and Dave would pack his computer into his bag and sneak it back into the DSS. That was our leap into the digital and technological age.'

The crew behind Middlesbrough's *FMTTM* took the rare decision to produce an issue for every single home game, each selling several thousand copies. It meant money enough for small editorial wages and an office. Robert Nichols – stepping up to the role of editor after a colleague 'went away to be an artist-in-residence at a tennis competition in Eastbourne', surely a Half Man Half Biscuit lyric – negotiated the use of a 'massive' desktop publishing machine 'the size of a small room'. It printed and produced booklets, meaning the days of nightclub begging were over.

While much mainstream football coverage was produced by a narrow cabal of ex-players and cosied-up journalists, fanzine contributors reflected a club's varied supporter base. Articles and cartoons cascaded from the terrace, not the press box. There were no inside scoops or sources; this was outsider information, and all the richer for it.

Most who conjured fanzine content had hardly written or drawn before. Often, motley bands of regular contributors populated most pages, their work topped up by occasional writers and frequent mail correspondents. Andy Groom's description of the eccentric blend of characters behind *The Peterborough Effect* summons a typical fanzine crew: 'Sean was really good at taking cartoons like Roy of the Rovers and substituting speech bubbles with his own speech bubbles. Mark wrote under an alter ego of "Norman Cross", which was a famous roundabout just outside Peterborough. We had a legend, John Smith, who everybody called Rupert. He was 35 stone and looked like Giant Haystacks. There was also Adi Mowles, who wrote as "The Sad, Sick, Senile Son of the Seventies", a rose-tinted take on hooliganism using humour to belittle it. And Adrian Durham, who went on to talk-SPORT, was an avid contributor as he started out in journalism.'

As Norman Cross and The Sad . . . knew, the pseudonym was a vital cog of fanzine life. By not giving their real names, contributors could be as spiky and occasionally scandalous as they wished. More pragmatically, using multiple aliases might disguise the fact that only a couple of people were sometimes populating entire fanzines. For the reader, it lent a mysterious air – exactly who *were* these nom de plume characters whose mordant words and caustic cartoons we revelled in? Did they stand among us behind the goal?

Even fanzine editors did not know who all their contributors were. Robert Nichols cites 'Teesside Tony', a ranting presence in early 1990s issues of *FMTTM*. He would push a brown envelope containing his articles through the office letterbox and then scarper. Then, says Nichols, 'We'd hear it clatter downstairs, run and burst out of the door to try and find him. He would creep up with real stealth, put it through the door and then absolutely hammer it away around the corner, down the street. And we never, ever caught him. We never knew who it was. And I met him for the first time a couple of years ago and he said it became a challenge, trying to run away without being seen. So it took thirty years to find out who it was, and now I've forgotten his name anyway.'

Other characters made more direct contact. 'Davey', a postman who has drawn the fanzine's Roofus the Boro Dog cartoon since the late 1980s, would phone before each deadline and pose the question, 'What's funny?' Another contributor, his name lost to time or never given, 'used to drop off these ideas for articles,' says Nichols. 'It'd be a whole page and he'd write the first sentence and he would say, "You just need to breathe on it a bit". One sentence! "Breathe on it a bit?" You mean write the whole bloody thing.'

Davey, Miniature G, Endy, Chopper, Lord Snooty, Richard Cranium; all were characters in the *FMTTM* cast who fascinated and tantalised me, and all whose pseudonyms I remember now. Yet even looking at old fanzines for the first time, I experience a similar level of wonder – who was To Loos the Trek in *The Pie* or PC Kostas Mavridis in *AWOL*, and why did they want nobody to know? Of particular intrigue is *Dial M For Merthyr*, with its 'Doctor Obnoxious', 'Chairman Mao', 'Llama', 'Taffy Fox' and more. Reading their words feels like being invited into a charismatic and funny gang for a little while. 'Well, I'm glad you like it,' laughs Mark Evans (Wolvesy in *Dial M* . . .). 'One fanzine once did a review, and called it "An incestuous church newsletter", which I thought was hilarious. Unless you know the characters, it is incestuous, and it looks like a church newsletter, so I thought it was perfect.'

Evans reveals that some pseudonyms covered the same two or three writers. 'Taffy Fox', though, is Jonny Owen, actor, producer and radio presenter. Writing for *Dial M* . . ., Owen explains in 2026, was a life-changing event. 'It was a huge moment. I was a working-class kid in a very working-class town in the 1980s, which was a really tough time in South Wales.' While '13 or 14', he met Evans and his friends on the terraces of Penydarren Park. Despite an age gap of several years, he was welcomed into their gang, joining them for those car safaris to matches in the West Midlands and beyond. When Evans announced that he was starting a fanzine, 'I'll never forget, he just said to me, "Write me something, something about the clothes you wear or the music you're listening to or what the football means to you."' Next, continues Owen, 'I shyly gave him some handwritten stuff at a match, and he was like, "all right, great." The following week, I met him at a home game and he came over to me on the terraces. I'll never forget it, he said, "That was really good what you wrote." Nobody had ever said that to me in my life before, no teacher or anyone like that from outside my family. I've no doubt that that moment put me on the path to what I do now.'

Whether or not contributors felt moved to write onwards and even forge a creative career, the utter thrill of seeing one's own words in print across a fanzine's pages was known to thousands. This democracy was simply unknown in the traditional media. Evans adds: 'You have something in your head, you put it on paper, and you send it to the fanzine. Then you see it in print. Wow. And people buy it, and they go, "that's a good article" and you think, "that was me!" There must be hundreds of people who wrote for the first time and then thought, "I could do this."'

Screenwriter Neil Forsyth concurs. His writing career was sparked by spotting editor Scott's name on *When the Hoodoo Comes*' opening page. Though only 15 years old, Forsyth 'got his phone number from Directory Enquiries – which my mum would have been furious about as that would have been 50p down the drain – and called him up. And he was so patient with me, him and his pal Norrie that ran it. And they said, "send in your articles."' The teenager did so and has never forgotten opening the fanzine soon afterwards.

'They handed it to me, and that moment of opening it and seeing my name in that dodgy font was astounding. I just couldn't believe that my name was in print. And I would sell the fanzine outside Tannadice and say to people, "I've got something in here." It was just so exciting. It has never been surpassed. I got more excitement seeing my name in print in the fanzine than I do seeing it on a TV screen now.' The future BBC writer was stymied, though, when his mum encountered a subsequent contribution, 'which was an extremely foul-mouthed diatribe about Dundee Football Club. She gave me a one-issue ban, but from memory I think I circumvented that by working under a pseudonym.'

Mrs Forsyth was not alone in her disapproval of fanzine expletives. To curse or not to curse was a production issue often resolved in favour of blaspheme. Editors faced the wrath of the offended letter writer, that most dogged of British types. 'The level of profanity is severe,' wrote Donald Smith after reading

Hamilton Academical's *Crying Time Again*, 'change this.' Another Smith, Andrew, complained to Middlesbrough fanzine *Ayresome Angel* of their 'four-letter words (six, two being F words). I asked myself why you keep them in when there is no reason to.' As he had bought the fanzine for his wife, he demanded a refund. 'The lad who was selling it was very apologetic and gave me my money back,' Smith continued. 'However, since he seemed so sincere, I decided to buy it anyway and keep it hidden from my wife.'

If not for their vile oaths, then fanzines were also upbraided for their spelling mistakes. This was especially true in the early era, when even a liberal attitude to Tipp-Ex could not hide all mistypes. If anything, typos became *part* of the fanzine fabric, a tolerated and even fondly regarded idiosyncrasy alongside upside-down pages and wrong issue numbers. Many errors were caused by decrepit equipment – missing keys and sticky space bars – and some by decrepit humans. 'The most striking feature of early issues was the occasional and inexplicable disappearance of words,' wrote Chris Salt of the Lancastrian *Rodney, Rodney!* fanzine. 'Our word processor could have benefited from a slightly more thorough operator. The readers entered sweepstakes to see how many mistakes would appear in the next issue. The contributors seethed and some left.' An anonymous Dunfermline supporter writing to East Fife's *Bayview Bulletin* was similarly uncharmed by such habitual sloppiness. 'The most cursory perusal of your fanzine,' suggested its author, 'reveals some rather embarrassing orthographic bloomers, VIZ: P3 – specimin; P28 – precense; P28 – frought.'

Perhaps the *Bayview Bulletin* editor should've blamed a pet. In the early 1990s, Simon Wright, embracing a new technological era, bought a £500 laser printer for *Grorty Dick*, 'only for our ginger cat to urinate in it and wreck it'. Sunderland's *Wise Men Say* apologised for early fanzine layout, pleading that 'an allergy to Letraset doesn't help matters, nor does a cat who insists on sitting on the proofs'. From one-finger typing to all-night stapling, the editor's lot could be wearying. Next, they had to brave foul winds and dismal rain to foist their fanzines upon the crowd.

Front covers with their recognisable and often intricate title logos magnetised passing supporters. Colour summoned eyes, especially on dank January afternoons. Sparky, inventive design helped, as did scathing speech bubbles attached to doctored images of those running football or scurrilous jokes about club figures. They looked like no other media attached to the game, rebellious and defiantly unofficial, somewhere between pop art and *The Beano*. Still, though, all fanzine sellers faced the same question before every match: 'Is that the programme, mate?'

As that enquiry inferred, early purveyors faced a considerable problem: very few people knew what a football fanzine was. Police and stewards regularly approached, leafing through suspiciously while sellers attempted to explain the concept. Further, persuading fans to part with coins for something alien would require persistence. In the fractious environment of 1980s football, selling could be an intimidating pursuit. Adrian Goldberg remembers he and Steve Beauchampé attempting to push *Off the Ball* on the terraces of St Andrew's. 'We were engulfed by these Birmingham City supporters wanting to know what this thing was,' he says. 'I was terrified. If they hadn't liked me, there were no police around. I just managed to talk my way out of it, even though the content of the fanzine wasn't all about Birmingham City. They kind of realised I wasn't there causing trouble.' In what appears something of a fearless move, the pair travelled to games across the country continuing to peddle, 'just literally standing outside grounds initially having to explain to every potential purchaser what they were buying'.

Approaching supporters on the terraces or standing outside a ground, facing the oncoming hordes, did not come naturally to the often-shy fanzine breed. Dave Knight of *The Leyton Orientear* wrote about his first selling experience, in 1986. He and a co-founding friend, Stef, had waited 'in the pouring rain, feeling like a right pair of wallies, trying to flog them off to O's fans for 30p a throw. People were quite rightly a bit suspicious, but we sold 76, and the rest went on the Tuesday when we were at home again. We were amazed that we had sold out, and our joy was complete when the *Ilford Recorder* gave us a review and said it was sold by "rain soaked youths". Being 30 at the time, I took this as a compliment.'

Flogging *Blue Print* for the first time, Mike Kelly realised 'that selling could be enjoyable' when a slightly worse for wear City supporter 'staggered' towards him offering two palms' worth of change. 'Hands open,' wrote Kelly, the man invited him to "'Just take what you need, son."' Guy Havord of the *Arsenal Echo Echo* recalled in a later issue selling his debut copy. The Gooners were playing Chelsea on a November evening in 1987. He and a friend arrived at Highbury two hours before kick-off, sharing 'similar thoughts – How do we sell it? It was dark, everyone was rushing about' and no one knew about the fanzine. Also, 'with a picture of Lester Piggott on the front page, I think even Victor Kiam would have struggled to flog it.' The pair sold around a dozen of 700 copies at 30p each and squeezed through the turnstiles with the remainders. At half-time, Havord attempted to attract sales on the terraces of the North Bank. 'Someone bought one. . .', he wrote, 'and then the bloke behind wanted a copy . . . and the bloke next to him. Suddenly it's "ere mate, I'll 'ave one", and "ay, over 'ere". Things were looking up. What's more, Arsenal beat Chelsea 3-1.'

Selling could even induce euphoria. 'There was magic in going to the ground with a lot of these fanzines and people buying them from you,' says Jonny Owen of *Dial M For Merthyr*. 'That was an amazing buzz. I remember how the first one sold out and we were hugging each other as if Merthyr had won a match.'

Also in a seller's armoury for attracting custom – once timidity had been overcome – was the holler. Soon, shouts of 'Fanzine!' or their titles strafed the air. It became a competitive pastime, something that extended to inter-fanzine howling. 'Nobody ever out-shouted us,' claims Simon Wright of *Grorty Dick*. 'We were the loudest sellers anywhere, much to the horror of many people.' A bellowing victory away at Maine Road is remembered particularly fondly. 'There were four different fanzines there,' says Wright, 'all sold in a line. But they stood there silently as if they were going to a funeral. We were surrounded but we out-shouted them. Some of them were a bit pissed off.' Other incidents included awakening an irate night-shift worker outside The Valley, and forcing a ranting Bobby Gould, Baggies' manager, to burst from his Hawthorns office.

Irked managers, possible violence or the programme question were not the only perils of selling. Boredom was the most common nuisance. For a Saturday 3 p.m. kick-off, sellers might arrive at the ground close to 1 p.m. After sales to early arrivals there would be long gaps spent perched by lamp-posts or turnstiles. Andy Ford of Gillingham fanzine *Brian Moore's Head . . .* wrote of suddenly feeling the cold and becoming 'so bored that you find yourself listening to the pre-match musical entertainment coming out of the Tannoy. This is usually fairly dire stuff.' Then, with 3 p.m. ticking near and thoughts of finding a terrace spot gathering, a seller would be 'suddenly besieged by a dozen or so late arrivals, all wanting a copy and all waving fivers and tenners at you (in fact, anything apart from the correct money) and you're desperately short of change'.

With the game begun, the opposite problem to a coin shortage struck many an editor. Tom Davies' stewardship of *The Leyton Orientear* involved collecting money from sellers and then having to take it all to the match. 'You'd end up with 300, 400 quid in pound coins,' he says, 'and that'd be with you for the rest of your evening sometimes. That's quite a precarious existence – East London after a few pints with loads and loads of petty cash on you.' Dangers lurked during the game too. 'I nearly managed to give myself a nosebleed from banging all the 50p's from the fanzines in my face,' wrote *The Fox*'s Gary Silke of celebrating a Leicester equaliser. 'But who cared?'

HE'S BACK!.... DUE TO 'POPULAR DEMAND

. . . COPYRIGHT IRREGULAR-ITES WHICH HAVE ARISEN AFTER PRINTING HAS FORCED US TO REMOVE THE HEADING FROM THIS ARTICLE. SORRY.

When Saturday Comes

are looking for poverty stricken football fans to sell their monthly magazine outside home games this season. You get 20 % of sales revenue, but for the first two months, if you order 50 they will guarantee you £7 commission even if you don't sell out.

If you are interested or know someone who might be write to

WSC, 1-11 Ironmonger Row, London, EC1V 3QM or phone 01 253 6776 ASAP.

JUMA PUBLISHING

PRICE £5·95

ISBN 1 872204 00 7

AVAILABLE AGAIN JULY 1st

AFTER A LONG ABSENCE........

OUR FANZINE COMPILATION IS

THE FIRST- PUBLISHED JUNE 1989

THE BIGGEST -210 ACTION PACKED PAGES

THE MOST ETHICAL!- PROFITS SHARED AROUND CONTRIBUTING FANZINES

THE MOST ECOLOGICAL- PRINTED ON RECYCLED PAPER

THE BEST!- WELL....WE'RE BIASED

AVAILABLE FROM SPORTSPAGES, SOCCER BOOKSHELF AND OTHER FANZINE OUTLETS, ALSO BRANCHES OF W.H.SMITHS SHEARATT & HUGHES AND WATERSTONES PLUS OTHER GOOD BOOKSHOPS, OR BY POST FOR £5·95 + £1·50 P·P FROM THE ADDRESS BELOW.

COMING SOON- "WHERE'S THE BAR?"

THE ALTERNATIVE GUIDE TO NON-LEAGUE FOOTBALL ON SALE MID-AUGUST 1990

AND

"GET YOUR WRITS OUT" (OR EL TEL Vol-2)

ANOTHER DOSE OF THE ALTERNATIVE FOOTBALL PRESS ON SALE AUTUMN 1990

JUMA PRINTING

PRINTERS OF "THE FOOTBALL SUPPORTER" AND AROUND 40 FOOTBALL FANZINES

• VERY LOW PRICES • GOOD QUALITY •

FAST TURNAROUND • NATIONWIDE DELIVERY

• 11 YEARS INVOLVEMENT WITH FANZINES •

• FREE INFORMATION AND ADVICE •

WE ALSO UNDERTAKE ALL SORTS OF BUSINESS PRINTING

• PHONE FOR QUOTE OR PRICE LIST •

— JUMA PRINTING & PUBLISHING - 44 WELLINGTON ST. SHEFFIELD S1 4HD. Tel: (0742) 720915 —

TWO FOR JOY

The Independent Fanzine of Chorley F.C

TERRY O'CONNOR

BANNED!! - WHY THE HELL SHOULD WE CARE?

TEA BAR SOUP SHOCKER

ISSUE NO.3

50p

CHAPTER 9: SELLING AND BANNING

You're like a Ban The Bomb lot, aren't you? That's what you are. You're Ban The Bomb people.

— DEREK PAVIS, NOTTS COUNTY CHAIRMAN ADDRESSING *THE PIE* FANZINE

Once fanzines reached their audiences, sales thundered. There were curious one-time customers but more importantly legions of loyalists, impatiently awaiting another issue. Buyers were electrified by these punchy, incendiary, funny, daft pamphlets. The game had never appeared like this before; their clubs had never been written about in this style. The dull days were over. A new ritual had been added to matchday routines and for a certain type of football fan it felt like experiencing a fresh dawn. The voice fanzines had found spoke loudly to them, reinvigorating how they felt and firing thoughts that the worst aspects of match-going could be campaigned against and in time overcome. The downtrodden, demonised fan had found hope in typewriter print.

In the late eighties and early nineties, fanzines attached to big clubs sold in excess of 5000 copies of each issue. Some skirted closer to 20,000. Per capita, lower division publications often did even better. Many fanzines of Division Three and Four clubs comfortably made between 1000 and 2000 sales per issue, meaning that often a third or even a half of those attending games were buying. Postal purchases bolstered numbers.

The Sir Norman Chester Centre for Football Research made a 'conservative' estimate that 'over one million' fanzines were sold over season 1988/89. Nationwide, mainstream coverage boosted sales. Early on, *The Observer*'s magazine supplement ran a feature with the editors of *WSC*, *Off the Ball*, *Terrace Talk*, *The Leyton Orientear* and others. There were mentions on television documentaries about the state of the game, and *Saint and Greavsie* items.

No wonder those who ran football grew scared. Their boneheaded mismanagement of the game had been exposed in glorious Letraset and read about across the land. Locally, chairmen and boards were being held to account and ridicule for the first time. That, or the irreverent nature of fanzines had stoked offence. It made for tumultuous relationships between clubs and editors. *Cheers*' Meadowbank Thistle frictions, and the *Terrace Talk* duo with their Inspector Hartley encounters, were precedents rather than curiosities.

Clubs often banned the sale of local fanzines on their premises and berated editors. Much antagonism derived from the clash between worlds old and new – spiky fanzine upstarts pitched against an older, suited world. Meadowbank's J.P. Blacklaw was again behind one early example, in January 1988. 'He was actually a lovely old man,' explains *AWOL* co-editor Colin McPherson. 'He was a retired squadron leader from the Second World War, a Spitfire pilot, very decorated for his bravery in keeping the Nazi hordes away from the British Isles. He let us sell at the ground. But I think his patience finally snapped when we published the Shoplifter's Guide to Edinburgh.'

In keeping with *AWOL*'s approach of mixing football articles with those about music and other, apparently random, topics, the guide had nothing to do with Meadowbank Thistle and instead offered tips on thieving from retail outlets across Scotland's capital. Safeway in the suburb of Balerno was 'Paradise. Delightful high shelves providing maximum protection from curious glances', while the Co-op in Tollcross offered 'Wonderful apathetic staff who couldn't give a toss what you do as long as it's not too blatant'. It would not do for such material to be on sale at Blacklaw's club. 'He hauled the four of us into his little office,' says McPherson. 'There we were in our leather jackets and ripped jeans. As an example of our backgrounds, Angry Al had been kicked out of the civil service for signing official documents "Angry Al" with an anarchist sign. And Grant Collie owned the most dysfunctional pet shop in the world because it didn't actually have any pets in it.'

Blacklaw held the fanzine open at the Shoplifter's Guide and 'asked, "What is this? What do you say?" He must have been thinking, "What the hell did I fight the Second World War for?"' Somehow, the quartet's mumbled explanations saw them excused, naughty boys spared the cane. Although there would not 'be a Spitfire coming along London Road, gunning for us any time soon', it was clear that *AWOL* would now be scrutinised. Regardless, McPherson remembers Blacklaw as 'a very honest and humble man, greatly respected amongst the supporters.'

During the same month, over in Glasgow Iain Campbell received a letter from Queen's Park secretary J.C. Rutherford. *The Web*'s most recent issue, it said, had gone 'beyond the bounds of reasonable journalism and contained references which could well be construed as being defamatory'. The fanzine would now be banned from sale in the club shop and anywhere 'within the boundaries of the club's property'. Rather than criticism of Queen's Park, offence had been caused by the fanzine's disparagement of other clubs. Campbell faced his own boardroom summit. 'The President went off his head,' he says. 'He said, "It's the worst thing I've ever seen in my life, it's an absolute disgrace. How's this ever been allowed in the first place?" He'd obviously never heard of fanzines.' Peace was later brokered, but the refined ways of Scotland's answer to the Corinthian Casuals had been ruffled.

Jim Cooke of *The Pie* was another editor to experience the cultural clash that fanzines unleashed. Relations with the Notts County boardroom were volatile from the start. In issue 1, published in February 1986, the fanzine stated that any profits made would be donated to the club through player sponsorship. The following week's club programme, however, says Cooke, 'warned fans that they did not know who these "*Pie* people" were and that no money had been donated.' Yet mutual understanding was accomplished and by issue 4 *The Pie* was being sold in the club shop and sponsoring reserve and youth team players. Then, following an article in issue 9 which resulted in the barring of the fanzine from club property and necessitated a printed apology 'for the reference to a player's wife', and an offence-causing *Viz*-style cartoon strip in issue 14, the editorial team were summoned to a meeting at Meadow Lane.

In attendance too were players and Magpies chairman Derek Pavis. 'The chairman asked us what we were *really* about,' recalls Cooke. 'I said, "Well, have you ever heard of *Private Eye*?" And he hadn't heard of *Private Eye*. So I said, "Well, what about *Spitting Image*?" He looked at us with a blank face, and then he said: "You're like a Ban The Bomb lot, aren't you? That's what you are. You're Ban The Bomb people." The players looked at us with blank faces, apart from Gary Mills and Aidey Thorpe who were grinning away.' Cooke agreed to destroy the remaining 700 copies of issue 14. Further, future *Pies* would now be subject to the approval of club captain Phil Turner. 'It was bizarre,' says Cooke. 'I used to arrange to meet him and he'd flick through it and say, "It's okay." He didn't really want to read it. He was only doing it because Mr Pavis had nominated him.' In return, *The Pie* was once more permitted on club property and sold in the club shop. Soon, trust flourished and Cooke was able to build a friendly relationship with Pavis.

Co-operation between clubs and fanzines, though, remained rare. Hostilities flared across the land, and at all levels of the game, from the early years into the 1990s. Matchday brought flashpoints. Early in that crackdown year of 1988, Guy Havord's *Arsenal Echo Echo* barked a dramatic front-page headline: EDITOR ARRESTED. While selling again on the North Bank, the future Sky Sports reporter had been detained by a police officer and taken to Gunners' assistant secretary David

Miles. Miles, wrote Havord, 'took one look and said "No, we don't want this sort of thing sold in the ground."' Havord was then ejected from Highbury. 'So what Arsenal are saying,' he continued, 'is that they don't want our views. They are happy to warmly embrace each £4 to £11 fan on a match day onto their private property. But allow them to say anything but "Up the Arsenal"? No thank you.'

Police intrusion became a regular occurrence. 'We started selling at the Torquay game,' said an editorial in issue 2 of Grimsby Town fanzine *Sing When We're Fishing*, 'and were mistaken for everything from programme sellers to Jehovah's Witnesses before we slowly but surely got people to understand – everybody that is except the police.' Co-editor Lloyd Wright was detained and had his copies confiscated. The police made several justifying claims – reports Wright was selling 'bogus' match programmes, obscenity, copyright infringement, the need for a selling licence. 'The potential charges came rattling off but all were unconvincing and the result was just pointless hassle,' continued the editorial.

There must have been something in the bracing Cleethorpes air. Similar militancy – though this time dispensed by a club official – plagued Robert Nichols as he attempted to sell *Fly Me To The Moon* before a Grimsby Town versus Middlesbrough fixture. 'There was an old guy in a club blazer,' recalls Nichols, 'and he saw me selling fanzines so he told me to move. I moved back a bit. Then he came and he marched me to the end of the street, then finally let me sell it 100 yards away. He said that near the ground it was competing with the programme.'

The selling of fanzines outside other teams' grounds was a widespread feature of the growing movement. Not all customers were visiting supporters. There existed a rich and open culture of discovery in which fans enthusiastically bought their opponents' offerings. Curiosity abounded, as did a sense that no matter where a fanzine sprouted from, its values and themes would be shared. The police did not always embrace this ethos. In 1989, Stephen Gleghorn reported on his experience of selling

Newcastle United fanzine *The Mag* close to the away end at St James' Park. Watching 'the visiting fans being herded like cattle into the ground', Gleghorn had seen how 'not surprisingly quite a few have wanted to buy a copy of *The Mag* but are always stopped from doing so by the police'. He wrote how a Liverpool fan 'was actually trying to give me the money for one when I was pulled back and told to piss off by a member of the constabulary', and then before a match against Aston Villa 'a policeman told us that there was no way he was going to allow us to sell any copies to their fans – Why not?'

The boys in blue were often assisted by a fluorescent squadron: stewards. 'The response we receive from the stewards has been none too friendly,' stated an article in the December 1988 issue of *Jackmail*, a Swansea City fanzine. 'Threatened, sworn at and accused of conning people into thinking this was the official matchday programme we were selling!' *King of the Kippax* editor Dave Wallace remembers a Maine Road where 'The stewards were awkward. Selling was awkward. You had to duck and dive. Sometimes we had the bags of fanzines taken off us.' The local council added to this hostile environment, citing a by-law that banned the sale of anything other than ice cream in the streets surrounding the ground. Another City fanzine, *Electric Blue*, responded with a front cover proclaiming its latest issue to be an 'Ice Cream Special'.

The catch-all concept of 'licensing' was frequently used as the basis to halt sales. Fanzine editors suspected that football club officials were leaning on local authority allies to force the banishment of their dissenting pages. In September 1990, Trading Standards departments across London informed sellers that they would need a £322 licence to operate. They were now, apparently, likely to cause obstructions and congestion, especially during crowd emergencies. Tottenham's *The Spur* vowed resistance, pointing out that 90 per cent of its 5000 sales were made on matchday outside White Hart Lane. Purchasing 10 to 15 licences for its regular sellers would render the fanzine unviable, a fate that could be repeated across London.

Alongside editors from other fanzines, *The Spur* representatives attended a council meeting to present their case. They had found a loophole – as fanzine purveyors did not use a 'receptacle' to sell, a licence was not legally required. Their argument proved victorious. Onwards and louder hollered the sellers of Seven Sisters. It was sweet revenge for proceedings a year earlier, when Companies House had blocked their application to register the name *The Spur* due to objections from the club.

The activities of smaller clubs' fanzines did not dodge bureaucratic gunfire. Also in 1990, rivals had found harmony in Lanarkshire when Airdrie's *Only the Lonely* and Albion Rovers' *Over the Wall* united to oppose similar licensing threats. With its 'uncensored criticism', *Only the Lonely* had been greeted, reported an editorial, 'less than enthusiastically' by the club's board – 'they blew their tops and the police moved us on.' *Over the Wall*, meanwhile, irritated Albion directors by mocking the meagre £1 prize on offer for winning Rovers' Lucky Number matchday lotto. The club had 'badly misunderstood the idea behind the fanzine' and appeared to be 'hypersensitive to criticism'.

The presence of both publications was banned at their respective grounds and police informed sellers that traders' licences would be required for any further sales. An appeal was made to Monklands District Council, however, who agreed that no such permits were required. Both fanzines suspected that their clubs may have plotted the licensing ruse.

Those behind Stockport County's *The Tea Party* grew similarly suspicious two years later. In conjunction with the local council, the club had used a clampdown on merchandise stalls to bar sales of the fanzine outside Edgeley Park. From then on, *The Tea Party* could only be sold on 'unrestricted streets'.

Fans may have found their voices but many who ran football clubs did not want to hear them. Banning and bureaucracy helped them put their hands over their ears.

Not all fanzines wished for a harmonious relationship with their subject. Clubs permitting sales in their official shops, as happened for *The Web*, *The Pie* and others, was considered by some to compromise editorial independence. Even sneakily selling on the terraces brought problems and uncomfortable contradictions. 'You want to be independent, so you probably don't want to sell on club property,' feels Robert Nichols. 'I remember an instance at Stoke City with the *Oatcake*. I bought a copy in the ground and looked at the back page and it had a cartoon of the chairman being hanged.' Tom Davies of *The Leyton Orientear* says that an unspoken compromise suited both parties: 'Clubs at that point were pretty intolerant of the idea that fans could do anything other than give them a fiver and stand in squalor on a Saturday. So they didn't let us sell inside the ground, but we never really wanted to.'

Where fanzines did attempt – and even succeed – to broker club shop shelf space, what happened next often unveiled official hostility towards them. Director Tony Willoughby used his Colchester United programme column to detail why U's fanzine *Floodlight* would never be sold in the shop. *Floodlight*, he wrote, was merely 'page after page' of negativity and moaning about club affairs. 'More important,' he argued, 'is the free usage of unnecessary language that we all recognise is detrimental to the game as a whole and to supporting families in particular . . . And could we possible [sic] have some of the larger words spelt correctly?' Further north in 1989, issues 1 to 4 of *The PNE View* – a fanzine by Preston North End supporters in London – were available in the Deepdale club shop. However, said a *PNE View* editorial, issue 5 was banned – 'The reason? Too contentious!'

The Tricky Tree experienced a similarly brief stint in the Nottingham Forest club shop. 'An old friend from school's mum was the manager,' explains co-editor Andy Lowe, 'so she agreed to sell them for us. That didn't last very long because we did a back page which was extremely critical of Ron Fenton, Cloughie's assistant. It was a pastiche on Ronald McDonald with Ron as a clown. He wasn't happy, so that was the end of us in the club shop.'

An angered Clough had himself attempted to have *The Tricky Tree* banned from another of its retail stockists, a newsagent close to the City Ground. He'd visited owner Mike West, held up the fanzine and asked, 'What are you selling this rubbish for?' The fanzine had made the mistake of daring to question God. The Forest manager demanded West cease selling or he'd cut Forest's lucrative daily newspaper order. However, says Lowe, 'Mike wouldn't budge. Clough picked up the fanzines off the counter and threw them on the floor.'

Sheffield Wednesday's Trevor Francis was another manager vexed by a fanzine. One day in 1993 Peter Holmes, editor of *A View from the East Bank*, received a call while at work. The fanzine had criticised team selections and to Holmes's disbelief, Francis sought to argue his case. 'For half an hour,' remembers Holmes, 'I had Trevor Francis on the phone talking to me. He says, "You've got some good points, but there are reasons I can never tell you of why I can't select these players due to contracts, transfers and other things."' Holmes must not have been entirely perturbed: in 2025, he started up another Sheffield Wednesday print fanzine, *Everywhere & Nowhere*.

In match programmes and elsewhere, club directors frequently leaked their feelings towards this upstart phenomenon. Despite his reputation for modernisation and innovation (albeit much of it unwanted by fans), in 1988 Jimmy Hill – then Fulham chairman – could not encourage *There's Only One F in Fulham*. His reasoning, according to the fanzine, had been given as their 'comments made about "one or two of the players". He does concede, however, that "this is a free country and you must do what you feel you must do." It was rather surprising, therefore, to learn through various third parties of possible action being considered by the club to restrain us from selling the magazine inside Craven Cottage.' The perennially pompous Hill would soon sneeringly label fanzines 'these so-called supporters' magazines'.

Non-league fanzines were not spared. Late in 1989, Chorley's *Two For Joy* proudly boasted that it had 'now joined the ranks of banned publications such as *Spycatcher* and *Lady Chatterley's Lover*'. In a letter enforcing the restriction, Chorley chairman Raymond Thomas stated that *Two For Joy*'s 'attacks on other clubs' and Vauxhall Conference officials were 'unwelcome' and 'contrary' to League rule 18C. As such, the fanzine could not be sold or distributed on club property or mentioned in the club programme. Nonetheless, no one briefed the Victory Park PA announcer who at the next game proudly pronounced a new issue of *Two For Joy*. In any case, reported the fanzine, sales had climbed 'considerably' due to the ban.

Also making a virtue of censorship in non-league football was *The Elmslie Ender*, a Wealdstone United fanzine started by Martin Lacey. 'Britain's most banned football magazine' boasted its cover, after a complaint by Dagenham led the Vauxhall Conference Management Committee to block the selling of *The Elmslie Ender* at 234 non-league grounds. 'It was a tongue-in-cheek thing really,' says Lacey now. 'We never actually got banned from attending matches or anything, but it was good for publicity.'

Whether from police or boardroom, the obstacles fanzines faced merited recognition in the House of Commons. On 5 February, 1990, an Early Day Motion was tabled by Harry Barnes, MP for North East Derbyshire. It reflected how the fanzine movement was 'generally a healthy development' that demonstrated that many fans wished 'to have a say in the running of their football clubs and to comment more widely on their game'. As such, the Motion called for 'football clubs and the police to make arrangements for these fanzines to be sold at matches in the same way as club programmes are and without causing any obstruction'. It attracted only a dozen signatures, all from Labour MPs, but parliamentary acknowledgement of fanzines was testament to a thriving movement.

Beyond clumsy bans, another menace to that movement emerged. Many fanzines pushed at the walls of free speech. Little was off limits. If something could be said in the pub, it could be typed in a fanzine. Some club officials, however, were reading keenly. Combined, thin skins and attention to detail could lead to legal threats. Numerous editors received letters on the kind of headed paper that made spines shiver. Or, chilling phone calls were made, some bleakly funny as mums called upstairs to beckon sons from their bedrooms to talk with the nice man on the telephone. Begging forgiveness helped, although fanzines having scant assets to plunder via lawsuits was also a factor. Sunderland chairman Bob Murray was a typical example, as Martyn McFadden of *A Love Supreme* now casually recalls: 'He tried to sue us on six different occasions or at least start off litigation. That was his way of trying to control us when he didn't like letters in the magazine. None of them ever came close to fruition, but he was just trying to kind of clip our wings.'

Some warning shots flew further. Stapled in the centre of the third issue of *When Skies Are Grey* was a small tab of grey paper entitled 'EVERTON FOOTBALL CLUB – Apology and Retraction'. In the text that followed, a *mea culpa* conceded that an article in the previous issue had contained 'inaccurate and defamatory' statements relating to Everton's published match attendance figures. The figures used, it confessed, 'were inaccurate' and inference that taxes were being avoided wrong. Graham Ennis recalls that this first was not the last: 'We were sued about five times by various organisations including Liverpool F.C. as well. Thankfully, settlements were reached and apologies given, and charitable donations were made to avoid any damaging legal action.'

In January 1990, issue 21 of Brighton & Hove Albion fanzine *Gull's Eye* wrongly accused three directors – Dudley Sizen, John Campbell and Ray Bloom – of various misbehaviours that had contributed to the club's £3m debts. Their allegations included drunkenness, dishonesty, fraud and – as at Everton – the under-reporting of attendance figures. Subsequently, *Gull's Eye* was the first fanzine to be sued for libel, with editor Peter Kennard and writer Ian Hart defendants. *Gull's* profits were not large – around £130 per issue in 1990 – and neither man was wealthy. Following a solicitor's advice, they agreed to an out-of-court settlement. An apology and retraction would be printed, and £6000 costs paid.

In late October, the cover of *Gull's Eye* issue 30 led with the capitalised words 'An Apology', with further clarifying lines contained within. On 7 December, 1990, in the Royal Courts of Justice, during a three-minute hearing to confirm the settlement, club lawyers stated that the fanzine's accusations had 'caused the Plaintiffs considerable distress and embarrassment and they felt they had no alternative but to bring these proceedings to clear their name'. For Kennard and Hart, now began the monstrous stress of finding £6000. To do so, a *Gull's Eye* Fighting Fund was launched with FSA assistance. It invigorated solidarity and support from fanzines across Britain. Donations, bucket collections and benefit gigs saw the money paid within 18 months. While outwardly defiant, editors elsewhere did now fret about future intrusion and litigation.

Proving that fanzines rattled football clubs at all levels, Boston United's *From Behind Your Fences* was another to receive legal warnings. Its editor, Richard O. Smith, now an acclaimed comedy writer, reported that the club had barred sales of the fanzine 'from anywhere near the ground' and 'threatened all sorts of nasty legal follow ups' for non-compliance. Smith was not even clear what exactly had inspired the curb, sarcastically wondering whether it was 'Our savage request for more people to attend matches'. In a bizarre episode soon afterwards, the Kettering Town manager Peter Morris and his chairman Cyril Gingell confronted contributors to *Poppies at the Gates of Dawn* fanzine at the club's player of the year awards. They claimed its pages were overly harsh in their mocking of the club. Further, *Poppies* was 'in league' with *From Behind Your Fences*, and together the two sought 'to undermine our respective clubs in some kind of anarchic way'.

For *When Saturday Comes*, life as a nationwide fanzine provoked boardroom wrath from high-profile figures. One Premier League chairman instructed his lawyers to sue over a satirical line describing him in unflattering terms. 'Our lawyer wrote back and in effect said "Come off it" in legalese,' says Andy Lyons. 'They wrote back again and said, "Well, we've looked at your accounts at Companies House and we see you haven't got any money anyway, but we'll be watching you."' Another top-flight chairman undertook the menacing himself, calling the *WSC* office to complain about an article concerning his club. However, 'he was on a car phone and he kept going out of range for a few seconds and then coming back. It was like a comedy sketch,' adds Lyons. 'He'd go under a bridge and he'd be saying, "So I just want to say that . . .", and then there'd be this silence. We had no idea of much of what he'd said except at the end I remember him saying, "I just wanted to get a debate going, that's all."'

Truly, fanzines and football clubs inhabited very different planets. That the former shared so much in common meant a movement of unprecedented solidarity between followers of different teams was blossoming.

CHAPTER 10: A MOVEMENT BUILDS

> *It was a way to connect with like-minded people … like being invited into little gangs all around the country. It was this amazing little portal into these far-flung places.*
>
> – NEIL FORSYTH, SCREENWRITER AND FORMER FANZINE CONTRIBUTOR

As the 1990s began in a muddle of anxiety, optimism and bad trousers, there were around 250 football fanzine titles available in the United Kingdom. Most league and many non-league clubs were covered, some by multiple publications. Early on, when only a handful of different fanzines existed, *Off the Ball* had championed the idea of an Alternative Football Network. Adrian Goldberg hoped that by printing details of other fanzines and championing the FSA, fans would be 'brought together right from the start. Instead of seeing other fanzines as rivals, the attitude was: we're all in this together. We're in this struggle to get football fans recognised by the mainstream media as not all being thugs.' That vision had now been realised.

Its spread happened not only through the endeavours of editors and contributors, but because of a voracious reading public. Everywhere, previously myopic supporters now feverishly bought up fanzines concerning apparently random teams. Many purchases came outside of matchday as curious collectors sent off their coins to the addresses listed in *When Saturday Comes* or club fanzine review pages. There was excitement in doing so, a thrill in opening up an envelope and sliding out unique designs from across the country. Editors swapped fanzines with opposition counterparts not only on matchdays, but via the post too. In the creative democracy of fanzine culture, this frequently resulted in the sharing and adapting of feature ideas.

Dedicated fanzine distributors also launched, publishing their catalogues and sending titles to curious readers across the country. Bundles sprouted in garages and bedrooms. Neil Forsyth still treasures his. 'Look at this,' he says, plucking a fanzine from his collection at random now. '*A Miller's Tale*, Fareham Town. An English non-league fanzine that I was reading when I was 13 in Dundee. Amazing.' Forsyth's hoard came mostly from Alternative Football Network Distribution, run from South Wales by a man named Steve James. 'I remember his address sounding so glamorous to me,' adds Forsyth, eyes glazing over in recollective joy, 'because: Mountain Ash! Mountain Ash, Mid Glamorgan. It sounded like he was up in the American Badlands or something. He was very kind. He would take these phone calls from a squeaky-voiced 13-year-old in Broughty Ferry and advise me what he thought were the best fanzines.'

'I just found it incredibly exciting,' continues Forsyth. 'I loved reading about other teams. I loved the humour of it. The kind of punk ethos, the fact that these were just fans and they put it together.' It made him, and tens of thousands like him, feel part of something bigger. 'In that pre-internet time,' he says, 'it was a way to connect with like-minded people all around the country. You buy some English lower division fanzine and you think, "this humour is my kind of humour. My outlook on football and life is the same." It was like being invited into little gangs all around the country. It was this amazing little portal into these far-flung places.

'It's such a shame that we've lost that sense of wonder with the internet, and the sense of discovery and the idea of places seeming impossibly exotic. Sunderland and Coventry and Cardiff, they seemed like these glamorous outposts that you could connect with through fanzines. And I think it was a way to find kindred spirits that you would never meet, but you'd follow them through the pages of the fanzines.'

While Forsyth's community was remote, those able to visit London found a physical base. Sportspages – a bookshop solely dedicated to sport – opened in September 1985 on Caxton Walk, a courtyard off Charing Cross Road. In a time of so much sound and fury, its founder, New Zealander John Gaustad, was determined to show that football fans – and those of other sports – had a thirst for literature. Speaking to *WSC* a decade after opening, Gaustad summarised the shop's ethos: 'Over the last ten years we've been trying to say that you don't have to be stupid to follow sport.'

'John always saw fanzines as part of the same movement,' says former Sportspages staff member Rob Bagchi, today a journalist with the *Telegraph*. 'He felt that sport had been so maligned by publishers and that they felt that it was a niche for thickos. He was an evangelist who felt that sports writing in Britain was lagging behind and the customers deserved better. He used to talk fondly about seeing the first fanzines and thinking, "These people are our people, this is our tribe" and wanting to be part of that. John always felt that it was an essential part of the shop's identity that he had them in. But once he had one, he couldn't stop.' A pile of titles for sale became a display unit's worth. The unit overflowed on to the floor. By the middle of 1988, 1000 fanzines per week were being sold. Soon, that floor was carpeted with pillars of fanzines, Sportspages customers tiptoeing and rummaging among them.

On Saturday mornings, the fanzines room teemed with visitors hungrily buying up new and favourite titles. Many were fans visiting London for their team's away fixtures. Others had travelled further. 'Sportspages was a mecca for us,' says Archie MacGregor of *The Absolute Game*. Before opening at 9.30 a.m., remembers Bagchi, 'You would get people from Scandinavia and Germany in particular queuing outside the shop. Some of them had got off overnight buses from Europe and come straight to us.' The morning rush subsided as customers floated away to their games. Then from 5 p.m., some would return to read the day's scores as chalked on a blackboard by Gaustad, right until 7 p.m. close. Bagchi recalls one last-minute customer – 'some kid who'd been to Charlton' – arriving after seven: 'We were downstairs in the basement getting ready to leave, and we just heard this plaintive wail from the letterbox: "Have you got issue 39 of *Grorty Dick*? Have you, please?" He wasn't even a West Brom fan. So we let him in.'

One other eccentric customer lingers in Bagchi's memory. An Arsenal follower, he would appear every day at 3 p.m. and 'on a pad copy out verbatim *The Gooner* and then *One Nil Down, Two One Up*. And then he'd get very agitated if the next issue wasn't here by the time he'd finished taking his manuscripts down. And I don't know what he ever did with them. He never did buy anything, though.'

Fanzine editors and contributors become misty-eyed when recalling the shop. 'You could just spend hours in there because you'd obviously have these fanzines laid out on the floor,' says Tom Davies of *The Leyton Orientear*. 'You could just pick up and browse, and you'd buy a few, and there'd be like-minded people in there doing the same sort of thing.' *The Peterborough Effect*'s Andy Groom remembers seeing fellow editors bringing 'satchels' of their stock to be sold, 'and you would bump into guys and say, "Oh, you must be Rob from *What a Load of Cobblers*", or you must be so-and-so from wherever. You knew them by name, you didn't know them by sight, and you'd bump into them in Sportspages.' Groom relished Saturday mornings spent encountering 'nefarious characters from the fanzine world . . . For editors, it was like getting drugs down in there. You'd go and get your fix and come out with an armful of fanzines that you didn't really need but you desperately wanted. It was a magical place.'

For Groom and so many like him, the appeal of reading fanzines went beyond the social and into the cultural. They were a window into the type of football others were watching, 'the grounds they were visiting and the habits that they were going through on a Saturday. It was an eye-opener for us 20- and 30-somethings. And beyond football we discovered the bands others liked, and the clothes they were wearing. So it was a whole culture built on shared experiences.' Given the treatment and demonisation of football supporters, it was tremendously heartening and unifying to find in fanzines 'people who weren't your supposed average football supporter who wanted to fight and shout racist chants at black players. It was such an empowering time. You look back on it now and it seems similar to the punk movement, but for football fans.'

A second Sportspages branch, in Manchester, opened in 1992, spreading the love north. Other cherished shops also offered eclectic piles of fanzines, creating more clusters of like-minded customers. Edinburgh had Football Crazy on Spittal Street and Dundee Groucho's record store. In Nottingham, Jim Cooke's Selectadisc boasted a fanzine wall selling around 60 titles.

Fittingly, the regular wares of Groucho's, Selectadisc and other record shops would overlap with fanzines on several occasions. In September 1989, the Confection label launched a double L.P., *Flair*, which boasted songs about 46 different football clubs. *Flair*'s album sleeve included a fanzine directory and contributions from *WSC* and *The Absolute Game*. Similarly *Rodney, Rodney!* released the 12-track *Bananas*, whose numbers included an ode to Altrincham F.C. by Frank Sidebottom and Half Man Half Biscuit's *I Was A Teenage Armchair Honved Fan*. Profits were donated to the Football Supporters' Association.

From club fanzines fell the occasional flexi disc, which gave the world aural novelties such as *And David Seaman Will Be Very Disappointed With That*, included in issue 24 of *The Spur*, and the Sultans of Ping single *Give Him A Ball and A Yard of Grass*, courtesy of the Nottingham Forest fanzine, *Brian*. *AWOL*, equally fixated on music as it was on football, went further, pressing 1500 copies of a 7" single, which had to be transported from London to Edinburgh. 'Then outside the ground,' remembers Colin McPherson, 'you would be handling this 60-page tome with a piece of vinyl in it. People walking by would be asking,

"What am I going to do with that, at the match?" So we sold more by mail order.'

While midnight hours with scissors and glue had seemed lonely pursuits, now a community had emerged. Its members were part of a counterculture that viewed football in a certain way and defied the stereotyping and besmirching of supporters that had characterised the 1980s. Many travelled to away games differently, swapping tip-offs of pubs that did half-decent food and real ale. Outside of the game, as evidenced by flexi discs and vinyl tie-ins, they shared musical and other cultural interests.

Perhaps conspiring to formalise this baggy union, two events were held in May 1990 – a fanzine convention in Birmingham and a first National Fanzine Fair, in Stoke-on-Trent. Prior to those gatherings, however, a more organic phenomenon had begun to foster togetherness: inter-fanzine football.

'On arrival at York station at 1015,' reported *The Leyton Orientear* in April 1989, 'we were met by Frank of *Terrace Talk*, the York fanzine. "Neither Washington, nor Moscow, but York City," he commented as we were escorted to the venue, which was a pitch in the middle of a racecourse.' The *Orientear* XI were beset by woes. 'The freshly scalped Tim Hewitt,' continued the match report, '. . . left the pitch saying he felt sick, poor lad . . . Young Mark in goal was without his glasses, gloves and a defence. We were also distracted by a pitch invasion involving a mad horse.'

It was *The Web*, in Glasgow, who inaugurated these meetings of short-sighted fanzine footballers with grumbling knees. They had played other supporters' club teams, and then *AWOL*. Having picked up *The Web* in Sportspages, *Orientear* contributors made contact and an unlikely alliance between the Glasgow Southside and East London formed. The two organised games, as did players from *Dial M For Merthyr*, *The Peterborough Effect* and others. All arrangements were made by post and phone, with players lodging in one another's houses. Regular tournaments, whether for teams full-sided or of seven or five players, were instigated. Andy Groom remembers *The Web* team's arrival for the first Chaos Cup, contested between several sides in London. 'They came on a bus that had been going for 12 hours from Scotland to Leyton Orient,' says Groom, 'and they got off drunk and beat us 3–2.'

Friendships that have endured were sparked. Importantly, the idea that supporters of different teams could not mix without violence flaring was shown to be hokum. On Saturday mornings the matches were played and in the afternoons fans bonded in the pre-match pub. Tom Davies speaks of 'A whole camaraderie building. You got to know lots of people. That created the network's solidarity. People doing fanzines backed each other up and we got to make friends with fans of other clubs. So it was kind of genuinely fraternal in that regard.' Groom adds, 'It was music, football, anti-racism, anti-violence. All the stuff that mattered. It was like-minded people from different parts of the country, coming together.'

In a further manifestation of solidarity, Andy Lowe of *The Tricky Tree* and Jim Cooke of *The Pie* formed Fanzines United, a Sunday morning football club. They remain a thriving entity on the Nottinghamshire amateur scene now, with various veteran, senior and youth sides – quite the legacy for two men of different tribes who met over the counter in Selectadisc.

This unity of purpose and fanzines' vibrant and droll way of covering football began to invite positive coverage from the mainstream press. Regional newspapers dedicated much space to their local titles. Nationally, the *Guardian*'s Stephen Brierley spoke for many when, in February 1989, he described fanzines as 'one of the delights of soccer in the past few years, glorious pulsating beacons of irreverence, wit and real information'. Later that year in the *Independent*, Patrick Barclay gave deep praise for the way fanzines had eloquently struck back against the linking of football with hooliganism and inspired a vast improvement in literature about the game.

Still, though, a sneering undercurrent festered. In October 1989, Michael Henderson wrote in the *Observer* about fanzines' 'feeble or naïve' content. Despite performing a 'useful task' by 'attempting to establish a bond among their peers and rivals', there was an 'underlying strain of inverted snobbery in much of them, and the perils of tribalism and perceived superiority are worryingly clear'. *WSC* and *Off the Ball* tackled 'common issues' but were 'let down by hot-heads'.

In the presence of regular journalists, Graham Ennis of *When Skies Are Grey* and colleagues often felt like 'these little ne'er-do-wells who are doing this little grubby magazine. I think some of them saw us as the unruly younger brother. Journalists are the Fifth Estate. We were the Sixth or the Fifth-and-a-half Estate.' Andy Lyons adds, 'I think some journalists were sceptical because they felt it was intruding on their terrain to an extent, like they were the gatekeepers, they wanted to be the sources of information between the clubs and the fans, now they felt they were being bypassed.'

Fanzines, however, were not created to attract media praise. Editors and contributors wished to strike against the mainstream rather than crowbar their way into it. Positive coverage, though, demonstrated that they had made significant progress in changing perceptions of football supporters. Their articulacy and wit had been noticed.

Often through campaigning via FSA branches or endorsing their messages, there had also been victories on a local and national scale. *The Leyton Orientear* played its part in successful campaigns to have the club reinstate its full name from the disliked Orient F.C., refurbish toilet facilities, launch a Football in the Community programme and oppose racism at Brisbane Road. Further north, suggestions made in *Hull, Hell and Happiness* had been adopted, wrote Martin Lacey in his book *Get Your Writs Out*, 'including the removal of red from the match strip, the opening of a souvenir shop in Hull city centre and improvements to the match programme'. Proving that gains counted no matter how marginal, Steve Beauchampé hailed 'the success of persuading Cowdenbeath F.C. to put a light in one of their toilets'.

More widely, the ground moves and hated club mergers plotted by the men that *Bolton Wanderers Worldwide* called 'Hooligans' were defeated, and anti-racism campaigns were now firmly entrenched. Inter-fanzine solidarity had been integral to these advances. In tandem with growing Sportspages mounds, envelopes of joy and Saturday morning kickabouts, it had grown among the struggle and sorrow of contemporary events.

WISE MEN SAY

THE INDEPENDENT SUNDERLAND FANZINE

40p

ISSUE 8 – MAR/APR 1989

THATCHER IN IDENTITY CRISIS!

PART THREE

THIS IS A LOW

CHAPTER 11: ID CARDS TO HILLSBOROUGH

We'd been pushed around for so long. We'd had to put up with hooliganism, bad policing and club officials slagging us off. ID cards were the final straw.

— DAVE WALLACE, EDITOR OF *KING OF THE KIPPAX* FANZINE

As fledgling editors finalised fanzine content, government ministers drafted legislation that would change going to the match forever. The Football Spectators Bill 1988 was the consequence of how supporters had been policed and perceived throughout the decade. For Margaret Thatcher, Colin Moynihan and their singalong politicians such as David Evans, it represented an opportunity to constrict fans as never before.

Should the Bill in its proposed state become law, spectators would only be permitted to access stadiums by scanning a registered photographic identification card. Supporters were once more being steered and cattle-prodded by figures who had never pushed turnstiles. Opposition to the scheme unified fanzines like nothing before.

Multinational hooliganism on the streets of West Germany at the 1988 European Championships gave the government impetus and cover to launch their domestic proposals. In a parliamentary speech on 14 June, Thatcher had called England fans partaking in violence 'a disgrace to civilised society'. According to Liverpool fanzine *When Sunday Comes*, 800 Germans and 300 English were arrested, and only 39 of the latter charged with criminal offences. Yet it was enough for the government to propose law changes that would attempt to control millions of match-going fans. The legislation would initially apply exclusively to clubs in the English Football League, though the Bill contained provisions for extension to Scotland and Northern Ireland.

The ID card system was to be called the National Membership Scheme. It would launch at the start of season 1989/90 and see supporters pay between £3 and £5 for one-club photo passes, which would be checked by computers at every turnstile. Those computers would link to a national database able to vet 250,000 fans per hour, barring known miscreants from entry. The idea of clubs employing such technological prowess in a world of Victorian stands and roofless toilets was but one snag in the concept. The scheme would be overseen by a new state-commissioned Football Membership Authority (FMA), a profit-making PLC with the power to confiscate ID cards and ban supporters from attending games. The FMA would also approve or reject applications, maintain the national database and ensure clubs installed 'approved machinery'. Falsification of cards and entering a stadium without one were to be criminal offences.

Tellingly, the National Membership Scheme provoked a spectrum of opposition. Although their resistance was the most strident, this was not merely the cause of fanzines and the FSA. Opposing also were the Police Federation, the Professional Footballers' Association and most clubs. Further hostility came from The Football Association and the English Football League, who estimated that implementation would cost up to £38m. Clubs, they said, would lose a similar amount in revenue as unregistered, casual fans stayed at home.

The increase in costs and losses caused by installation of an ID card system would, agreed all opponents, push smaller clubs towards bankruptcy. In its very first issue, *Dial M For Merthyr* warned that 'This scheme will destroy the backbone of the game – the small club . . . Merthyr will have to install new computerised turnstiles to join the Football League if we are successful in our march. The turnstiles cost money, and large sums of money at that – not to mention the amount of casual supporters that Merthyr will lose.'

Fanzines like *Dial M* . . . placed their own dissent in the context of the era. 'Thatcher had taken on and beaten the miners,' says Jim Cooke of *The Pie*, 'and now she was going to take on the football fans.' Adrian Goldberg adds: 'Football for her was purely a law-and-order issue. There was no nuance in it. It was as black and white as a *Sun* or *Daily Mail* editorial. That was a wrong-headed notion and it united fanzines.' It was also mooted that intrinsic in Thatcher's clampdown was electoral strategy. 'There was an "othering" of the football fan about ID cards,' according to Andy Lyons, 'which fitted in with the Tory government's perception that fans were all thugs. Clamping down on thuggery would be a vote winner.'

Whether forcing all football fans to carry cards would practicably work and prevent violence was almost a side issue for fanzines and their readers. Their opposition was visceral, sharpened by years of maltreatment. 'We'd been pushed around for so long,' says Dave Wallace. 'We'd had to put up with hooliganism, bad policing and club officials slagging us off. ID cards were the final straw.' That the scheme was being proposed just as English football was hauling itself from the doldrums of 1985 also smarted. Attendances were rising and fanzines had played their role in a brightening of mood. Should the Bill pass, said Millwall's *The Lion Roars* fanzine, it 'would cause such irreparable damage to the fabric of the game that it could alter the whole structure of football in this country as we know it'.

Once again, supporters felt victimised and that they were being singled out. Aggression resulting from other pursuits seldom induced similar government interference. As a piece in *When Sunday Comes* sardonically put it, 'The worst thing about all this is that there will still be fights at discos, pubs, town centres, rugby, cricket, young Conservative balls, Mrs. Thatcher throwing the cutlery at Denis for coming home drunk again.'

Important too was the 1980s mindset. Where now we may glumly accept that we will be caught on camera many times on the way to swiping our season cards through electronic turnstiles, *1984*-steeped worries of a coming surveillance society dominated. 'At that time,' says Simon Wright, 'we were just not used to being marked and stamped and registered.' Stating its own case for opposing ID cards, Lincoln City fanzine *The Deranged Ferret* summarised the texture of the times: 'Remember that Big Brother is watching you. Since the introduction of close-circuit television cameras into grounds our every movement and every gesture is likely to have been spotted by Officer Dibble in his control room. What is more, simply because you are not in the ground does not mean that you are safe from their beady eye.'

Nonetheless, the fanzine campaign against ID cards could not be based purely on emotion. To change politicians' minds, practical opposition arguments were required. Thankfully, they existed in abundance.

Beginning with a lived experience, fanzines cited the failures and discrepancies of the existing 50 per cent membership system. 'For most clubs,' said an article in Sunderland's *A Love Supreme*, 'they were irrelevant, impractical and where they had been introduced in an ill-considered way, could be dangerous.' *The Chelsea Independent* labelled the 50 per cent scheme a 'total failure, with the membership enclosures half-empty while non-membership areas are packed. This has almost led to injury and potential riots at many grounds.'

Further, fanzines posed doubts over the new system's ability to curb violence. Hooliganism, pointed out a hundred or more titles through 1988 and 1989, almost always took place away from football stadiums. It was the preserve of violent firms in their pre-arranged meets, as amusingly portrayed in *The Bill*. The swiping of a card through a reader could not stop the slashing of a casual's pen knife in some shabby car park.

Strenuously trying to justify the new measures, sports minister Moynihan released what the tabloids called a 'League Table of Terror'. Purporting to show the shocking levels of violent crime that resulted from football fixtures, its intention was to justify the National Membership Scheme. Fanzines, though, forensically slaughtered the table's offerings and then picked at its carcass some more. It was underpinned by two feeble suppositions: that arrests for offences committed in and close to grounds amounted to guilt; and that offences cited had anything to do with football – Moynihan's figures included, for example, the theft of car radios from vehicles parked near stadiums. Within those suppositions, the table's claim that 6000 arrests were made across the 1987/88 season only translated to 0.03 per cent of all match attendees being detained. There were no details of how many were later found guilty of offences.

As one of many fanzines offering examples of the table's worthlessness, Chesterfield's *The Crooked Spireite* took one fixture, Southampton versus Portsmouth, and revealed that only three of 100-or-so Pompey fans arrested were later charged. Closer to home, continued the article, 'If you live on St. Margaret's Drive, opposite the front door of the Recreation Ground, and you don't have a television licence, then you are committing a football-related offence, for geography appears to be the only criterion.'

Through their experiences as unwilling witnesses to football violence, fanzine contributors offered solutions of their own beyond criticising the new scheme's anti-hooligan credentials. 'This needs to be solved by prevention, not punishment,' stated the *Chelsea Independent*. 'By prevention we mean the catching and conviction of those who have caused trouble. If hooligans could be caught now, then (by Attendance Orders) they could be stopped from attending matches.' Crucially, powers already existed to ban the guilty from football for five years. The legislation was not only poor; it wasn't even required.

Arguments concerned with the scheme's impact on match-going were also raised. There were fears that clubs may use their powers to seize ID cards from protestors or those questioning boardroom affairs – perhaps even fanzine editors. Certainly, turnstile queues to swipe through as yet untried technology would be lengthy. 'Apparently,' wrote Robin Jeeps in *A Kick Up The R's*, 'one company . . . claimed that the card reading would only take an extra half second for each customer. Even if we believe this fairytale, my calculations tell me that this would add nearly an hour and a half on to a crowd of 15,000.' Beyond the boredom lurked danger – the Police Federation cautioned that delays at the card-checker could lead to fatal crushes.

Once fans had been registered and approved, it was not clear who had access to their data. On several occasions, politicians and supporters of the scheme suggested that personal details should be sold to marketing companies. An article in *Terrace Talk* claimed that the Economic League – known for blacklisting left-wingers to prevent their employment – had offered to provide a similar service for football clubs, scouring newspapers to provide information. 'If they're as accurate about football supporters as they are about "troublemakers" of the industrial kind,' it concluded, 'we'd better all watch out.'

Data concerns overlapped with fanzines' opposition to ID cards on the grounds of civil liberties. The peaceable majority that comprised a football crowd were already subject to what the *Chelsea Independent* called 'the oppressive instruments of crowd control' (police escorts, fencing, CCTV) and would now be 'expected to pay for the privilege of getting state permission to go to a game'. Further, 'individuals could be punished (and to a football fan, not being able to attend a match is a severe punishment) without due process of law via the courts'. In *The City Gent*, Alan Mountford worried that ID cards would be 'a subtle form of cultural and sporting apartheid', while Wendy Michallat wondered if football was being 'used as a testing ground; more precisely that the introduction of compulsory ID is a step towards a national identity system' as deployed in continental Europe. An article in Torquay United fanzine *Mission Impossible* supposed the same: 'I do not like the idea of soccer being used as an "experiment" for a universal ID card scheme for the UK population. I accept that this is an alarmist viewpoint, but it is an important point that needs making.'

With their arguments of heart and mind trenchant and polished, it was time to mobilise. The anti-ID card campaign needed to leak from fanzine pages into football grounds. Petitions were key. The first was launched before a West Bromwich Albion game by Simon Wright's *Fingerpost* and the West Midlands FSA branch, chaired by Adrian Goldberg. With the club's support, says Wright, 'We had people with clipboards at pretty much every turnstile block – a combination of fanzine sellers, people we knew and FSA members.' Fans signed and then took copies to their local pubs and workplaces. Within a week, 10,000 signatures had been gathered.

Then, the Albion activists began to picket other grounds across the country and encourage supporters to do the same when not following their teams. 'Everyone was great,' remembers Wright, 'apart from when we did the League Cup final, Forest against Luton. There were complications with Luton. They were very, very hostile.' Goldberg and the local FSA persuaded Aston Villa, Birmingham City, Walsall and Wolves to support the campaign. Fans harbouring fierce rivalries stood together. 'It gave people a cause and made the idea of unity amongst fans a reality,' says Goldberg, 'and it demonstrated that supporters could come together from different tribes and not kick seven bells out of each other.'

It was a model replicated outside grounds in every nook and cranny of the nation. Inside their fanzines, readers would find articles deploring the Bill and pull-out petitions to circulate. Other supporters were engaged and energised by editors, contributors and FSA volunteers manning stalls and brandishing clipboards. It helped that clubs themselves often facilitated their efforts and publicised opposition to the scheme. On FA Cup third round day 1989, over the Old Trafford Tannoy fans attending a tie with QPR were asked to wave 'for' or 'against' ID cards. Masses of the 36,222-strong crowd voted in opposition.

Beyond their open-air presence, fanzines instructed supporters on how best to lobby their local MPs. Template letters were provided, plus contact lists and procedural explanations. 'Please bear in mind,' read one note in *Wise Men Say*, 'that MPs are far more likely to be swayed by reasoned argument than a torrent of abuse.' Public meetings were heralded, their messages often delivered thunderously. 'Football is the sport of the working-class people in Britain,' ran one in Middlesbrough's *Ayresome Angel*. 'Thatcher and the Tories are trying to make football fans the scapegoats for the problems in society that their policies have caused. We won't stand for it. We won't let Thatcher destroy our game . . . Come to the meeting and show the Tories what you think of their plans.'

Fanzine figures attended MPs' surgeries or badgered their representatives into meetings. Jim Cooke and his *Pie* crew met Kenneth Clarke, their MP and then Minister for Health. 'We booked an appointment and went down to see him because he goes to the County, he goes to Forest, he goes to the cricket,' says Cooke. 'But he was just toeing the party line, saying it's definitely going to happen, it's what the game needs. We couldn't believe his response.'

Enthusiasm and righteous arguments frequently encountered such deaf ears. Against all apparent sense, the government's position was entrenched. Time and again, Colin Moynihan was sent out to champion the National Membership Scheme. All good campaigns need an enemy to rail against. Moynihan resolutely fitted the bill. His became the face of numerous lampooning fanzine covers, articles and spoof cartoons. 'Forget the Headhunters, Zulus, the I.C.F. and the 6.57 Crew,' seethed

Off the Ball, he 'is the most dangerous football hooligan ever let loose on our national game . . . Moynihan's jackboot is fashioned in the guise of commonsense, bears the pattern of "reasonableness", and is laced with the illusion of democracy. It is a jackboot nonetheless, one which stomps on football's fragile recovery and threatens to trample on our civil liberties.' Over-heated, even hysterical language perhaps, but certainly in keeping with tense times and the mood of fanzine contributors.

Fanzines and the FSA co-ordinated a 'Send Moynihan Off' protest, in which red cards were waved by thousands of supporters attending televised matches. On one occasion – a game between Aston Villa and Manchester United – commentator Brian Moore dismissed their actions. The fans were, said Moore, waving their cards due to the excitement of being on television. His suggestion that the ID card scheme 'was welcomed by many fans for its many great merits,' said an article in *The Crooked Spireite*, 'only served to indicate his own complete absence of knowledge of the way the average fan feels about the way that the game is going.' Happily, Moore's highlighting of the card-waving meant that eight million viewers had now heard of the FSA.

Across the segregation fences of Villa Park that day and vaulting the physical and imagined barricades between fans everywhere, opposition to the ID cards project had unified those who paid their money and took their chances. In its creation of new obstacles to accessing stadiums, the 1988 Bill would make attending matches an even riskier pursuit. That was the last thing football supporters needed.

Going to football should have become safer after the ghastly events of 1985. Following the Bradford fire, High Court judge Oliver Popplewell led an official inquiry. It heard only five days' worth of testimony from 77 witnesses yet still concluded that changes were needed. Popplewell's report recommended the banning of wooden stands, the provision of guarded safety gates in terrace fences and improved access to grounds for emergency services. It led to legislation requiring local authority approval for football stands' fire safety measures.

The cause of most deaths and injuries at Valley Parade that day, wrote Popplewell, had been locked exits and turnstiles, which prevented escape. The main stand's lack of fencing saved many hundreds of lives as spectators were able to flee on to the pitch. Popplewell acknowledged that fences polarised 'the respective factions' and created 'a worse standard of behaviour because the fans feel they are being treated as violent people'. However, 'For practical reasons,' he continued, 'it is not possible to allow rival fans to be present at a game unless they are both segregated and penned in.'

Where pens and fences remained, they were not merely a view-sapping irritant, as fanzines had warned (see chapter three). Knitted with hostile or careless policing, they could manufacture terrifying incidents. The result was a shared sense of inevitability that English football tiptoed on the precipice of further horror. Flashing an ID card would do nothing to quell the causes of those fears.

Supporters reflected on their near-miss experiences in numerous fanzine articles. In the *Chelsea Independent*, Peter Collins recalled a March 1985 Milk Cup semi-final second leg tie with Sunderland. Police prevented access to the Shed End until north-easterners had passed by, meaning a gathering throng of home fans in which Collins 'spent an uncomfortable 20 minutes or so fighting for breath until the cordon opened and we burst through'.

Two years later, he had been at White Hart Lane when police were determined to maintain an empty terrace pen between home and away supporters. 'The crushing was appalling,' wrote Collins, 'but the police took no action until well into the second half when the empty pen was opened up.' *When Saturday Comes*' Mike Ticher, a Chelsea fan, wrote of his own experiences that day in the same fanzine. 'People were so crushed that many lost their shoes; one barrier towards the back of the section collapsed; those attempting to get out of the crush by climbing over the fence to the adjacent section were beaten on the hands by police.' The Chelsea Independent Supporters Association, of which he and Collins were members, had written to Spurs demanding answers as to why this perilous situation had developed. No answer was received. 'Tottenham couldn't care less about the safety and comfort of away fans in the Park Lane End,' concluded Ticher. 'What they have learned and put into practice since Heysel . . . is nothing.'

The 'low and shallow, mainly below pitch level' pens of Stoke City's Victoria Ground were highlighted by *Fingerpost* in that same year of 1987. 'Fronted by a ten foot fence', continued their report, they offered 'no crush barriers to prevent packed crowds swaying' and exit could only be made via 'a narrow tunnel which would become a death-trap in the event of a fire and of course, you can't possibly go into the empty pen next door'.

A further, prescient incident unfolded at Loftus Road in January 1988. For that afternoon's FA Cup fourth round tie, too many Hammers fans had been wedged into a restricted away end. There were visible, empty areas in nearby parts of the ground: seated gaps reserved for participants in QPR's 50 per cent membership scheme. The overcrowding became uncomfortable and then alarming. Three minutes after kick-off, West Ham supporters began hauling themselves from the terraces and on to the pitch. The game was suspended. Mounted officers responded, wrote Paul Caulfield in *WSC*, by riding 'onto the pitch before lining up, paramilitary-style in the centre circle. This show of force was ridiculous and totally unnecessary, and was undoubtedly aimed at impressing the watching German police.'

Injured fans were stretchered to hospital and displaced away supporters moved to empty areas. The game recommenced and, true to 1980s media form, in radio reports 'crowd trouble' was cited as the cause of delay. 'No one was killed, or even seriously injured at Loftus Road,' continued the *WSC* article, 'although they almost certainly would have been if there had been fences in front of the terrace. Ironically, there is a sign at West Ham's own ground, warning people to leave slowly, which says, "Remember Ibrox". Do they? Or Bradford? Or Heysel? Are we really waiting for yet more disasters? Or, even worse, creating the conditions in which they are likely to occur?' Although itself fence-free, West Ham's Upton Park was an apt ground to mention for an additional reason. Airport-style security metal detectors had recently been installed outside its away end, causing delays to entrance and dangerous crushing.

That same month of January 1988, Everton visited Hillsborough for a third round tie which would be replayed three times. Around 10,000 Toffees travelled and many in the Leppings Lane End, said an article in *When Skies Are Grey*, 'were herded into the two central pens behind the goal where a most uncomfortable crush occurred'. As the game proceeded, fans pleaded for the opening of gates to other, less populated sections of the stand. The police, however, 'didn't seem interested'. Blackpool supporters had faced similar nonchalance when visiting Hillsborough for a Littlewoods Cup tie later that year. According to *Hit the Bar*, a national fanzine based in the seaside town, 1500 fans had been squashed into a pen with 'acres of open terracing all around. The police were not interested in our opinions or our comfort and safety and when a coach load of late fans arrived there was a totally unnecessary crushing down from the one tunnel being used.'

In *Not the View*, Celtic supporter Jam C asked of an Old Firm derby in April 1988: 'Remember the Celtic End fans spilling out onto the trackside? Remember them trying to get into the Jungle and most being refused? Remember them walking calmly along the track and into the Rangers End?' Stoke City's *Oatcake* offered a similarly portentous recollection of a recent match at Oakwell, Barnsley: 'The Police kept asking the Stoke fans to move along but there was just no room, so at half-time they just opened the gates and let the remainder of our fans in.'

Arsenal fanzine *An Imperfect Match*, meanwhile, cited a November 1988 League Cup game against Liverpool, when 'there were the faces of panicky young kids, holding onto their fathers' sleeves in the almighty crush at the corner of the Gillespie and St Thomas Roads half-an-hour before kick-off'. The writer, Martin Smith, recalled how desperate people had been to get into the ground, with 'only an occasional' police presence that had 'no real control as people pushed and jostled in their attempts to head towards their respective entrances.' There was, he wrote, elation as fans surged into Highbury. Smith noted that, due to its lack of fences, the Arsenal stadium had recently been dropped as an FA Cup semi-final venue.

A year after their Hillsborough scare, Evertonians travelled to South Yorkshire for an FA Cup fixture once more, this time at Oakwell. *When Skies Are Grey* recounted 'a severe crush' with fans 'screaming at the police to open the gates at the front, as people were clearly hurt'. A sole officer had stared back at the swarm, before finally, after 'several minutes', he 'deemed it necessary to earn his keep and get something done. Several hundred EFC fans were allowed out through the gate and into the quieter wing sections.'

On 11 April, 1989, Liverpool visited The Den for a league fixture. Following the game, a 2–1 Reds victory, according to Millwall fanzine *The Lion Roars* there had been frightening crushes outside the ground. Fans were 'carried down' an alleyway 'by the surge of bodies'. 'Cold Blow Lane was smothered,' wrote Mark Nottingham, 'and people were climbing onto the ten-foot wall to walk past, whilst I'm told police stood idly by at Ilderton Road. Men were tightly clinging to their sons, afraid they might stumble.'

It was nothing compared to what some who had been at that game would encounter four days later.

FLY ME TO THE MOON

ISSUE 15

DEDICATED TO THE VICTIMS OF THE HILLSBOROUGH TRAGEDY.

CHAPTER 12: THE HORRORS THROUGH FANZINE EYES

Peter Beardsley cracked one against the bar, Barnes went on a run that beat two men, and not 50 yards away people were dying.

— *WHEN SUNDAY COMES*, LIVERPOOL FANZINE

There was no doubt about it, things were getting better. Despite the ID card menace and away end flashpoints, and in the face of rank toilets and belligerent policing, going to the match was, in 1989, a better experience than it had been in 1985. Hooliganism appeared to be in decline or at least hidden. Some said that many of those who had been fond of throwing fists had opened their palms to the mellowing balm of ecstasy tablets.

Attendances were up. Some clubs had even removed their grounds' fences. If the mood could not be termed cock-a-hoop, then it was at least fair-to-middling. Fanzines made an immense philosophical contribution to that shift, and also a visible one.

They were held up, dangled, wobbled and punted in the air on terraces everywhere: a menagerie of inflatable fruits and animals, brightly telling the world that football had cheered up. It all began in August 1987 when Frank Newton, soon to be of *Blue Print* fanzine, took a 5ft 6in inflatable banana with a face scrawled on to it for a Manchester City home fixture against Plymouth Argyle. The banana began to travel to away games. At The Hawthorns in November, City fans began to sing 'Imre

Banana!' to the tune of "Hava Nagila" as it was hoisted, in reference to their forward Imre Varadi. More bananas appeared at City games, plus inflatable gorillas and crocodiles.

Eleven months later, when City returned to the Black Country, the phenomenon had spread. 'At West Brom,' wrote *Blue Print* founder Mike Kelly, 'we were treated to a fight between two Frankensteins, a giant dinosaur, a Lilo wearing a City shirt, a 6ft diameter paddling pool, a 5ft Newcastle Brown Ale Can and a 4ft diameter fried egg, whilst an authentic 7ft long rubber dingy looked on.' For City's final game of the 1987/88 season, at Crystal Palace, *Blue Print* urged its readers to bring their bananas – around 50 obliged.

As 1988/89 began, inflatable mania spread across England. Some supporters chose objects that pertained to their clubs or local areas – West Ham United fans brought hammers, Brentford bees, Hull City tigers, Norwich canaries and Grimsby fish. The Bury club shop stocked 3000 inflatable black puddings while followers of Lancastrian neighbours Wigan Athletic waved baked bean tins, a nod to the local Heinz factory. Others were more obscure along the lines of Newton's banana, such as Stoke City's flaunting of Pink Panthers and Leicester City's dinosaurs. Many were random and brandished according to what street sellers had on offer, with skeletons and parrots particularly common.

Fanzine *Rodney, Rodney!* named their aforementioned album – *Bananas* – after the craze and stated that inflatables had 'tremendous significance in the fight against ID cards'. Now a country presented with the notion that every football follower was a fervent thug could see that a lot of fans were, well, harmlessly daft. *Rodney, Rodney!* gave an inventory of 50 inflatable varieties that had been witnessed on the terraces, including pterodactyls, cigarettes, toucans, astronauts, Father Christmas, A.L.F. (Alien Life Form), USS *Enterprises*, rowing boats, ocean liners, double-decker buses and more. The fanzine retailed its own exotic range (from 'airplane (Top Gun)' to 'Large Zebra' via 'Hamburger' and 'Spitfire').

In March 1989, *When Saturday Comes* temporarily exported the blow-up fad to communist Albania. On an organised trip for readers to watch England play in Tirana, Andy Lyons noticed members of the party had packed their inflatables. 'The Albanians looked very baffled,' he recalls, 'because people would carry these big inflatable fish and bananas and things. I don't think we tried to persuade them that this is what it was like in the West, but I think one of them had a mask of Thatcher stuck over the top of a banana.' Lyons remembers too the change in mood inflatables brought to domestic games, citing a visit of Grimsby Town to Wimbledon. The away side scored but 'none of their fans seemed to have inflatables. Then they turned away from the pitch, pulled them from under their seats and they all appeared like a synchronised performance.'

Perhaps wishing to diversify, having launched this mass trend, *Blue Print* and Manchester City began to accompany their displays with fancy dress. On Boxing Day 1988, 12,000 Blues invaded Stoke. Few were wearing normal outfits. Of the journey south, Frank Newton wrote how 'it seemed that every car had blue scarves flying out of the windows or contained a rabbit sitting next to Henry VIII . . . whilst a taxi arrived at a house in Manchester to be greeted by four gorillas and the muffled words "Take us to Stoke".' Then having arrived, 'Three musketeers walked past complete with swords and frilly hats. A gladiator was munching a hamburger on a street corner and a Christmas tree was walking in the general direction of the ground.'

Home and away fans drank and laughed together, and in the Victoria Ground Newton observed, among others, 'a very official looking Postman Pat and a Humpty Dumpty who insisted on sitting on the wall'. As they ran on, each Manchester City player threw an inflatable banana into the crowd. 'It was as if we had just won the cup, cheering and celebration as far as the eye could see . . . There were balloons floating in the air, thousands of bananas waving and other weird and wonderful inflatables bobbing up and down in the crowd.' Predictably for the late 20th-century incarnation of City, Stoke won the game, 3-1.

After the final whistle, said Newton, 'A rather cold looking fan wandered past wearing a snorkel and flippers and not much else, a group of pixies were spotted heading towards the car park, whilst Rambo complete with machine gun (with a City scarf tied round it) walked the other way.'

Perplexed, some clubs reacted to the inflatable craze with suspicion. Further, it was claimed that 6-foot inflatables being held in the air could block other fans' views. Bans were announced at Everton and Charlton Athletic. For a short while, Arsenal sold inflatables in their club shop but barred supporters from taking them into Highbury. Such isolated actions did not detract, however, from the transformative effects these spectacles of the terraces were having. In the eyes of an indoctrinated public, they helped rehumanise the alien species that was the football fan. The blow-up hammer suddenly removed from that fan the fear of the truncheon, and Postman Pat had come on as substitute for Sergio Tacchini. Yes, things were definitely getting better.

At 2.30 p.m. on 15 April, 1989, Julie Pritchard was selling her fanzine, *Brian*, outside Hillsborough. There were not many takers. Most of her fellow Nottingham Forest supporters were inside. 'And why were we all in so early?' Pritchard wrote in the next issue of *Brian*. 'Because there was such a crush to get in last year.' In the previous season's FA Cup semi-final, the same two teams had met in the same ground. As well as facing their own uncomfortable arrivals, from across the pitch followers of Forest had seen cramming and ebbing. The difference was that, somehow, in 1988 no Liverpool fan in the Leppings Lane End had been killed.

Nineteen eighty-eight was not even the first warning from recent history. Pritchard had been in the Leppings Lane End four years earlier to watch her team play Sheffield Wednesday. 'I saw nothing of the first-half,' she wrote, 'as I was crushed up against the back wall with half-a-dozen armpits in my breathing space, and I was scared.' Andy Lowe, editor of another Forest fanzine, *The Tricky Tree*, was there that day too. Lowe and his cheerful gang of 16- and 17-year-old friends had tried to enter the Leppings Lane End's middle pen but, 'It was absolutely rammed. Just so packed. Bear in mind that we were young and pretty fearless, but we actually came out of it because it was so frightening and went and stood around the side. There'd been problems at the Wolves v Tottenham semi-final in 1981 as well. That lack of crowd management going into Leppings Lane was obviously a regular occurrence.' As Pritchard simply wrote: 'Hillsborough was waiting to happen.'

Eyewitness accounts of that day written for fanzines were a first draft of monumental history from the bottom up; the view from inside the death-trap terraces and the other end as Forest supporters looked on in helpless horror. They were complemented by the reflections of those who had been at matches that day across Britain. These urgent fans' eye views could not be read elsewhere. They burned with bewilderment, loss and rage.

Kevin Howson, a Liverpool supporter with a ticket for the Leppings Lane End, told his story in Lancastrian fanzine *Hit the Bar*. He and his brother had arrived early and chosen a spot in one of two central pens on the paddock. By 2.45 p.m., 'the crush where we were was becoming unbearable, one man was desperately trying to get his daughter who had passed out away from the crush, another man next to me had his arm broken back in the pushing and shoving.' Howson continued: 'Apparently the two side sections were well under capacity at this time, but no attempt was made by police, stewards or the Public Address to move people into these areas.' From the other end, the Kop, Andy Lowe recalls noticing that those same side pens remained 'quite empty. But you could see the middle pens were unnaturally full. We thought they were going to delay kick-off, but they didn't.'

The game began and the crush intensified. 'Because of the fencing,' continued Howson, 'there was nowhere the fans could go, escape routes to the front and both sides were cut off by 7ft of iron railing. Fans who were climbing over the top of each other to try and escape over the fencing at the front were being pushed back into the crowd by the police.' He and those around him heaved fellow supporters 'up into the arms of supporters above us . . . again without the help of the police'.

Meanwhile, on the pitch, reported Liverpool fanzine *When Sunday Comes*, 'Peter Beardsley cracked one against the bar, Barnes went on a run that beat two men, and not 50 yards away people were dying.' Attacking drama had caused fans to surge forwards, worsening the compression. Of Beardsley's effort, recounted Andrew Saxton in *Rodney, Rodney!*, 'the cheers came from only one section of Liverpool supporters. Behind the goal, they were concerned with escape.' They had already begun to clamber over the fence and cascade on to the pitchside behind Bruce Grobbelaar's goal.

'Everything started to unravel,' says Lowe between pauses, an ebullient man suddenly overwhelmed by sadness 37 years on. 'You're just stood there and you don't know what's going on. There were quite a few people around us calling out Liverpool fans – "Oh they're always causing trouble" and "Get off the pitch". But I genuinely remember saying at the time "Something's not right here." So almost as it happened, we're going "this isn't crowd trouble."' Saxton, another Forest fan, recalled his own 'fury as [Liverpool] supporters began scaling the perimeter fencing. As that policeman ran on to tell the referee to stop the game, frustration was widespread.'

When it became clear that hell had been unleashed, anger turned to silent disbelief. Then, there were scuffles among Forest fans eager to clamber on to the Hillsborough turf and offer help. A horror film was spinning and reeling in front of them: 'More people flooded onto the pitch,' wrote Saxton. 'Only when bodies were brought and placed on the grass in front of us did we, collectively, realise what was occurring. Ambulance sirens wailed in the distance. A friend suggested that some people were dead. I refused to believe him. Fans, laying prostrate on the pitch, dead, in front of me? No way.'

Similarly disbelieving, in *Brian* Steve Hanley wrote, 'Even when the ambulances came on, it didn't click that people had died. I saw someone having their chest pumped, and someone said they could see a fan with their head covered. The penny began to drop but we still didn't *know*.' In the same pages, editor Julie Pritchard saliently asked why police 'were ordered to line up in front of our end with the fucking dogs?' Perhaps instead of forming a pointless cordon, she suggested, they might have utilised their first-aid training.

Advertising hoardings were being torn away for use as stretchers, but still no information was given until, remembers Lowe, 'an announcement came out: "Can any qualified medics come to the front of the fence?" You just stand there and eventually you start to acknowledge what's happening and the fact that there are people who've died. And it lives with you now.' Saxton recalled hearing nothing for 'at least 40 minutes' and then on the Tannoy 'Kenny Dalglish muttering something about co-operation with emergency staff'.

Those impromptu stretchers were needed in the absence of the real thing. 'The emergency services took *so* long,' said *When Sunday Comes*, 'seeming to confirm that the authorities aren't, or certainly weren't, concerned about our safety, treating us as just a law and order problem. Well, are they happy the problem's not as bad as it used to be? Ninety-five [now 97] people not as bad.' Kevin Howson of *Hit the Bar* noted more official tardiness as the police failed to unlock gates opening on to the pitch until after fences had been ripped away by desperate fans. Then, even open 'it was apparent that they were far too small to be of much use, one 3ft wide gate for a whole pen hardly constitutes a viable escape route'.

At 4.15 p.m., the match was finally, formally abandoned. 'Someone's coat pulled over their head,' recorded *When Sunday Comes* of the Hillsborough scene, 'you know what that means. Then a man indicating with his hands: 50. That could only mean one thing. Sitting in numbed silence, dragging ourselves home, tears as you make the most important phone call you'll ever make. MUM – I'M OK!' In his article, Howson thanked locals for letting fellow Liverpool fans phone home, and Lowe recalls 'big lines of desperate people at phone boxes'.

From the Forest stands, he and 20-odd thousand others shuffled away, desperate to awaken from the nightmare they had watched powerlessly. 'Pathetically,' recounted Saxton, 'we were told to keep our tickets.' The tie would be replayed, even if football now had no meaning. With few words worth sharing, those fortunate enough to be leaving walked past ambulance jams and through silent Sheffield streets towards cars, coaches and trains. 'We went to see Liverpool F.C. get hammered,' wrote Steve Hanley, 'and we saw people the same as ourselves die. Those of us at Hillsborough on 15 April 1989 spent 100 minutes staring at the most awful event of our lives.' By the time some of them arrived at Sheffield station, *The Green 'Un*, that fine city's Saturday evening sports paper, was on sale. '50 DEAD', cried its headline.

There were league matches in every corner of the land on that vile and sunny Saturday. As they were played, bleak rumours and snippets bounced from terrace to main stand and back again. Club officials muttered partial news from stadium public address systems. Then, after the final whistle, that sainted ritual of listening to the scores arrive from elsewhere was replaced by something altogether more sinister. It was as if a dark figure had entered stage left and turned a gentle drama into a ghastly horror.

Reading their accounts, it is possible to imagine a black and hissing serpentine cable spreading devastating tidings to grounds and motorways from Pittodrie to Plainmoor. 'The first I heard of the disaster was from a policeman inside Moss Rose,' wrote Barney in Dartford fanzine *Light at the End of the Tunnel* of an away trip to Macclesfield Town. He 'said that a stand had collapsed at Hillsborough, killing five people.' An editorial in Glasgow Rangers fanzine *Follow, Follow* related how 'We began to get garbled accounts about "the trouble" . . . at first, it seemed as though there had been a pitch invasion and fighting was taking place, then we heard two were dead, then four. . .'

That afternoon, Manchester City fans and their bananas saw a 4-0 reverse at Blackburn Rovers. 'But were any of us in the 7,000 or so strong following of Blues that day really bothered?' asked R. Neale in *King of the Kippax*. 'I, for one, wasn't.' Dire tidings had begun at half-time. 'The rumour was that there had been some trouble and unbelievably five people had died,' wrote Neale. 'We were shocked but when the full report came over the radio driving home, we were numb with disbelief.'

With misinformation spreading, not everyone was dumb-struck into silence. *The Spur* reported on its team's fixture at Wimbledon, and a half-time announcement 'implying that there had been deaths due to pitch invasions in Sheffield'. In 'ignorance', sections of both sets of supporters had chanted, 'We hate Scousers, we hate Scousers. . .' At Old Trafford, half-time Tannoy messages during a home loss to Derby County provoked similar reactions. Appalled United fans wrote to *Red Issue* to express their anger. One was 'sickened' and 'ashamed to be a Red . . . I just hope those bastards feel as guilty as hell'. Another had been 'disgusted . . . I would just like to send a message to them: "You are sick and need help." I don't know how anyone can start cheering because innocent people have been killed.'

There was, of course, another FA Cup semi-final played on 15 April – Everton v Norwich City at Villa Park. Scousers in blue would have known – and loved – many Reds who had journeyed that day to South Yorkshire; whispers would be particularly agonising.

On a terrific spring day, Norwich fans made for the colossal Holte End. There, at 2.15 p.m., they faced a scare of their own. 'Someone tripped as new arrivals irresponsibly caused a crowd surge,' wrote Brian Spurrell in Crystal Palace fanzine *Eagle Eye*, 'and another person was being helped away after an apparent faint.' An article in Norwich fanzine *The Citizen* reported how '10,000 inflatable canaries were hoisted proudly as the teams came out, and at this moment we were blissfully unaware of the carnage that was going on 70 miles up the road in Sheffield.'

Spurrell was present to take notes for a forthcoming book following that year's FA Cup through the rounds. He watched 10 minutes into the game as the stadium scoreboard flashed the message: 'Game suspended at Hillsborough – more news later'. Then, Spurrell turned on his radio for what initially sounded like 'the all-too-familiar Hooligan Incident scenario', but soon became something altogether different. 'Overcrowding, ticket allocation controversy, Graham Kelly being interviewed,' he continued, 'serious injuries, advertising hoardings used as stretchers. During this report Pat Nevin scrambled a botched clearance into the goal to put Everton into the lead. The match no longer held my full attention.'

News of unconfirmed fatalities drifted in at half-time. The second half began and five people were known to have died. Norwich pressed for an equaliser, and from every stand came songs. Rumours were not enough to prick the atmosphere. The final whistle, though, heralded 'a subdued walk back to Aston station, with fans around me stopped in their tracks as they heard the news for the first time. Norwich had lost a game of football; at least fifteen people had lost their lives. As *Sports Report* began, the figure 74 came loud and clear over the airwaves, like a hammer blow between the eyes.'

Toffees only began to understand the devastating happenings at Hillsborough as they left Villa Park, their victorious swaggers immediately giving way to intense worry. 'Instead of the party atmosphere,' reported *When Skies Are Grey*, 'the journey home was a morose affair as thoughts turned to friends/relatives who had made the trip to Sheffield. Being Evertonians the disaster affects us all. We all know a Kopite. Be they good or bad, they are still the people who we meet in all walks of our lives.'

Final whistles peeped everywhere and legions of shell-shocked fans drifted from grounds big and small. What they half-knew from radio reports, Tannoys and rumours was bad. The truth was worse. 'It's a long time, if ever,' commented Sunderland fanzine

Wise Men Say, 'since we've watched a game with so little involvement as we did at Oldham. The news coming through from Hillsborough rendered meaningless all else that was happening. Numb, we left the ground still listening as the latest on the disaster was being relayed, and travelled home to be confronted with full visual horror. It's hard to describe our feelings. Grief, sympathy, shock, helplessness, frustration, anger. How could it happen?'

Peter Collins of the *Chelsea Independent* had been at Filbert Street as his side surrendered their 27-game unbeaten run. Collins left the ground in disappointment, but as the scale of Hillsborough became clearer, 'a tremendous, irrational guilt' swayed through him. 'Guilt that I had even presumed to take that afternoon's events in Leicester so seriously,' he explained, 'guilt that I had stood on a terrace screaming blue murder at the unfairness of it all when people were dying – dying?!? – on a similar, bigger stretch of terracing further north. Guilt that I had anything to do with football at all.'

Many now stumbled to their transport home. 'We got back to our buses,' wrote Ian Kelly in Hamilton Academical's *Crying Time Again*, and were 'hit with the feeling that people had been killed doing what we do every Saturday: watching football. It could so easily have been us.' An editorial in *Follow, Follow* related how 'On the bus we sat listening to the radio about what had happened. Slowly everyone began to realise just how serious the situation was. The usual banter and mucking about went by the board as Peter Jones gave a very graphic account of the events and their aftermath. On other buses we passed, the same air of sadness seemed to prevail as they too sat stunned.'

Jim Cooke of *The Pie* travelled home via train after a Notts County game in Preston. At Manchester Piccadilly, supporters of both United and Derby boarded. At Sheffield, they were joined by distressed Forest stragglers. 'We were all in the carriage like sardines,' says Cooke, 'and we thought, "Something could kick off here". There was one big guy who stood up and said, "After what's gone on today, there's going to be no trouble anywhere on this train." And it was brilliant. And I thought on a normal day, that would not have happened, would it? I think people realised what solidarity there should be between fans.'

Some fans supped post-match pints in near-silent pubs, with Hillsborough footage flickering away on corner televisions. The death toll kept rising like some devil's ticker tape. An article in Leeds United fanzine *Marching Altogether* recalled, 'That sinking feeling in your guts . . . the slow horrific realisation that nearly a hundred people had died, suffocated under the weight of their own fellow fans . . . We stared at each other in the pub afterwards and let the horror sink in . . . It could have been us.'

Sunday morning arrived with Liverpool now a city blind to the blue spring sky. Diane Collinson typed her feelings, which would soon be published in *Hit the Bar*. 'I went to the match yesterday and am still feeling sick and disgusted by it all,' wrote the Liverpool fan. 'I'm sick because I saw dead bodies being carried out, and left in the goal area.'

Collinson was clear: 'ID cards, all-seater stadiums and tearing down fences won't solve the problems. Treating supporters like human beings, instead of animals, would be a start.' Switching on the television would not have been a good idea. Shortly after 1 p.m., Luton Town chairman David Evans MP appeared on BBC One's *On the Record* to demonstrate how ID cards would have prevented the previous day's tragedy. The government were not for turning.

As fans spent the day and much of the week to come in horrified reflection, one reaction – as expressed in *Marching Altogether* – was common: it could have been us. 'It was a situation that any of us could have been in at any time at any away game and has chilled us all to the bone,' said a *King of the Kippax* editorial. In *The Mag*, editor Mark Jensen concurred: 'This could have happened anywhere at any time as it is the culmination of years of abuse directed at football supporters, 99% of whom would never dream of getting involved in any so-called "football hooliganism".' Fanzines and the FSA had offered both warnings and preventative measures; at every turn, deafness to their pleas once more reigned.

In tandem with anger, a sense of pointlessness draped itself over fans. Some despaired that the Liverpool versus Forest tie would be replayed, and the season completed. Many found the idea of going back to a match unpalatable. In *Rodney, Rodney!* Andrew Saxton reflected that 'It is all trivial. 1988/9 as a season is nothing, and I am annoyed at that. Isn't there a sense of falseness about everything now?' Bristol City's *Bountyhunter* felt for a while that it was 'pointless to carry on with something as trivial as this fanzine . . . When people die at a football match, it makes our complaints with the board of directors seem pathetic. What have we got to moan about?'

Yet understandable melancholy quickly gave way to positive action or, at least, doing the only remotely helpful thing possible: raising money for Hillsborough victims' families. From the Saturday following the disaster, header and footer declarations began to appear on fanzine covers – 'Includes 20p Donation to Hillsborough Disaster Fund' or 'All profits donated to Hillsborough families'. In pubs and outside grounds, buckets were trembled and coins and notes tossed in generously. It meant renewed, tightened solidarity between fanzines and fans from different clubs.

One viewpoint of the Hillsborough disaster seldom sought was that of Sheffield Wednesday fans. The setting for this terror was, after all, their beloved ground. It is startling to think that within a fortnight they were back there to watch their team, with the buckled crush barriers and breached fences of the Leppings Lane End cloaked in tarpaulin. In their fanzine, *Just Another Wednesday*, the lyrics to Cole Porter's 'Don't Fence Me In' appeared above news of a Hillsborough poetry anthology written by Liverpudlians, and the bank details of the disaster appeal. Through fanzine pages, we know that Wednesdayites mourned for those lost in their home.

Similarly moving, *The City Gent* published a Hillsborough Disaster Appeal Special Issue with all profits – £500 – donated.

'Yes, I'm mad,' wrote Mick Dickinson in its pages. 'I'm mad that 95 people had to die after the 56 at Bradford. . . I'm sick of being treated as scum just because I love football. . . I'm sick to the back teeth of being a scapegoat for somebody else's bloody mistakes.'

At the start of the 1989/90 season, *Blue Print* reported on a further display of solidarity. Following Manchester City's visit to Valley Parade, both sets of supporters chorused *You'll Never Walk Alone* together. Hands were shaken, hats, scarves and badges swapped. Typically, television crews were already dismantling their cameras and so missed this outpouring of goodwill. As a letter to the fanzine sighed, 'All the good things that are done generally receive little or no publicity and are undone in a moment by one mindless act.'

Impromptu shrines popped up outside many grounds. Fans of various clubs travelled to the Leppings Lane End or the Shankly Gates and left tributes. One account of a visit to the latter appeared in *Brian*. Written by 'The Universal Football Fan', the article poignantly depicted quiet streets where no children played. There were 'massive queues for the florists', who would 'accept no money but point to the collection boxes instead'. Having queued, the writer spent three hours reading every tribute, from 'long anguished letters' to those that just said 'Why?' There too was a group of weeping schoolchildren 'paying tribute to a departed classmate by scrawling felt-tip messages on the barrier by his accustomed place on the Kop'. Despite the profound sadness of the scene, 'the sheer spectacle of it all was remarkably uplifting, all those thousands of flowers, elaborate tributes to single red roses, all interspersed with scarves and programmes and bedspreads and teddy bears, whole lifetimes' collections of memorabilia, donated as much for the comfort and unity of those left as in memory of those departed'. Much of it had come from supporters of rival clubs.

'The Universal Football Fan' knew that what he or she had seen at Hillsborough – 'the small boy prostrate in his desperate father's arms. . . the fat man with his head covered and his arm dangling limply by his side' – could not be forgotten. Nor would there be 'dignity for those herded to die like animals'. Yet should the silent majority now 'be raised to protest, to ensure that this time it really won't be allowed to happen again, then perhaps all those people will not have died in vain'.

It feels remarkable – preposterous, even – that nearly a full card of Division One matches were played the week after Hillsborough. The exception was Liverpool's home match with Arsenal, moved to 26 May. In *Five to Three*, Reds fan Dylan Jones described going to games that were 'utterly insignificant compared to the misery inflicted on the bereaved families' in the weeks after the tragedy. Every Liverpool match 'meant increasing publicity and tension. I felt like an exhibit on show every time I watched a game, especially away from home. The opposing supporters would applaud us, the minute silences would be almost total and even the police would be much more accommodating than usual.' Then came 'the grand finale against the Arsenal. Everything about the game was so unreal – a Friday evening kick-off, a delayed start because of traffic jams (there's a new idea!), no fencing.' Running from the Anfield tunnel that night before their acclaimed victory, each Arsenal player carried a bouquet of flowers.

In the Kop, they applauded and thought about those who were not there.

A KICK UP THE R's

50p (OR MORE

HILLSBOROUGH SPECIAL

we've witnessed your triumphs...
...and envied them

now we've witnessed your sufferings...
...and we share them

A QPR FANZINE.

CHAPTER 13: AFTERMATH AND ALL-SEATERS

I find no logical argument whatsoever to suggest that as one is sitting, the art of punching one's neighbour. . . becomes any harder or easier.

— *GOLDEN DAYS*, MAIDSTONE UNITED FANZINE

The cover of *When Saturday Comes* issue 28 bears the headline, 'Hillsborough: Unanimous Verdict'. Beneath it in a square are four black-and-white photos, each with a speech bubble. 'It wasn't our fault' says Graham Kelly of the Football Association. His words are repeated by images of South Yorkshire Police chief Peter Wright and Margaret Thatcher. The fourth image shows a football crowd standing on a terrace, crammed rigid. Their speech bubble reads, 'Oh well, it must be our fault again.'

It is the most famous fanzine cover of all time and bitingly captures events immediately after Hillsborough. Fans, maintaining the decade's narrative to its conclusion, were blamed for what happened to them.

On the morning of Monday 17 April, Andy Lyons and three colleagues sat in *WSC*'s temporary office. 'It was very quiet,' he says, 'no one was really talking. We were all still a bit shocked.' Issue 28 was not due to be published for a fortnight, and so they had time to consider their cover. Lyons stuck with the usual process of drafting ideas and collecting black-and-white sample prints from a nearby picture agency, Colorsport, to choose from.

'In the intervening couple of weeks,' he adds, 'there'd been daily coverage of Hillsborough. There were lots of comments by politicians, football administrators and South Yorkshire Police. So we decided we needed to do some sort of representative cover of them all and a crowd shot. It was obvious that we needed to make a point about so much blame being attached to the fans on the day. We needed to kick back against that.'

The tabloid press was viciously certain of who to blame. On 19 April, *The Sun* published its heinous 'Truth' front cover, labelled by *When Sunday Comes* as 'sick, disgraceful, depraved and *not* the truth'. While the tabloids shrieked about robbed corpses, and while broadsheets hurled accusations at Liverpool supporters, fanzines formed the print defence.

The rattles of Hillsborough Disaster Appeal collection tins could not drown out fanzine contributors' outrage and anxiety. Defenders of the press reaction cited their right to freedom of expression. 'Freedom to stick cameras in the faces of the grieving,' responded Ranting Roger in Dartford's *Light at the End of the Tunnel*, 'freedom for reporters to lie their way into hospitals in order to try and get interviews with the injured fans. . . freedom to print unsubstantiated stories about supporters. . .'

In *Terrace Talk*, Frank Ormston despaired at papers 'competing to see who could publish the most harrowing picture of someone being crushed to death', and their hypocritical 'banner headlines proclaiming that the fences must be torn down. Well, of course they must, but could these really be the same papers who, 15 years ago, were saying things like, "Fence these animals in"? You bet they were.'

'Instead of trying to help the injured,' wrote Frank Newton in *Blue Print*, 'photographers' "professionalism" led them to take nice close-up photographs of people being crushed against the fences.' Cardiff City's *Bobbing Along* said their 'snapping away at the helpless dying' was 'voyeurism at its crudest level and sordid in the extreme'. A *Gooner* article asked, 'Can you imagine it? Trapped in that awful crush. It was all they could do to cry for help. And all they got was some press vulture pushing a camera in their face.' Fanzines noted that despite their skulduggery, no photographic evidence emerged of *The Sun*'s allegations that fans urinated on corpses and pickpocketed the dead.

Tabloid lies also included allegations of 'sporadic fighting' between fans. The only brawls Kevin Howson of *Hit the Bar* witnessed erupted when journalists and photographers 'pushed their way through the crowd of distraught fans and attempted to photograph the dead and dying who the fans were trying to carry away or revive'. Notably, Andrew Saxton's *Rodney, Rodney!* piece was followed by information about the new – and successful – 'Don't Buy *The Sun*' campaign.

The demonisation of supporters meant that they were repeatedly held responsible for what happened in Sheffield. It also meant that the scale of football's hooligan culture was wilfully embellished. In *Hull, Hell and Happiness*, an article by Kieran Burns asked, 'Was that 10-year-old lad who died a hooligan? Was the 62-year-old bloke a hooligan? Or how about those two sisters? Were they only there to cause fights? Unlikely.'

Fanzine anger frothed and was accompanied by desperate attempts to understand what had occurred. 'The $64,000 dollar question on all our lips this week has been *Why?*' wrote Ron Wylie in Ayr United's *Railway Ender*. '*Why* football? A pastime which is meant to be about enjoyment and fellowship. . . strong men wept last Saturday, but no one should feel ashamed of that.' Through matchday experiences, most contributors instinctively knew that dreadful stadium facilities, the police and authorities were more likely to be culpable than Liverpool supporters.

However, unsurprisingly given the misinformation being wafted out by the media, some blamed their fellow fans. In Norwich City fanzine *Never Mind the Danger*, one contributor wrote, 'The mud-slinging which followed was both disgusting and pointless. Quite simply, everyone was to blame – and that includes the supporters.' Others alleged – repeating mainstream explanations – that late-coming or ticketless drunken fans had forced the crush at the front of the paddock by pushing from its rear.

Red Issue printed a horrifying letter that epitomised negative attitudes to Liverpudlians still detectable now. Although its author, MUFC Derbyshire, felt sorry for 'the majority' of Liverpool supporters that day, much 'if not all' of the blame, he or she wrote, should be attributed to 'thousands of Scousers arriving too late, too drunk'. The pseudonymous author continued, 'remember Heysel I say. . . The people of Liverpool are blind to any criticism of their team or their so-called loyal supporters.' Replying, a *Red Issue* editor had, after 20 years of away games in Sheffield, 'already come to the conclusion that the South Yorkshire police were as much use as a one-legged man in an arse kicking contest'. The recently announced Hillsborough Inquiry (later known as the Taylor Report) would, he felt, put 'most of the blame' their way.

Football supporters knew that they would be held responsible, though perhaps not by their own brethren. Generally, they used fanzines to shape a different narrative, one that would eventually, decades later, come to be accepted as the truth. Further, they howled for change: Hillsborough must be, felt the angered optimists, a watershed after which the game could be realigned so that it served and belonged to the people that loved it most. The disaster *had* to be the moment after which they were finally listened to. Going to the match *had* to become safer. 'Years of mistreatment of fans finally culminated in the Hillsborough Disaster,' said *When Sunday Comes*, 'and now a basic requirement must be met, that the authorities actually *care* for the supporters.'

A fiery, strongly worded piece in Sunderland's *Wise Men Say* by Jack Hughes was typical: 'No longer can we accept the attitude of police which, hitherto, has regarded the football supporter as being nothing less than a criminal. No longer can we allow ourselves to be frogmarched from coach to ground. . . Only animals are put in cages. We are not animals, just people who love watching football. We must be treated as such.' An editorial in Derby County's *Mutton Mutineer* seethed in tandem. Supporters had been far too tolerant of 'violence, decrepit grounds, bubonic catering, medieval toilets, racism, corruption within our clubs and thuggish behaviour by the police'. *The City Gent* whistled a similar tune: 'There has got to be a shift in the emphasis within football. Supporters have got to be given more consideration. We pay to keep the businesses afloat, yet we have no access to shares, to decision-making, to comfort. We are never consulted about major decisions which affect our club. So far as most football clubs are concerned, we are a necessary, but troublesome, sort of revenue which must be kept at arm's length.' It was time to fight back.

Restrictions on the movement of away supporters should now end, felt the revved-up dissenters, and hardline policing be replaced with considered stewarding. Ground facilities must be improved starting with the ripping down of fences, altering the material circumstances of watching football and encouraging more families to attend matches. An age of supporters being considered humans, not suspects, could begin. As Liverpool fanzine *Through the Wind and Rain* put it: 'The days of sitting by while we are treated like scum are over.'

Margaret Thatcher disagreed. Within days of the tragedy, she reaffirmed her commitment to ID cards. Colin Moynihan was dusted down and wheeled out to extol once more the scheme's virtues. Fanzines despaired anew, with fresh and bleak weight added to their opposition. 'The ID scheme,' wrote Mike Baker in *Sing When We're Fishing*, 'is at best irrelevant, and has now been shown to be potentially lethal.' It may, said *A Love Supreme*, 'literally kill off fans. Not without foundation many people worry that the introduction of computerised turnstiles will make events like Hillsborough more common.' Even the most modern equipment could malfunction; a stuck gate would have horrific consequences. But 'why should a football tragedy get in the way of a government on the rampage?' asked Lincoln City fanzine *The Deranged Ferret*.

Then in January 1990 the Hillsborough Stadium Disaster Inquiry published its findings. Lord Justice Taylor was critical of the proposed ID scheme and pronounced that it would not have prevented what happened on that fateful afternoon in Sheffield. Reluctantly, *finally* the government abandoned its plan.

Although it was the pen strokes of an establishment figure that persuaded them to do so, there can be no doubt that the key-taps of fanzine writers contributed to the ID scheme's abolition. It was '. . . a major turning point for football supporters in England,' said *The Mag*. 'For the first-time football fans have got together and fought a co-ordinated campaign . . . The work of the fans has undoubtedly influenced both the government and Justice Taylor.' Jim Cooke of *The Pie* agrees. 'The ID cards idea didn't work,' he says, 'because we all got together and stood up to it. The level of solidarity between fans of every club is unimaginable now, because everyone's on their own. We were trying to say that we're all members of the working-class game, it's our game and let's keep it that way. We don't fight each other; we fight the enemy and the enemy at that time was the government.'

By contrast to his declarations on ID cards, many of Lord Taylor's other findings were deeply unpopular. 'Taylor has made a cop-out by not recommending the removal of all perimeter fences,' said Watford's *Mud, Sweat and Beers*, '. . . as long as fences remain, there will always be the potential for another disaster.' In *Terrace Talk*, Steve Wyndham set this omission within a wider context of national disregard and decay. The decision, he wrote, 'should not surprise us. After all, the disasters of Piper Alpha, the *Herald of Free Enterprise* and Clapham show that safety is fairly low on some people's lists of priorities.'

In national Welsh fanzine *Five to Three*, writer The Practitioner said that Taylor had criticised 'the fact supporters are shepherded around like prisoners of war but made no recommendations to prevent this happening'. Further, he had ignored 'the main lesson of Hillsborough', that '95 supporters died not by virtue of police falling below their normal standards, but because of standard police behaviour. They treated the fans like animals, herding them into cages and then ignoring their pleas for help until it was too late.'

Elsewhere, Taylor's recommendation that racist abuse at matches should become a specific criminal offence was welcomed, although questions surrounded the police's credentials for enforcement. There were criticisms, too, of the report's failure to endorse supporter involvement in running the game and Taylor's lack of football insight and out-of-touch attitude to the game. In *A Load of Bull*, Dave Worton wrote how 'Justice Taylor shows that he doesn't understand what football is all about in one ludicrous quote from his report – "On scoring a goal a player often rushes straight towards the perimeter fencing and either affects to climb it or, with fists raised and shaking, goes on his knees to excite response from supporters. Little has been done to stop such demonstrations which are calculated to hype up the fans into hysteria."' It was a paragraph also highlighted in *Through the Wind and Rain*: 'how many supporters even see what footballers are up to when we have just scored? We're usually too busy jumping on each other to notice!'

The Liverpool fanzine felt Taylor's tone to be patronising. Down the years, supporters had 'become truly sick and tired of paternalism, of having our heads ruffled and told "not to worry, we know what's best for you".' The report felt like more of the same.

Another Taylor recommendation that induced bafflement among seasoned match-goers was the idea that clubs should provide more pre-match entertainment. This would, he wrote, entice fans to arrive earlier for fixtures. Yet those who had seen clubs' concept of such entertainment were unconvinced. 'Marching bands', said Shrewsbury Town fanzine *A Large Scotch*, are 'not popular with everyone.' The thought launched recollections of 'men on stilts, flame throwers, police dog displays and at Ipswich they had animals from a nearby zoo'. Bristol City once staged a pre-match monkeys' tea party. 'However,' continued the article, 'one of the monkeys dressed in a Bristol City shirt decided it would be more fun to hang from one of the posts.'

Of even greater concern than the likelihood of roving simians was Lord Taylor's recommendation that stadiums should become all-seater. Within days of the report's publication, the government announced that his proposal would be passed into law. Clubs would have to pay for stadium alterations themselves, finding funds to adapt concrete terraces to seating areas or construct entire new stands. It would apply across the game, meaning a lower division team whose lonely supporters stood in ample space on deserted terraces should redevelop on the same principles as top-flight clubs with bustling kops. *Five to Three* called the government's intentions 'a non-subsidised edict to convert early 20th Century theatres of football into 21st Century decency'. Fanzines opposed the idea vehemently and on multiple bases.

Most seriously, they repeatedly pointed out that rather than helping in an emergency, seating areas delayed evacuation. 'Do we really want to wait until people die in a fire, hampered by having to clamber over the seats meant to protect them?' asked *Sing When We're Fishing*. Nor would seating solve access and egress issues, the most likely causes of danger. There was an inference in the Taylor Report, and by politicians, that seats would combat hooliganism. Given that most violence now occurred away from grounds, it was unclear how such a conclusion was reached. Mike George of Maidstone United fanzine *Golden Days* was even more discombobulated: 'I find no logical argument whatsoever to suggest that as one is sitting, the art of punching one's neighbour . . . becomes any harder or easier.'

The financial implications of enforced renovation works were another cause of dissent. *Five to Three* also labelled the proposals 'crippling for smaller, poorer clubs . . . The government has said they won't help out and by that token they have condemned perhaps a dozen or more football clubs to death within the next ten years. Survival of the fittest? Or callous murder?' During the inquiry, several fanzines highlighted, Lord Justice Taylor had visited only two grounds of clubs outside the top flight.

Other fanzine contributors worried about rising ticket prices due to reduced capacities, and the hushing of matchday din. It was, *is*, an ageless truth that the loudest voices belonged to standers. Atmospheres would be lessened further still if directors chose to embrace the executive box cheque over the turnstile fiver. 'It appears that they are now trying to price fans out of the market,' wrote Mark in *Fly Me To The Moon*, 'replacing cages with directors' boxes.'

A contributor to *Depleated*, a Luton Town fanzine, had already lived this sound-sapped, sanitised future. While noise had still emanated from the Kenilworth Stand terrace, those who wished to join in from other parts of the ground were trapped by neighbours and seating area conventions. 'Everyone around you is made of stone,' said the writer, 'but you still can't move closer to the chanting few or jig up and down with them harmlessly, because you're a prisoner in a world of crammed-in plastic seats. It's a goal! You enjoy what is traditionally among the best moments of your life, jumping up in the air – and back down to earth onto the seat in front, grazing both legs and tripping over the seat rest at the same time.'

There were other pitfalls. On a terrace, said Albion Rovers fanzine *Over the Wall*, 'you can, when need be, move away from bampots'. Seating meant confinement; being trapped next to reeking drunks, bigots, wailing moaners or foul-mouthed bores. It also meant knees rammed tight against the ridge of the pew in front, and borderline hypothermia from perching motionless for 45 minutes rather than toe-hopping and wandering around on a terrace. In *Against the Tide*, a fanzine for female supporters, Sheila Seacroft detailed the joys of terrace life. 'You can move around,' wrote the Sunderland follower, 'change your view, fetch a drink or go to the loo without forcing a whole row of other people to stand up for you.' Moreover, 'You can jump up and down, sit on the ground in despair, hug your friends (and strangers!). There aren't many places where women can stand and shout to their heart's content.'

Should compulsory seats clutter Maine Road, *Electric Blue* pledged rebellion. 'When we've forked out an arm and a leg to sit next to the psycho with the airhorn and the bad breath, behind a stanchion and under the hole in the roof for a whole season, I know what I'm going to do. I'm going to get on my seat and stand up. . . and scream probably. Like we did in the old days.' The communal delights of standing areas were imperceptible to those who had never sampled concrete and crush bar. 'We like to laugh and joke with each other when we're playing well and grumble together when we are not,' said *No One Likes Us*. 'Taylor doesn't really understand the terracing wit and mateyness, or realise people speak to friends in different places or change ends so they are closer to the goal [their team are attacking].'

The Shankill Skinhead, a Manchester United fanzine, saw the potential eradication of standing as a leap towards a purified, Americanised version of football. It was being driven by those who could not understand terrace culture and feared its 'passion, togetherness and power' and were 'trying to destroy it. It is vital for us all to kick up as much fuss as we did over the ID card if we want to preserve our right to stand.' The key was to make standing safer rather than abolish it – 'a terrace with a carefully monitored capacity, adequate barriers and clear exit routes'. As *Through the Wind and Rain* highlighted, terraces per se had not been responsible for Hillsborough; people had died due to 'bad organisation, bad policing, unfair ticket allocation, fences, poor medical facilities'. Seating would do nothing to make these failures 'harmless rather than lethal'.

Fanzines steered campaigns against the all-seater tide and were buttressed by the support of the FSA. 'We didn't accept Taylor's assertion that admission prices wouldn't be affected,' says Craig Brewin, chair from 1990 until 1994. 'We thought it would inevitably be a first step toward gentrification and exclusion, particularly of young people. You couldn't just put seats on the terraces either. We didn't accept that standing up is inherently unsafe. It's a design problem. But we recognised that supporters behaved differently from the time of the White Horse Final [1923 FA Cup Final]. We, including the fanzines, were raising issues of crowd management and stadium design well before Hillsborough, including the use of fences.'

Both fanzines and the FSA recognised the need for radical modernisation but demanded the right to choose between sitting and standing. 'It is not that we are traditionalists clinging to our terrace origins,' wrote Endy in *FMTTM*, 'we want the standards improved but we demand changes that are necessary, not that cut across our needs.' Once again fans' views had not been solicited, and more diktats from those who had never heard of Bovril were raining down. In Birmingham City fanzine *Tired and Weary*, David Parker suggested that money designated for seating areas should be spent on all-round improvements that would 'provide safe, habitable, covered accommodation' with 'decent refreshments and social facilities that encourage fans to arrive earlier'.

Petitions objecting to the all-seater mandate appeared within the pages of fanzines and as flyers. 'All-seated stadiums,' read one widely circulated in Scotland, 'will do little to combat the problems they are designed to.' Instead, they would '*ruin* many clubs because of reduced crowds', 'bring admission costs to an *even higher* level', and fail to make football safer or combat hooliganism. Messages were also localised, and petitions applied to particular grounds. 'We the undersigned,' read *FMTTM*'s version, 'believe that MFC has blatantly disregarded its supporters in its decision to make Ayresome Park an all-seater stadium. We feel it will be detrimental to the character of the stadium, and the enjoyment of the game for many people.'

Across in Liverpool, even before the Taylor Report was published *Through the Wind and Rain* predicted that Anfield's Kop would become 'full of those cheap, red plastic efforts we've seen in other parts of the ground. No, not inflatable flamingos, seats.' The stadium as it was had become meek enough – seats in the Kop would muzzle it further. Over the next few seasons, *Through the Wind and Rain* and others supported anti-seating crusades. In the spring of 1993, *Another Wasted Corner* advertised the No Kop Seats campaign's 'Stick your seats up your arse!' sit-down protest at a forthcoming match against Spurs.

Not all Liverpool supporters agreed. Three years earlier, R.J. Roberts wrote to *Through the Wind and Rain* arguing that the Taylor Report should be heeded. 'There is nothing beautiful about being crushed against barriers, walls or fencing,' said Roberts' letter. 'Ducking under barriers, crawling between people's legs is not comfortable. . . Being pushed and shoved constantly throughout a game is annoying.'

Certainly, standing on congested, unregulated terraces with their swarms and surges and barbed fences seemed, in the wake of Hillsborough, a grotesque relic. Disturbingly, near-miss incidents recommenced only months after the tragedy. Halifax Town fanzine *The Sound of the Shay* peered up through the divisions to report on the opening weeks of the 1989/90 season. Half an hour before kick-off on its first day, intense pressure at the turnstiles at Plough Lane had seen 'children being crushed from all sides' and 'no announcements about when the gates would open'. A week later at Highfield Road, Everton supporters faced a 'crush' and 'pandemonium' while entering the stadium. One supporter approached a policeman and asked, 'Haven't you learnt anything from Hillsborough?' The officer had replied, 'You bloody well got in, didn't you? Go and sit down.'

In December, scores of visiting Leeds United supporters attending a fixture at Middlesbrough purchased tickets for the home end from touts. Identified by police, they were escorted to the already full away end terrace, where displaced fans stood in gangways, with children crowded at the front. The enclosure was now, estimated Leeds fanzine *The Square Ball*, 400 to 500 people over capacity. In *The Hanging Sheep*, another Whites fanzine, it was reported that 'whilst young children were being lifted over the fence, the police were still putting more fans into the section via one of the gates in the fencing'. According to *The Square Ball*, 'the overwhelming feeling was that Middlesbrough could have been another Hillsborough. That it wasn't is due to luck rather than sensitive or intelligent crowd control.'

Later that month, a letter in Boro's own fanzine, *FMTTM*, highlighted another of Ayresome Park's dangerous defects – the hazardous nature of exiting the Holgate End. 'First battle your way out and down the pathetically narrow exits and stairways,' wrote Mad Dog of Billingham, 'then squeeze down the alley picking your way through the horseshit, dustbins, potholes puddles, cobbles and rubbish. Then dodge the parked cars and flying police cars in Ayresome Street. If all that isn't hard enough, do it in the dark. There isn't one light at this part of the ground. It only takes one person to slip and someone at the back to push and we all go down in the shit together.'

There remained a sickness about how football was governed and policed. Yet supporters had long lived with that chronic malady. Improbably, indefatigably they had continued going to the match and maintained the warped kind of love only a fan knows. On fanzine pages, their experiences of the game were uniquely and richly chronicled.

ROUGH GUIDE TO EASTER ROAD

(1) Our Alex. (2) The Gruesome Twosome. (3) Peter "Bad Boy" Cormack. (4) Drunken Hacks who would rather be at Ibrox. (5) "Hibernian" supporters (G-reg Volvo in the club car-park) (6) Winners of competitions in the Matchday Magazine (behind a pillar) (7) The more distinguished visiting scumbag. (8) North Stand rumbletums. (9) "Miller Must Go" faction, (ex Auld/Stanton/Blackley must-go) (10) Lazy coppers who get paid for watching the match.
(11) Police control box resembling one of the pie huts.
(12) Hibs Kids.
(13) Terracing Tams: "I remember the days when...'
(14) Sadistic Hibbies here for the sole purpose of slagging corner takers.
(15) Terracing Bams.
(16) Archie "candy-floss heid" Mac-Pherson.
(17) The now famous Easter Road pie hut home of Scotland's only chilled pies.
(18) The Neil Orr fan club ?
(19) Non-colour wearing loonies.
(20) Scarf & badge seller (does he ever watch the match ?)
(21) Gaping hole in the back wall of the terracing (a Kenny Waugh idea maybe ?)
(22) Those bloody pillars.
(23) McEwans Lager sign to make the Huns feel at home.

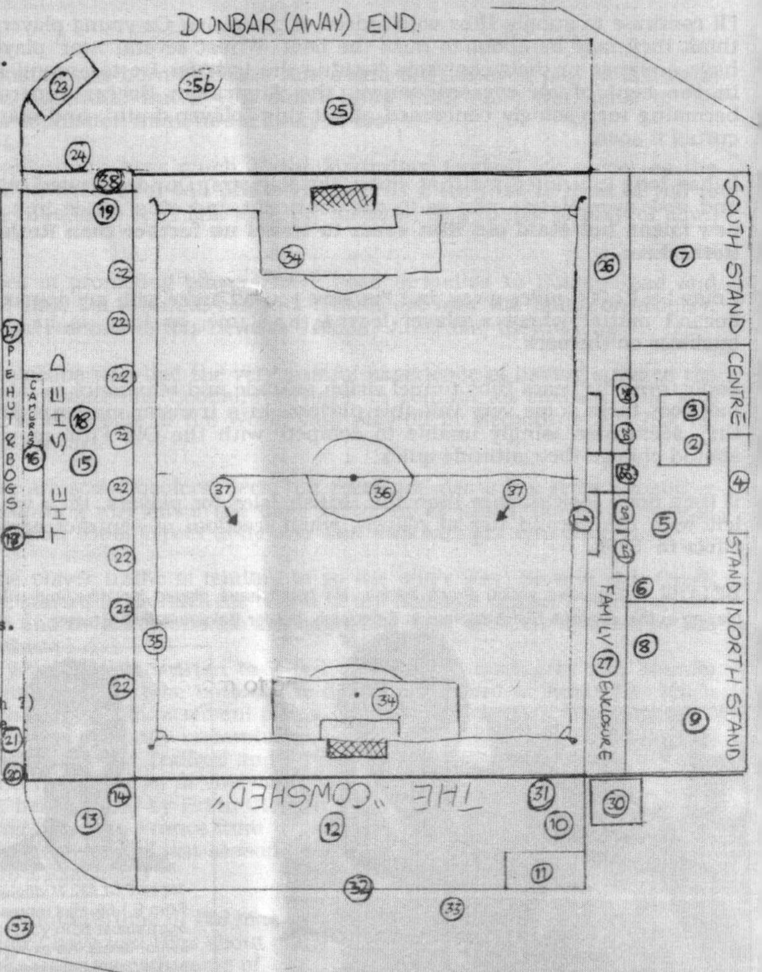

(24) Opposing non-colour wearing loonies (who usually depart around half-time). (25) Unwashed hoardes of scumbags. (25)(b) Where the three St Mirren supporters stand. (26) Green seats to make the Huns feel at home ? (27) Family Enclosure which left many "Enclosure" regulars homeless. (28) "Radio Hibs" DJ who grows more unpopular by the week, with his Stock,Aitken and Waterman crap. (29) The Executive Yuppie Hibernian supporters, who pay for the privelege of sitting in a box, out of their loose change. (30) useless block, with a mysterious cameraman on top. (31) Huns,Celts and Jambos who steal our tickets. (32) Stumps, where our infamous "Electroni scoreboard once stood. (33) Huge queues ("come early, and we'll open the gates at half-two for you") (34) Walters/McCoist diving zones. (35) Linesman who never fails to attract widespread abuse. (36) The Bxxxxxd in the black. (37) Beginning of the Dundee United passback range. (38) No Man's land.

PART FOUR

TURN AND FACE THE STRANGE

CHAPTER 14: GOING TO THE MATCH

It is a meeting place of cultures, a source of wit, a font of wisdom . . . It has a smell unique to itself – fresh beer, stale beer, fresh Oxo, stale pies, pipe tobacco, cigarette tobacco, illegal tobacco.

– *BEYOND THE BOUNDARY*, OLDHAM ATHLETIC FANZINE

Throughout hardship and in spite of all the danger, fans' devotion to football remained intact. For all the mud slung and hazards heaped in front of them, on a Saturday afternoon they knew where they wanted to be. Perseverance and doughty affection for their teams kept them going along to games and reporting in fanzines on what they saw, heard and ate. Their written observations offer a portal on to the terraces during a time just before football changed immeasurably, and an account of their role in that transformation.

For all their ranting, groaning and sarcasm, fanzine contributors were prone to bouts of affection. Being there, following, bawling, jeering, cheering *mattered*. Fans were, wrote Mark Evans in *Dial M For Merthyr*, 'Together as one. Drawn forward with one common aim. Blooded with a masochistic streak which to the uninitiated would seem pointless and pitiful . . . But to them it is life. The be all and end all of their mere existence.'

An article in *UTD/United* – unsurprisingly, the only joint Dundee United/West Ham United fanzine – further captured this spirit. 'Despite bad food, toilets, policing and all the rest,' said an editorial in June 1989, 'the game of football is ours, and enjoyed by many millions of people each week . . . it's not the surroundings that count, it's the fellowship . . . We put up with it because we love our game – we love our team and we love our respective grounds.'

Nothing expressed this gritty love more than supporters' dedication to attending away matches. Each fortnight they disregarded the police pestering and general hostility experienced last time to book coaches and board trains again. The football fan was cargo, fetid meat, a hostage in a bobble hat. He or she did not travel freely and whimsically, but was transferred, processed and jostled. And still they went.

Their doggedness was not completely unthinking, nor blind. Fanzine writers pondered the philosophy of it all. Few places were better venues for an existential crisis than away ends. In Oldham Athletic's *Beyond the Boundary*, a piece by James Barrett struck a contemplative tone. 'What strange phenomena, what untold mysteries of human behaviour motivates the away supporter?' wondered Barrett. Perhaps 'he is a nut, a misfit, a fanatic' or the 'backbone, the lifeblood and the very essence' of a club.

Venturing away could be a lonely pursuit, even when standing among fellow travellers. It seemed to invite incident and insecurity, farce and mortification. An article in Oxford United's *Raging Bull* by Andy Urban-Smith trickles with typical angst: 'A cold wind blows onions out of my hot dog and sprays the man next to me on the terrace. It's ten past two and United supporters are still outnumbered 2:1 by the Vale stewards who huddle behind the corrugated iron cladding and stare gloomily into the distance across the rooftops and chimneys of industrial Stoke. A splatter of rain comes and goes . . . Later, at the other end the net suddenly bulges sickeningly. Deep sound around us while two sides of Vale Park effervesce in waves of relief. Final whistle. A long return journey stretches ahead.'

Away ground guides were a golden staple of most titles, describing and forewarning readers about imminent trips. Helpful, snarky and often beautifully illustrated, they represented the concerns of all away day regulars and perfectly encapsulated the fanzine ethos of being simultaneously serious and useful, and wildly caustic and sardonic. The guides covered all elements of the away day – travel and transport, food and drink, ground description and local police temperaments. They demonstrated that football was a social undertaking in the face of media slurs and governmental suppression, and reflected the fact that to follow your team in other towns and cities required a certain level of adventurism. Match destinations were very rarely tourist towns, and it was in this manner that the average football fan saw a real version of Britain in the 1980s and 90s untroubled by guidebook devotees.

Portrayals of others' home grounds were rarely flattering. They made for some of the best pithy fanzine writing. Carlisle United's *Foxy Ferret* said of Feethams, 'Darlington has no place in the Football League, and their ground should be bombed.' The main stand at Airdrie's Broomfield Park, said Dunfermline fanzine *Walking Down the Halbeath Road*, 'looks like the Munsters House', while Cappielow was 'The most god-forsaken place on earth, perpetually raining, foggy and cold.'

Of Vale Park, Chester City's *Hello Albert* advised, 'the only way to keep dry is to try and get arrested.' Halifax Town's Shay offered away fans 'the enviable choice of either standing behind the goal in the rain, gazing forlornly across the wide expanse of the speedway track . . . or, if the Pennine torrent reaches epic proportions, huddling under a corrugated iron roof to look through the gaps in the most closely meshed fence you've ever come across.' Town's own fanzine, *The Sound of the Shay*, said of Scarborough that 'The arc in the fencing behind the goal gives you double vision'. Another seaside club, Blackpool, was even less hospitable, said Torquay's *Mission Impossible*: 'The visitors' enclosure is separated from the rest of the ground by vast areas of empty space resembling no-man's land between East and West

Berlin. I half expected to find a machine gun nest on the floodlight pylons.' Molineux's South Stand, said *The Fox* meanwhile, 'is a thinly disguised mountain. Take sandwiches and a YHA card if you're thinking of walking down to the front.'

Architectural appraisals were accompanied by food and drink reviews that occasionally read like witness statements. Beyond standard issue bad-mouthing of ropey pies, words showed that there was a desire among fans to enjoy eating and drinking on matchdays, and to be treated humanely; to be, in short, bestowed with the same courtesies as cinema-goers or followers of cricket.

The culinary ordeal often began pre-match with a catering van visit. Seductive fried onion scents did not always mean ambrosian fayre. Hygiene was rarely a priority. In *The Fox*, Matt the Mod described a visit to an unnamed wagon near Filbert Street. There, the owner 'picked up his prongs and dipped them into what can only be described as a primaeval swamp and pulled out what looked like a soggy circle of carpet'. The carpet, it transpired, was the burger Matt had ordered and now, 'with a deft movement of his right arm', the van man 'shook off a couple more droplets of grey water and slapped it between two pieces of stale bread . . . he started fishing about in the washing up water for the onions, eventually finding some he threw them on top of the burger along with a spoon of water. "Ketchup?" he threatened. I shook my head glumly.'

To dodge the van meant risking the in-ground food hatch or hut. An anonymous writer in *Terrace Talk* was not a fan of Bootham Crescent's, 'where you are served at length by someone with dirt under their fingernails' and food was 'usually lukewarm and there's not exactly a wide choice'. The experience grew worse in retrospect as, looking up to the club's lounge windows, 'very warm and well-fed large groups of people' could be seen carrying 'sandwiches, cups of tea and coffee, pints of ale and glasses of Scotch'.

Most focus, however, fell not on grubbily aproned or tabard-sporting servers, but on what they supplied. Pastry mattered. Many fanzines published pie ratings and league tables. In East Fife's *Bayview Bulletin*, a series named Taste Tests set out the typical intentions of these pastry dossiers. 'Armed only with our trusty notebook,' wrote intrepid compilers Sam and Ellis, 'a napkin, a packet of Rennie's (spearmint flavour) and a stomach pump . . . we'll tell you which pies are most likely to be edible and even enjoyable, and which ones aren't even fit to give to the dog (and taste like they've been made from a dog).'

Words matched ambitions, with Cowdenbeath's pies lauded for offering 'Hardly any gristle at all', Queen's Park's bemoaned for their saturation levels ('I wouldn't say it was greasy, but when I bit into it, I thought that I was drowning') and away supporters warned against trying their own East Fife pies: 'Stodgy and disgusting . . . an absolute disgrace . . . You just have to look around at the amount of half-eaten pies lying on the terracing to back this up.' Grease was the word north of the border. Hamilton Academical's *Crying Time Again* proposed that a Motherwell pie contained 'So much hot fat' that 'I turned it upside down to drain it, and to my total disgust, the fat just kept on running . . . and running . . . for ages. It was like going for a pee after 10 straight pints.'

Middlesbrough's *Fly Me To The Moon* warned ahead of a trip to Blackburn Rovers, 'Don't touch the pies – especially meat and potato – they're permanently too hot to eat, full of spud with a bit of corned beef in the middle.' Hartlepool's 'bright pink sausage rolls which almost dare you to eat them' also received an honourable mention. In *The Peterborough Effect*, sacrificing himself to the nation, Botulism Bob constructed a comprehensive Good Pie Guide. Rochdale's possessed 'a crust that would do Ketton Cement justice', York City's was 'A deep round, undercooked gristle bonanza' and Doncaster's 'A treat for lard aficionados'.

If the stereotype that football supporters were slightly obsessed with pies echoed among fanzine pages, so too did a love of Bovril. Stoke City's *Oatcake* ran an Away Day League in which the 'Bov' at each ground visited was reviewed. Newcastle were guilty of putting 'Pepper in the Bovs yet again', while thankfully at Watford 'The Bovs were superb (and only 30p a throw), being the real draft stuff'. In *A Love Supreme*, a feature named 'The Bovril Beat' rated refreshments liquid and otherwise. Due to the 'inconsistent temperature of the Oxo', Hereford had lately suffered 'a slight fall from grace'. Craven Cottage confirmed that the 'capital city is a cultural desert as far as half-time snacks go', their own Mackem Bovril continued to be 'state of the art', while down the Durham coast, Hartlepool's catering hatch had 'the dubious distinction of having the rudest old woman in the Football League'.

Refreshment was a serious business on Wearside. In fellow Sunderland fanzine *Wise Men Say*, Brian Matthews concocted a lexicon of the tea bar. 'Grimples' were 'the white furry lumps only found in half-time pies, which you can't decide whether or not to chew, and usually end up swallowing whole.' The 'inevitable scalding of your fingers from the plastic tea cups no matter how carefully or slowly you walk' was named 'Tipcup', while a 'Scurb' was 'the not inconsiderable lump of congealed matter that is revealed upon draining your cup of Bovril'. A. Mitchell of *Brian Moore's Head . . .* was another hot drinks connoisseur. 'You can actually taste the Domestos in the coffee here,' wrote he or she of Cardiff City's offering, 'If left for 10 minutes it can be served in slices.' Brentford offered the 'worst' tea in the Football League, which Mitchell likened to 'Stagnant swamp water with tsetse fly topping. No taste – if tested by eminent scientists, will probably prove radioactive.'

In Meadowbank Thistle's *AWOL*, a piece named 'When The Going Gets Tofu' tackled a very different dietary issue – the famishing, occasionally revolting existence of being a vegetarian on a football away visit: 'I do remember the early season game up in Forfar on a lovely hot day, with everyone getting stuck into mammoth steak bridies. That was almost acceptable but the wafting smell of dead sheep from the adjacent slaughter-house and the humid stifling atmosphere made it a nauseating experience in the extreme . . . Maybe someday we'll be able to turn up at a few grounds expecting at least an alternative.'

Beyond the burger queue lay the pitch and an actual sporting contest to consider. Previewing fixtures, opponents' deficiencies were given much fanzine page space both collectively and individually. Descriptions departed majestically from those found in club programme 'meet today's visitors' features and regularly employed stereotypes, regional or otherwise. Blackburn Rovers fanzine *Many Miles from Home* called Bristol Rovers 'Patchy, rustic and slightly simple', Barnsley 'Brassy. Gauche. Proletarian . . . Training sessions consist of kicking lumps of coal around back streets. . .' and Portsmouth 'Spitters, shirt pullers and pickpockets'. As 'the second division's most bestial presence', Millwall merited special attention, not least because their 'offside trap consists of barbed wire, Semtex and a trip switch'.

The highest vituperation, however, was reserved for a fanzine writer's own darlings. Nothing said 'I love you' like a description of a full-back as a 'brainless tube' (*Hibs Monthly* on Neil Cooper) or a centre-forward as 'a total shiter in the tackle' (*Killie Ken* on Gordon Smith). *The Leyton Orientear* boasted a particularly fine line in such demolitions. During one game, 'Foster tackled like he was wearing hush puppies. . . Sitton was a disaster area. . . Cornwell dropped back to bring his own particular brand of play (i.e. whacking the thing whenever it comes near you) . . . Wells played as if he had something in his eyes or had had one too many at lunchtime.'

Beyond individuals, collectives were also bemoaned. 'The midfield would hardly have been missed had all three locked themselves in the toilet', said West Ham United's *On the Terraces* of a 1–0 *victory* at Fratton Park. 'Five-nil to fucking St Johnstone,' fulminated Aberdeen fanzine *Northern Light*. 'An utterly spineless display. . . Abject, craven, gutless.'

Fully recognising the slings and arrows of following most football clubs, the same Mark Evans, who so beautifully captured the delights of being besotted with a team, summarised just a few weeks later the abject pain loyalty could cause. After a 7-1 loss to Gloucester City, he used his *Dial M For Merthyr* editorial to morosely philosophise how 'We've all had times when we've sat and wondered what we were doing with our lives. Just such a moment for me was during the Gloucester disgrace.' That afternoon, he'd contemplated the logic behind his support and 'couldn't think of one concrete reason, just an insane need to belong I guess. All around me my fellow Martyrs seemed to be in the same resigned trance.' Perhaps it was best to concentrate on the bleakly funny as Darlington's *Mission Impossible* often did. 'Coatsworth had a particularly impressive game,' said its match report of a 1-0 defeat to Tranmere Reserves (Attendance: 19), 'and provided the match highlight when, with a mighty clearance, he knocked the first "S" off the Sports Centre sign.'

Contrasting with a newspaper's fixation on sporting action, fanzine match coverage revelled in telling us about sign breakages and other occurrences left unobserved elsewhere. Fanzine writers' minds wandered and they found themselves watching the tea hut queue or buses passing behind the goal end. They were distracted by minutiae and peeves. Why did no one throw toilet rolls on to the pitch anymore, mulled Pompey fanzine *More Dead Wood Than the Mary Rose*. Theories included 'the introduction of those stupid new machines that dish out one sheet at a time' and the demise of Football Special trains with their 'extra tough long distance British Rail bog rolls that always seemed made for throwing'.

In *Jackmail*, on a grisly afternoon at the Vetch Field, one writer became suddenly perturbed by Swansea City's 'waddling' ball boys in their '70s bobble hats and rain macs the size of your average tent'. Their attempts at catching the ball made it 'suddenly turn into a slippery bar of soap; throwing it back it turns into a heavy cannon ball and when they are chasing the ball it adopts this magnetic forcefield around itself that won't let them get closer to it however much their little legs are pumping'.

As two teams heaved around the pitch, idle minds also set fanzine contributors studying their surroundings and the tribes that dwelled within. In *Beyond the Boundary*, Timmy Barrett described Oldham Athletic's Chadwick Road End as 'more than just a covered enclosure on a football ground. It is a meeting place of cultures, a source of wit, a font of wisdom . . . It has a smell unique to itself – fresh beer, stale beer, fresh Oxo, stale pies, pipe tobacco, cigarette tobacco, illegal tobacco.' He could have been writing of 200 other such terrace ends.

Standing upon them, fellow fanzine writers observed the regulars who populated these environs and immortalised them in print. These characters – whether specific people or generic types – were unrecorded elsewhere. Fanzines preserved them in print and four decades on we can meet them at a safe distance.

Late in 1988, Steve Beauchampé introduced readers of *Tired and Weary* to 'the loony in the seats'. Beauchampé had first noticed 'the loony' in the 1970s as he took up his usual St Andrew's perch close to the dugouts and began berating 'every refereeing decision, embellishing each incident with leaps, gesticulations, mock applause and runs to the edge of the pitch'. They would sing for him from the Kop, 'Grandad, grandad, give us a wave', a plea never indulged. He had chosen a season ticket seat by the steps, 'six or seven rows from the front, allowing him the space his performances demanded. His use of the gangway was inspired and provided him with easy access to the touch-line from where he could harangue with gusto.'

After years of surveillance from on high, Beauchampé decided to spend a match in close proximity and purchased a main stand ticket. For the first quarter of an hour, Grandad Loony remained placid. 'I began to feel disappointed – cheated even,' wrote Beauchampé; but when a Blues player was fouled 'he was off – up, up and away to the front, the sense of injustice etched in his face'. Then, 'as the match got dirty he became shirty. His dander was up and there was a fire in his belly.' When he did sit, he was 'agitated, forever fidgeting, ready to rise, obviously a nervous and irritable man, always anticipating the foul, the offside, the bad decision'.

A year later, in *A Kick Up The R's* Dave Thomas profiled a motley crew of Shepherd's Bush regulars, giving them handy epithets. 'One Man Kop' was a solo fan who raised and swayed his scarf alone and greeted opposition goals 'with a sag of the shoulders, like a dagger to his sorry heart'; 'Sid the Sage' sported an 'ever-lit cigar and rakish trilby' and was known for calling over young substitutes and offering them 'a spot of advice and encouragement'; and 'Fred the Head', a pensioner who could be 'relied upon to sicken visiting be-suited Arsenal yuppies on leave from the City, with his incessant dogmatic and voluble references' to their 1933 FA Cup defeat to Walsall.

A similar band were invoked by Millwall's *The Lion Roars*, though this time as *away* end regulars. Favourites included 'The Old Boy In The Grubby Mac', a non-league obsessive who 'asks ridiculous questions about old Wimbledon Southern League players from the sixties'; 'The Bobble Hatted Man', who on the bus 'always takes a food hamper with him, and talks to you whilst eating, which normally results in you arriving at your destination covered in chicken legs'; and 'Jellyneck', a 'walking dollop of lard in a dirty mac, always carries a massive wood panelled Goodman's radio with no batteries in it, but this doesn't prevent him from constantly bellowing out hugely inaccurate scores to anyone within earshot'.

For some, the all-seater fear of being snared next to bores, or worse, had already been realised. As the Premier League arrived, Alan Fitter, writing in *The Spur*, described 'Laurel and Hardy'. The latter was 'a self-opinionated Scotsman who had more hair growing out of his nose than he had on his head', the former 'a little man who had no opinions of his own'. Sitting together, the two were unmoved when Spurs scored and visibly satisfied when opponents did. The pair 'spent most of the match rubbishing the Spurs players', and fixed Fitter with a vacant stare when he asked why they bothered attending matches.

Millwall's radio man was not alone, although most others deployed batteries in their transistors. *The Absolute Game*'s Archie MacGregor dedicated a whole article investigating their breed. They were, he said, 'Courageous, fearsomely single-minded, prepared to risk long-term hearing disabilities or even deafness' on behalf of all fans. Relaying goals, red cards and all the rest from elsewhere, their collective efforts created 'a truly global terrace'. Yet, highlighted MacGregor, not all transistor men spread their news. Some guarded their radios or deftly 'lowered the volume, causing much gnashing of teeth: a sort of airwave equivalent to the offside trap'.

Generic species like the Transistor Man were often identified in fanzines. *Tales from the Riverbank*, a 1994 London football fanzine, profiled The Tactics Man. Wearing an Umbro or Adidas padded bench coat, he could be seen 'arms folded tut-tutting at bad passes' or 'gesturing frantically and barking out complex instructions to the players'. Unsought advice would be issued for players to 'Load the box' or 'Give him some options', as he waved 'his arms to usher the players forward'. In Carlisle United fanzine *The Cumberland Sausage*, Richard Nixon categorised further universal types. The Old Crone could be identified by the key phrase 'they're not as good as they were in my day'. The Loyal Club Man wore a 'Snorkel jacket, NHS specs with lenses like paving slabs', whereas The Labourer came straight from work in his 'Black duffle coat and workmen's jeans which show off half their buttocks'.

Flatteringly or otherwise, matchday sartorial choices were also noted by fanzine observants. As early as January 1985, taking a break from enraging the local police, *Terrace Talk* noted that 'bleached jeans have been replaced by split cords' and 'ski-hats and flares' had emerged. Over in Bradford later that year, *The City Gent* reported that the terraces were 'alive with people in pink cardigans', the colour 'adopted by those with the greatest macho pretensions'. Reassuringly, more traditional, seventies-hangover styles were also in evidence, from 'greasy denim, scarves and lumberjack coats' to 'fur-lined parkers', flares 'still waiting to be taken in' and 'the wing collar brigade with those razor-sharp lapels'.

Five years on, reported Taffy Fox in *Dial M For Merthyr*, 'the fashion among football fans seems to be finely balanced between that of the London look and the Manchester way'. From the capital came rap-influenced 'multicoloured Kicker or Timberland boots along with bell-bottoms' and 'Naff-Naff baggy coats'. Starting to dominate now, though, was aping of the Stone Roses and Happy Mondays' baggy look. Echoing Mancunian music's sprightly, carefree mood, optimism could be discerned on the terraces if fans lifted their floppy fringes and looked hard enough. Yet fanzines still had an almighty role to play in extinguishing from crowds a stench that was a million times worse than rancid pies.

WEMBLEY

— VENUE OF ~~LEGENDS~~ —

TERRIBLE VIEWS

EXORBITANT TICKET PRICES

SALMONELLA BURGERS

TOILETS FROM HELL

A GREYHOUND TRACK

PISS BEER

United Colours of Football

A free fanzine for supporters by supporters

CHAPTER 15: ANTI-RACISM AND OTHER CAUSES

Racism is a disease that we don't want in our football grounds. Make sure it doesn't inhabit your club.

— *OVER THE MOON*, ANTI-FASCIST FANZINE

If you went to football in the 1980s and early 1990s, you probably heard the monkey chants. Visceral, hateful, sonorous. A cacophony of 'ooh-ooh-ooh' noises howled over and over. The odd armpit-tweaking simian gesture. A sinister and medieval charade. When a black player ventured to the byline to take a throw-in or corner, that part of the ground took its cue – such a violent, menacing, othering sound rising as the footballer, the *human*, approached to do his job. What must it have felt like, glancing up at that baying pack?

The poison could take on other flavours. The hurling of bananas – supposed to be witty, perhaps? – and other missiles. Flying darts and pig's trotters were not unknown. Black players on your own team being nicknamed 'Sambo' or 'Sooty'. The individual, audible cries of 'Get back to the jungle'. Some that partook claimed such abuse had equivalence with chants of 'You fat bastard' or taunts of 'You bald twat'. As Barnsley fanzine *South Riding* put it, 'When was the last time you heard of someone having their house fire-bombed because they were bald or fat?' Some dismissed it as 'a laugh' and all part of the match-day pantomime. It was telling that the National Front (NF) and other fascist groups saw football matches as ideal recruitment fairs. Fanzines became depositories for witness stories but also instigators of the fightback.

In 1987, John Barnes signed for Liverpool and Mark Walters for Rangers. Although both had been professional footballers for six years, these high-profile moves emboldened racist supporters on the terraces. 'The real acid test was always going to be how the Everton fans reacted to Barnes in the derby,' wrote Graham Ennis in that December's *Off the Ball*. Depressingly, 'They attacked him with joyful abandon, booing every time he touched the ball', hurling bananas as he jogged to take corners and chanting 'Everton are white'. Despite Liverpool being home to Britain's oldest black community, the terraces of neither Anfield nor Goodison could be labelled diverse, and few black players had passed through the city. Yet, says Ennis now, it made for a 'narrative which we felt was undeserved. No one ever denied that Everton had a race problem. Every club had a race problem. But we as fanzines needed to change the mood music about the club, and to start saying that there's lots of people who are anti-racist and oppose those who were racist.'

Across Stanley Park, a *When Sunday Comes* writer observed similar prejudice in the Kop. Racism was 'abundant', said a 1988 article. 'You'd have thought that the arrival of John Barnes would at least shut up the racists' but 'lots of mindless idiots still join in'. In common with Graham Ennis, the writer struck a note of defiance: 'They can be silenced, so don't just stand there, say something. All mankind are equal. Racism is sick and unfunny, tell the racist near you how wrong they are, and you should get through.'

Walters too faced resounding verbal abuse and missiles. In *Not the View*, Celtic supporter Donald Murdoch deplored Hoops fans' treatment of the winger. 'It seems to be getting worse as more people appear to be joining in,' wrote Murdoch. 'Just because we were playing badly and losing there was no reason to resort to this.' *Follow, Follow*, the Rangers fanzine, published a stinging editorial attack under the headline 'Blue – The Only

Colour That Matters', while *The Falkirk Unofficial Fanzine* noted that 'the Celtic support succeeded only in humiliating themselves'. Predictably, after signing for Celtic in 1989, centre-half Paul Elliott faced similar treatment to Walters.

Much fanzine denunciation of racism came from writers deploring their fellow fans. They, after all, walked and stood among these Neanderthals. In *Wise Men Say*, writer A. Fan described the totemic hypocrisy of a Roker Park bigot. Two black players – Sunderland's Gary Bennett and Noel Blake of Leeds – had been competing in a challenge. Momentum took Blake into the hoardings of the Clock Stand Paddock. 'Offensive and inane monkey chants' were discharged by fans 'too blind or stupid' to recognise that both were black. 'The ironic stupidity of these chants is obviously lost on these idiots,' continued the article, 'and goodness alone knows what Gary himself thinks about it all.' It was now time for 'the powers that be at Roker to speak out against these racist thugs'.

Editorial words in the April 1990 issue of Swansea's *Jackmail* regretted that the tunes 'sung with most enthusiasm in recent games' had been racist ones. It was now 'essential to make a stand against racism'. In a December fixture with Brentford, visiting left-back Roger Stanislaus 'suffered some venomous verbal attacks and got so worked-up he was making reckless challenges and the frustration was written all over his face'. *Jackmail* apologised to Stanislaus and any black Swans fans despite its own vehement anti-racism. Meanwhile, in Barnsley, Keith Norman of *South Riding* fanzine had witnessed children of 'no more than eight or nine making monkey noises at a black player'.

Entrenched racism made terraces repellent for many ethnic minority supporters. Where they did brave the brickbats, an intimidating afternoon often awaited. In a 1991 issue of *Through the Wind and Rain*, an anonymous black Londoner wrote of his short time living in Liverpool and attending fixtures during the 1989/90 season. 'Nearly always,' he wrote, 'a heavy atmosphere of racism hung over the game.' At Anfield, while not suffering direct racial abuse, 'it still hurt when black players did; indirectly

I felt I was abused also. I felt a mixture of emotions; embarrassment, hurt, anger.' Goodison Park meant being forced to 'put up with some abuse, but you got used to it and learned (as much as possible) to blank it out. I just went with the attitude that such morons weren't going to stop me from enjoying myself.'

In *Flashing Blade*, an Asian supporter reflected upon his experiences watching Sheffield United during the 1970s and 80s. 'Standing on the Kop,' wrote Abid Rahim, 'it was commonplace to hear black players being subjected to a constant stream of racial abuse, this becoming worse if the Blades were losing. Imagine the feelings of a single 12-year-old Asian boy surrounded by this type of behaviour.' Taking coaches or trains to away matches, Rahim would find himself in a throng of fellow fans who abused any black person they passed with 'pure hatred and filth'. Queuing at the Bramall Lane turnstiles, several times he had been 'told that the ground was for whites only'.

Fanzines regularly bewailed the absence of ethnic minority fans in their teams' grounds, especially those set within multicultural areas. 'Pop into your local park,' wrote Peter Shaughnessy in Crystal Palace fanzine *Eagle Eye*, 'and see how many black people play football for leisure. Yet they would never dream of going to a football match, why? Because every time they turn on a TV and see John Barnes touch a ball he is booed simply because of his colour. They pick up a paper and read of Nazi thugs in support of the England team, sieg heiling to the national anthem.' In *Saddle Sore*, a Walsall fanzine, editor Graham Doe reflected on abuse of black players at home matches. 'Any racism is too much, and too loud,' wrote Doe. 'Racism isn't funny, or clever, or hard. It's sick, it's dangerous, football doesn't need it and Walsall certainly doesn't. Yet still it goes on. No wonder you see so few non-white faces in the crowd at Fellows Park.'

Often, Jewish supporters felt similarly besieged. Leeds fan, magazine editor and writer James Brown recalls the terrorising atmosphere at mid-1980s Elland Road. 'When we were still at school, if you stood on the Kop the National Front would hand out Holocaust denial leaflets and stickers,' says Brown.

'There was such a prevalent NF presence in Leeds and a lot of it around the football club.' In particular, he remembers a 1985 game against Oxford United as 'just horrible. There was open hissing and anti-Jewish songs and it was vile.' Tor Johnson of *Wise Men Say* endured similarly diabolical conditions when visiting in 1989. On sale were 't-shirts promoting Leeds United fans' affinity to violence, racism and fascism etc' and during the game a 'recital of the NF song book in full' could be heard. As Brown and Johnson witnessed, the NF made infiltrating football a priority, whether at club games or England internationals. Their publications included 'louts leagues' – lists of clubs whose fans were supposedly ripe for recruitment.

In May 1991, *Blue Print* reported that some Manchester City followers had made hissing sounds – mocking holocaust gas chambers – as Jewish forward Ronnie Rosenthal entered the field for Tottenham Hotspur. Their fans regularly faced antisemitic chanting, most notably through use of the word 'Yid' (still a debated topic for Spurs supporters now). In *The Boleyn Scorcher*, Jewish West Ham United supporter GP reflected on its derogatory use at Upton Park during a recent London derby. 'I know that language changes according to how people use it,' said the writer, 'but as a Jew, I also know that I'll always find "yid" offensive. And when it's yelled with venom by thousands of fans around me in a stadium, it's more than that. It's sickening and terrifying.'

Beyond their eyewitness laments, fanzines were the vanguard of the resistance. Anti-racist campaigning and raging against terrace numbskulls became a core value of the movement. As individuals, readers were asked to challenge racist language whenever they heard it at a game. Collectively, they would come together around the fanzine and link with others across the land to howl that racism was never acceptable. Fanzines were strong, brave and bolshie, and could talk in terms unseen and impossible in matchday programmes and newspapers.

The tone of anti-racist fanzine writing was furious and belligerent. 'Could I just pass on a message to a certain gang of lads in the East End seats,' demanded a piece in *Fly Me To The Moon*, 'the chanters, the part-timers, the bottleless shits . . . Get your heads out of the *Sun* for a while and get wise.' Under the headline Racists, Racists, Get Tae Fuck, an editorial in the Aberdeen fanzine *The Northern Light* let fly: 'They are fundamentally gutless wankers who are terrified of being identified for the feeble-minded excuses for human beings that they really are . . . If any of our readers feel that they disagree with our stand on this then I suggest that they keep their 50p pieces from now on – AND SHOVE THEM UP THEIR RACIST JACKSIES!'

Get A Grip, Ref!, a Scunthorpe United fanzine, burned with righteous anger against fellow Iron fans and urged a club response to terrace racism: 'There are still a few amoeba-brains who seem to find it funny to carry on with this infantile behaviour. Why do they do it? Well, at Glanford Park it seems to be a case of follow-the-leader – black player gets the ball, wall-head starts "Ooh, ooh, ooh", rest of sheep think, "Good idea let's join in" . . . Whoever you are, either grow up or get out.'

Airdrie fanzine *Only the Lonely* concurred: 'The people who make monkey noises and neo-Nazi songs are ignorant, scared and prejudiced. They toy with philosophies their infantile minds do not understand. Preying on the weak is not big, it is absolutely pathetic. They are a disgrace to their club, country and to the human race as a whole.' Under the booming headline 'Pompey Against the Nazis', *More Dead Wood Than the Mary Rose* linked racism inside Fratton Park to events in wider society. 'The Nazis attempt to scapegoat black people and others for the economic problems we face,' said the fanzine. 'They attempt to sow disunity where unity is the only answer. On the terraces they chant their racist filth at black players – but how does this help our team?'

That fanzines were intrinsically, avowedly anti-racist owed something to the punk origins of many founding editors. 'Fanzines carried through the punk and post-punk ethos,' says

Adrian Goldberg, 'which was vehemently anti-racist. I don't think everybody in the fanzine movement was inspired by punk, but I think there were enough of us who were locked into that progressive wing of punk for it to become a part of the thread in the carpet.'

Sparking the fightback, fanzines strived to embolden readers so that confronting those guilty of racist utterances was not a concept laced with fear. Bravado, said *The Northern Light*, would soon ebb away as 'The people who indulge in this noise-making shut up very quickly when they are faced with a negative reaction from anybody nearby who chooses to howl them down'. By acting together, supporters could drown out and ostracise those guilty of racism, just as they had alienated hooligan groups.

Terrace Talk supported the idea of confronting bigotry. 'We can drown it out,' said a 1989 editorial. 'Tell those responsible to "cut it out". Ask the police what they are going to do about it.' There was a philosophical underpinning to this militancy. 'The interests and concerns of white supporters and players are the same as those of black supporters and players,' continued the article, 'and the more time fans spend abusing players because of the colour of their skin, the less time they spend questioning the dangerous and disgusting state of many grounds, or the way they are being treated by the police, or any of dozens of other problems affecting them.'

Facing up to a colossal skinhead infused with testosterone and other substances was a more difficult task than writing acerbic words. Fists might fly. Plus, as a contributor to Everton fanzine *When Skies Are Grey* explained: 'Tackling racists to their face would be beyond me. How can you tell an unemployed, ugly, pot-bellied, talentless idiot that he's not better than David Rocastle simply because his own skin is a pinky-white, blotchy hue? That kind of stupidity is absolutely impenetrable.' Concerted, organised initiatives were needed; actions that harnessed the unity already felt between fanzines from the anti-ID cards campaign.

Fanzines spread the messages and resources of external campaigns such as Anti-Fascist Action and the Anti-Nazi League. The Kick Racism Out of Football crusade sprang from and multiplied within the pages of fanzines. Individual publications were able to advance national anti-racist messages tailored to their club's situation. They could also shame that club should it have refused to sign up to Kick Racism Out of Football's Action Plan.

Most powerful, however, were local, grassroots actions. Outside St James' Park, 100 anti-fascist Newcastle United supporters regularly gathered to leaflet passers-by and shout down National Front agitators. *The Leyton Orientear* marshalled an Anti-Fascist Alliance presence at home games. Leeds United supporters were not passive through the soiling of their club. In December 1987, prior to a game against Bournemouth, 70 of them picketed the Elland Road turnstiles appealing for an end to racist chanting. Then, a further development: a dedicated anti-racist Leeds United fanzine. The swashbuckling, rowdy *Marching Altogether* was founded in the city's Trades Club as a response to the rising presence of National Front leaflet drives. From 1988, it was handed out, free, outside home games. The fanzine was aggressive in its anti-fascist polemic and illustration. It hit readers sleepwalking towards apathy with a baseball bat – the skinheads outside Elland Road were Nazis, infiltrating *your* sainted matchdays. Other actions were instigated, such as petitioning and out-singing, and then reporting, racist chants.

Remarkably, before a game in September 1988 *Marching Altogether* co-ordinated a joint anti-racist picket line with visiting supporters of Chelsea, another club bedevilled by far-right zealots. The fanzine ran a Racist Scum of the Season 'award' and reported on anti-fascist activities taking place outside of football across the region. In each issue a cartoon advised of 101 Things to do with a racist, including drowning them in Elland Road toilets. Crystal Palace player Ian Wright noticed the effect *Marching Altogether* was having: 'We went to Leeds the other week. It was brilliant. They've got a thing down there petitioning against the noises towards black players and the racial abuse that black players take. I think it's a giant step because Leeds were really bad. . . it's changed a lot. . . That's due to a handful of people who got together and said "Right, that's enough. We've got to sort it out."'

News of *Marching Altogether*'s achievements roused fans of other clubs. In 1989, *For Fox Sake* related that an Inter Racial Solidarity Campaign had begun leafletting outside Leicester City matches in response to player abuse. 'For far too long,' said the fanzine, 'us grassroots fans have acquiesced in letting racism coagulate into a particularly unpleasant mould, on the terraces and in the seats.' A few years later supporters created *Filbo Fever* with its tagline of 'The Foxes Against Racism Fanzine'. It had the firm aim of making Filbert Street a welcoming place for local black and Asian people to watch football.

Over the Moon, an anti-fascist football fanzine with no club alignment, was also established. In 1991, it helped explain how supporters could use the new Football (Offences) Act to their advantage when encountering racism. The fanzine encouraged direct action, and invited supporters to question the actions and inactions of their clubs: 'Racism is a disease that we don't want in our football grounds. Make sure it doesn't inhabit your club.' Down in Devon, *You Wot!* proclaimed itself an 'Anti-racist Alternative Torquay United Magazine' and donated a portion of its profits to Gulls Against Fascism and Racism.

Determined to speak up for Everton's anti-racist majority and reclaim a name that had been 'dragged through the mud', in 1993 *When Skies Are Grey* launched their No Al Razzismo campaign, employing Neville Southall as a T-shirt model. During the same year, Burnley fanzine *Marlon's Gloves* endorsed work to combat the British National Party (BNP) presence in their town. When the BNP attempted to shift their newspapers outside one Turf Moor home game, the fanzine handed out 4000 'Clarets Against the Nazis' leaflets at the next.

Marlon's Gloves writers had noted a resurgence in racist abuse at Burnley matches, and incidents elsewhere proved that fanzines could not retreat from vigilance. In another *Over the Moon* – a Kent-based general football fanzine whose co-editors included *Test Match Special*'s Andy Zaltzman – 'A. Scribbler' wrote that 'still lurking amongst the crowds are people who think it is acceptable to spew out the same guttural noises, and to utter their pathetic, narrow minded, and ignorant opinions'. *Filbo Fever* cited a January 1994 FA Cup tie in which Ian Wright was forced to withstand '90 minutes of monkey noises, chants of "kill the black bastard" and general racist filth from a very sizeable section of the Millwall crowd'. At the year's end Spurs fan Alice Kennedy followed her team to Filbert Street, where 'A couple of BNP recruits behind me spent most of the match spitting out racist invective, coming out with abuse I hadn't heard for a long time, seemingly unable to work out that Sol Campbell, who they liked so much, also has black skin.' It appeared that *Filbo Fever*'s anti-racist campaigners would be required to infiltrate the away end.

Reacting to this new wave of bigotry the FSA produced *United Colours of Football*, a 12-page mini-fanzine. A hundred thousand copies were inserted into regular fanzines or handed to supporters as they marched towards the ground. *Dial M For Merthyr* distributed 700 copies before a game against Yeovil Town, alongside anti-racist posters and stickers. 'We will continue to monitor the situation on the terraces,' wrote Chairman Mao, 'and racists will be shouted down.' Penydarren Park had anti-racism pedigree. In the late 1980s, remembers Jonny Owen, *Dial M . . .* editor Mark Evans 'started a campaign to stop racism at Merthyr, which was rife on the terraces. There was a lot of small-mindedness and ignorant thinking, and really nasty chants to players of colour who would play against us.'

In response, Evans 'started a campaign through the fanzine that handed out leaflets and talked to people on the terraces, saying "You've got to stop this."' Owen highlights that 'This wasn't a campaign led by the FA or anyone else. It was led from the grassroots. The fanzine was right at the centre of stamping racism out. I realised then that *Dial M . . .* had become something more important than just the scribblings of some teenage boys. It had actually become a force that we could use for some good.'

Though never entirely vanquished, that any racist utterances on today's terraces are met with almost universal shock – and, hopefully, the confidence to take remedial action – is palpably a legacy of football fanzines and other campaigning vessels. 'Fanzines did work that clubs weren't prepared to do,' says Rob Bagchi. 'They engaged supporters. Clubs then got savvier and I think they invested more in community relations as the years went on. Fanzines made a positive, lasting contribution to fighting racism in football grounds, and that should be recognised.'

The campaigning zeal of fanzines was also utilised to combat other forms of prejudice. In 1993, 19-year-old Angela Charlton from Teesside founded *Against the Tide*. Billed as 'The fanzine for women supporters who want an equal voice in a people's game', its opening editorial pledged to 'further the interests of women supporters and players' and 'air their views about the game'. Abiding by those pledges, contributor Nishat Adat shared her experiences of being a steward at White Hart Lane. Adat, who would go on to work as a BBC broadcaster for 30 years, despaired at how her footballing opinions were ignored in male company. It was, she wrote, 'Sickening. Pathetic. Grossly unfair. What do women have to do to be taken seriously?'

Another north-easterner, Jane Purdon from Sunderland, had already established *Born Kicking*, 'The fanzine for women who love football, because a woman's place is in the six-yard box', in 1990. The fanzine tenaciously publicised and celebrated women's football in an era when coverage barely existed. Indeed, one of the causes pursued by *Born Kicking* was the mainstream media's disregard. 'Even intelligent, sympathetic newspapers will do a once-a-season report on women's football,' wrote Purdon in issue 3. Later working in football governance and as an author, her work has contributed to addressing this imbalance.

Besides dedicated titles, women opined on matters of prejudices faced while following football in regular fanzines. Pre-match and half-time entertainment – even before the Sky Sports Strikers pom-pommed their way on to the pitch – was a frequent bugbear. In *On the Terraces*, A Female Writes took aim at the 'sexist, degrading, disgusting' Woodstock Homes All-Girls XI interval display. If West Ham wished to attract more female supporters 'as spectators, not objects of blunt comments and ogling machismo', then 'brains and integrity' would 'have to be removed from trousers'.

Sarah Tabor of *The Leyton Orientear* helped force her club's programme to drop a dubious advert for a local car insurance firm. She also reported vividly and with winning fanzine sarcasm on the occasionally depressing experience of being a female away fan. In April 1989, she advised fans not to 'go to Exeter wearing a skirt, unless you're a bloke of course, then you'd probably be alright'. Taylor supposed that 'all the chemicals those farmers come into contact with must do something to their brains, or their libido. I've never seen anybody go into such contortions to look up my skirt as a man in a pub in Exeter did. If I ever go to Exeter again, which I sincerely hope I don't, I shall wear a full suit of armour.'

In *AWOL*, Rachel detailed The Life and Times of a Female Football Supporter. In her earliest era of attending games, with boring frequency men had suggested she was interested only in footballers' legs. 'I did look at their legs, once,' she recalled. 'It was a long time ago. The game was boring . . . and nobody wanted to go to the pub. So I looked, first at Wattie Boyd, then Nipper, then Ralph Callahan. Then I spotted a blade of grass, and another, and another. I counted all the blades of grass. Far more exciting than the highly-acclaimed football legs.'

At Airdrie, an elderly fan 'wanting to tell me something thought it better to first approach my owning male. Apparently, I could get half-price admission by using the OAP/Boys' turnstile. . . Was I a boy? Was I an OAP? I stood there, perplexed.' The pensioners of Berwick Rangers, said Rachel, had been 'particularly helpful. Seeing that I was apparently alone they tried to make me feel welcome by offering to sit on my knee. There wasn't much grass at Shielfield, so I opted for watching the players' legs.'

Coverage of women's football could occasionally be found in those same fanzines. Late in 1991, Roger Deason wrote to the letters pages of *A Load of Bull* to express his belief that Wolves should 'adopt' Wolverhampton Ladies. It would 'help community relations' and 'may even help draw more female supporters to Molineux'. In *King of the Kippax*, Neil Mather set down the process of forming the Manchester City's women's team from scratch. On 31 October, 1988, 36 players had attended their first open training session, '50% reasonably accomplished players (one or two were very good) and 50% appalling'.

Having watched the 1990 Women's FA Cup semi-finals on Channel 4, Tony Scowcroft, editor of Plymouth Argyle fanzine *Rub of the Greens*, concluded that 'Football needs women. The game could only be enhanced by their greater involvement at all levels.' Enlightenment was a gradual process. In *Hibs Monthly*, also watching on television Your Raving Reporter had found 'the lassies attempting to play the game' to be 'absolutely hilarious . . . it beat some Monty Python sketches hands down'.

Fanzines occasionally articulated views on homophobia, another terrace ill as evidenced in cries of 'poofter' at any vaguely injured player and the absence of openly gay footballers. In the summer of 1988, *Terrace Talk* raised the case of Norman Redman, 'England's only openly gay football referee'. Redman had been selected to officiate a Sussex County Cup game. However, 'One of the clubs refused to accept him as referee on the grounds that he was a danger to the players; they were afraid of getting AIDS.'

Understandably aggrieved, Redman complained but was found guilty of bringing the game into disrepute for doing so. *Terrace Talk* highlighted how 'it is likely that something in the region of 200 professional footballers are gay, along with 40,000 regular supporters, perhaps 100 of whom have bought this issue of *TT*'. All of them would 'at some stage feel threatened by the hysteria whipped up by certain newspapers and politicians. Just as we urge readers to stand up against racism, *TT* hopes all football fans will unite to resist the coming tide of hogwash.' *More Dead Wood Than the Mary Rose* worried that the first footballer to contract HIV would face abhorrent prejudice. 'How will you react?' asked the Portsmouth fanzine. 'How will the media react? Hopefully positively but frankly that's unlikely. Can you imagine the chants and the exaggerations in the newspapers?'

The most seismic event related to this particular avenue of discrimination was the *Sun*'s outing of former player Justin Fashanu. Writing in his own *Elmslie Ender*, Martin Lacey condemned fanzine writers who had 'come out in their true colours with a spate of anti-Fashanu and anti-gay jokes . . . Anyone who thinks it's funny that the media should attempt to destroy somebody's career and reputation simply because they are gay is in serious need of a lobotomy . . . Next time you call a visiting goalkeeper a "poof" and think you've just delivered a heinous insult perhaps it's time you asked yourself, what are YOU scared of?'

In response to the Fashanu story, Dave Ansell decided to launch *The Football Pink*. Based in Manchester, it would reflect the views and experiences of LGBT football supporters. 'The fanzine press,' reflected Ansell on Fashanu, 'with a few dishonourable exceptions, were either positive, neutral or didn't cover it, while the tabloid press had obviously decided that they couldn't deal with the phenomenon of gay footballers and so decided to ignore the story altogether.'

The Football Pink continued to report on the struggles and resilience of LGBT supporters, and the rise of all-gay amateur teams. It seems implausible, given the game's progress in battling other prejudices, that the concept of an out footballer in the men's game remains an embarrassingly improbable proposition.

AMAZING FREE GIFT
You are now a shareholder
in the Brechin hedge

THE LIFE AND TIMES OF A FANZINE SELLER:-
'ERE, SONNY - YOU CAN'T GO IN WITH THEM - THEY COULD BE USED AS OFFENSIVE WEAPONS!!

FOOTBALL SUPPORTER

fSA

50p

Football Supporters Association

THE FSA's ITALIAN JOB FOR FANS

The 1990 World Cup Finals are now very firmly underway ... and it's time to forget the speculation, forget the hype, forget the forebodings: it's time to concentrate on events happening where it really matters – on the pitch; time to celebrate the ultimate extravaganza of the Beautiful game; time to feast on a month of the best football in the world ... time to get that fiesta feeling!

And while the majority of us are having to settle for a comfy chair, a copy of the TV schedules, and the company of Des, Jimmy and Archie, fans lucky enough to be travelling to Italy will find the FSA in the forefront of helping to ensure that they have an enjoyable and problem free holiday.

With the help of valuable sponsorship from the companies, fanzines and organisations listed at the end, the FSA has been able to set up a 'drop in' advice centre, open to all football fans.

Initially, the Football Embassy will be based in Cagliari, Sardinia, the venue for all three of England's First Round, Group F matches versus the Republic of Ireland, Holland and Egypt, and will be the focal point of the FSA's World Cup campaign.

The campaign, which enforces the Association's commitment to constructive supporter involvement, has four main strands:

1. **To provide advice, assistance and representation to fans on Sardinia.**
2. **To monitor the behaviour of fans in Italy.**
3. **To liaise with the Italian and World Cup authorities on behalf of supporters, as and when appropriate.**
4. **To liaise with the British and Italian media so as to promote fair coverage.**

The approach is strictly 'pro-supporter' rather than 'anti-hooligan' and it is hoped that this will lead to helping make the tournament as trouble free as possible, whilst minimising the predictable sensationalist and defamatory media coverage of fans in Italy.

The Football Embassy is staffed by four 'full time' FSA members backed by several other volunteers, some of whom speak Italian. The office contains telephones, a Fax machine, photocopier, video, television, typewriter and computer. It will be open between 1000 - 1300 and 1430 - 1900 local time every day between June 7th - 23rd. Fans will be able to drop in for any reason ranging from the need to get an important message home, to a casual enquiry as to the location of a good restaurant. There will be information and advice available on just about everything, be it a medical problem, an enquiry about how to trace lost property or the availability and location of camp-sites. (continued)

THE F.S.A.'s WORLD CUP CAMPAIGN

The address of the Football Embassy is:

First Floor, 45, Via Malta, Cagliari, Sardinia, Italy.

Telephone: (010 3970) 670 101
Fax: (010 3970) 668 461
7 - 23 June

Members who see or hear unfair or sensationalist press comment are urged to register a complaint with the Press Council. Their number is 071 353 1248.

Branches are asked to contact Head Office for regular updates of the World Cup Campaign. A reminder of the new address and telephone number: F.S.A., 4 Rodney St., Liverpool, L1 2TE. Tel: 051 709 2594, Fax: 051 708 0392.

CHAPTER 16: MONEY TALKS AND WORLD CUP '90

If that's how football should be played, well then you can shove it up your arse with a wire brush and Dettol!

— *FROM HOME TO HOME*, SHELBOURNE FANZINE

There are several contenders when trying to specify the exact moment or event after which modern football arrived. Paul Gascoigne crying at Italia '90, the publication of *Fever Pitch* and the Premier League's arrival are all candidates. Some fanzines, however, believed it was heralded by an 0898 number.

Although ClubCall launched in 1986, it came to prominence in the late eighties and early nineties. During that period, its reach stretched to a majority of teams in England and Scotland. Some of us can still recite our teams' numbers and the cries of our parents when the phone bill arrived. Two other ClubCall numbers also linger – 36p (cheap rate) and 48p (premium), the per-minute charge for phoning up. So too do we recall the universal format: a welcome message from a manager or player (and the enjoyment of saying 'Hello!' back); a presenter listing through the many and varied transfer exclusives soon to be thrilling our ears; and the dreaded words 'But first. . .' preluding a seven-minute conversation with the club groundsman about his new gardening fork.

Fanzine coverage was plentiful and scathing. To many editors and writers, this astronomical heist represented a new dawn in which clubs began financially and morally fleecing supporters even when they were not at games. Finally, they were talking to supporters about what was going on; it was just that those fans would have to pay £7.12 to listen. Thatcher's decline and fall was underway, but football clubs were only just entering their full embrace of Thatcherism.

Scores of fanzines published spoof articles that ran to a shared layout. At the top would be the ClubCall logo and slogan, or a bastardised version of it. Exponentially rising phone bill figures that usually began in the high pence and ended with several zeros appeared in the left-hand margin. Alongside them ran an increasingly ridiculous script parodying ClubCall's procrastinating tendencies – 'But before we exclusively reveal the identity of Exeter City's top transfer target, here's Gary with the lowdown from today's kit wash . . .'

Others relied on straightforward carping. In *What a Load of Cobblers*, the Northampton Town fanzine, Andy Cooper fumed at Cobblers Soccerline, a localised alternative. Particularly annoying was the service's habit of reminding callers what they had called and the number they had dialled to do so. Fans 'could do without the costly and time-wasting reminder,' wrote Cooper. 'Those who were hoping for Sexy Sonia and Her Black Suspenders will soon suss their mistake when they hear the details of Paul Culpin's latest groin strain (unless they're particularly perverted).' Sheffield Wednesday fanzine *Just Another Wednesday* griped at the production quality of the Owls' ClubCall service, suggesting that player interviews were conducted 'in Hillsborough baths during the local swimming gala.'

In *A Large Scotch*, Bob announced that Shrewsbury Town ClubCall was now providing full match commentaries. However, it would prove 'a damn sight cheaper to travel to these games, even if you are thinking of going to the longer away trips. For example, 90 minutes of live commentary on a Saturday would amount to around £34 (so make sure you phone from work).'

Bolton Wanderers' *Here We Go Again* summarised gripes felt by thousands and repeated in a multitude of fanzines. 'You somehow keep "hanging on" having hanged on for minutes on end just waiting to see or hear if anything remotely interesting is going to happen,' said an article headlined 'The Most Obscene Phone Call of All Time?' Persistence led only to 'dull, totally uninteresting conversation saturated with futile comments' with 'Phil Brown, he of much tanning'. A new version of this tease developed when Teletext flashed tantalising transfer rumours next to teams' names and ClubCall numbers – 'International star jets in' and 'Ace in Hartlepool link'.

In a strange twist, *Tired and Weary* were visited by 'Two strange men into 0898 telephone numbers,' reported Jim Bryant – representatives of a premium phone service asking to use fanzine content. 'Parade our wares on one of their lines,' continued Bryant, 'and we'd get to keep half the profits.' The 0898 men were dismissed. Stranger still was a call to the Swindon Town line made by a colleague of Paul Hawksbee's in search of tittle-tattle for *90 Minutes* magazine. 'He said, "I've just phoned and something's gone badly wrong because it sounds like an abattoir",' says Hawksbee, 'You could hear a kind of clopping of hooves and lots of mooing and some of it quite distressed as well. Maybe it was the early days of phone hijacking. Someone had got on there and had hijacked Swindon Town ClubCall with the sounds of an abattoir.'

ClubCall was owned by the recently privatised British Telecom. As they had sniffed, there was money to be made from football as its rehabilitation accelerated in the last days of the old decade and the earliest of the new. The game began to attract would-be investors removed from the stiff-collared, yellow-teethed local businessman of yore. Some were so different that they found themselves fluttering between clubs.

Robert Maxwell began his butterfly decade in 1983 by attempting to merge his Oxford United – whose board of directors included daughter Ghislaine – with Reading, creating the Thames Valley Royals. Defeated, he tried to buy Manchester United, then Watford, but settled for Derby County instead. In 1990, he placed the club up for sale. 'The noose has slackened!'

said Rams fanzine *Interesting, Very Interesting*. 'Annually we have stumped up our million pounds in season tickets and so showed our faith. This man did not return this faith. We have expected nothing in return bar pleasure in watching *our* team, but Maxwell expects only one thing from any business – *Profit*.' As 1991 began, Maxwell was attempting to purchase Spurs. 'Questions must be asked about his long-term commitment,' said Lilywhites fanzine *Off the Shelf*. They could find no 'reason to believe that if Maxwell does take over . . . he won't just discard the club when he has lost interest, or it has served its usefulness'. In protest, Spurs fanzines and the FSA staged a meeting and agreed that supporters should buy up their full share entitlement to limit the businessman's grasp. From Derby to North London, fanzines had again demonstrated their prescient tendencies.

While Maxwell had initially invested in football during some of its bleakest days, perhaps he wished to cling on now the game was showing signs of becoming trendy. Another figure who seemed suddenly determined to attach himself to the sport was moustachioed entrepreneur Michael Knighton. Resembling both Hale and Pace at the same time, in late 1989 Knighton stated his intention to buy Manchester United and performed keepy-ups on the Old Trafford pitch in order to prove it. *Red News* reflected that he had claimed to be a 'very emotional and shy person' before handing over a 13-page press release about himself and running on to the pitch and saluting the Stretford End. He had later addressed the players in the dressing room and blown kisses at them.

Knighton's newsworthy takeover, however, stalled, although he was given a seat on the United board. 'This once glamourous club has been treated with all the care and respect of a pub conman selling some dodgy goods,' said *Red News*, 'yet because it was all done under the glare of TV cameras – and with nice accents and dinky Paisley handkerchiefs – it took a while for the masquerade to fall apart.' Later that year, a rumour swept through Edinburgh that he was now eyeing Hibernian. With the supporters' and fanzines' battle to prevent a Hibs-Hearts merger not long won, *The Proclaimer* fanzine inserted a STOP PRESS sheet into their September 1990 issue. It encouraged vigilance. Knighton would eventually land at Carlisle United, who he owned from 1992 until 2002, a reign which included a spell as self-appointed team manager.

Football finance had entered a new age. In 1991, Arsenal announced a debenture bond scheme. Supporters could pay £1500 or £1100 for 'A' and 'B' bonds respectively, which would guarantee them access to season tickets in the newly rebuilt all-seater North Bank. Fanzines led a campaign on behalf of priced-out fans who would be displaced from their regular perches. Speedy initial take-up of bonds slowed. 'Indeed,' said Mike Cochrane in Stockport County fanzine *The Tea Party*, 'David Dein [Arsenal Chief Executive] became so worried that the board of directors issued writs to the fanzines to stop.' West Ham United followers showed similar militancy in 1992. With the campaigning of *On the Terraces* fanzine and others, they forced the Hammers board to abandon their own bond scheme. A series of sit-down pitch protests was particularly successful.

Whenever the new incarnation of football started, it had begun to entice people with big ideas and bulbous wallets. There was no doubt that the product – if football might be momentarily denigrated with that word – they courted was made more attractive by a recent reduction in violence and hooliganism. Ironically, this crumbling occurred as a hooligan fanzine, *Get Into Them*, launched. Its pages included written reconstructions of notable hooligan performances. 'We were left with about 100 lads to battle it out with 400 or so angry long-haired Vikings,' said an account of a 1986 visit to Sweden with England in issue 2, 'the north/south divide was forgotten as Cockneys, Mancs and a lad from Bristol in a smart ski coat refused to run.' Perhaps he was afraid of getting too hot.

The decline of the *Get Into Them* flock and general aggression was noted, pondered upon and cheered. In a 1991 issue of *A Kick Up The R's*, Rob Anderson related how watching football was certainly now a gentler experience, although police behaviour did not always reflect that shift. 'We may not exactly be exchanging bouquets of flowers with rival supporters,' he wrote, 'but the days of proving some sort of macho superiority over them have long gone.'

One year on, in *The Leyton Orientear* Tom Davies analysed the various factors cited by columnists and academics for this downturn, although he did caution that 'hooliganism hasn't totally gone away. There's still a Nazi fringe at England games, and you still have to be careful at times. Yet the dodgier places these days tend to be smaller provincial towns . . . Your biggest problem now seems to come from 15-year-old kids looking for something to brag about to their mates at school on Monday.'

Argument 1 in Davies' list was 'Raves, Ecstasy', the idea that hooligans had moved on to taking mellowing stimulants at raves instead of battering one another. This, however, was 'far too smug and bandwagon-hopping to be credible'. Secondly, Davies examined the notion that 'Seats and Removal Of Fences = Better Behaviour'. That fences had been removed at some grounds did not lead to 'the carnage once predicted'. However, 'you'd have to be seriously deluded to believe such idealistic rubbish about seats', and all-seater stadiums had 'nothing to do with concern for fans or reduction of violence, and everything to do with using the Taylor Report to force through the Premier League and price "undesirables" (i.e. people who can't afford a bond) out of the game.'

Next, the writer felt 'Stricter Policing, Better Crowd Control' deserved 'more credit than the woolly liberals among us are prepared to give it'. There was undoubtedly less chance of violence 'and the vision of fans fighting on the pitch exists only in nostalgia and pub anecdotes it seems these days . . . So, to an extent, the old bill have done their bit.' Finally, Davies scrutinised the role of fanzines and the FSA, both 'crucial in bringing to light the poor facilities and lack of consultation we have had to suffer over the years. This has also led to a much-more supporter-friendly standard of press coverage. Fanzines have, to an extent, changed the agenda.'

In the approach to World Cup '90, the antagonism of some England fans as noted by Davies had flared. Prior to a qualification match in Sweden, they had, said the tabloids, 'rampaged' through Stockholm. In *The Mag*, Gerry Lynch wrote that 'They are not football fans, they are hooligans who have no interest in our national sport'. Echoing a widespread feeling, Lynch argued that these aggressors seldom attended weekend league fixtures and instead used England internationals 'to come together in large numbers and cause havoc in the name of some perverse sense of patriotism'.

Scotland, with their supporters increasingly renowned for benevolence and dancing in fountains, faced no such qualms. Ever scarred from the hubris of 1978, they fretted instead about the deficiencies of their squad. 'We haven't got a cat in hell's chance of making an impression in Italy next year,' said David Beveridge in East Fife fanzine *Bayview Bulletin*. 'What is the point in asking players who play week-in, week-out at 100mph to suddenly change their style in midweek and start poncing around trying to be "continental"? It is totally alien to us.' With their 'limited talent', Scotland should instead be 'taking no prisoners and coming down the tunnel breathing fire'. Manager Andy Roxburgh, continued Beveridge, was 'far too nice. He lets the players call him "Andy".'

With their team's fixtures slated for Genoa and Turin, Scotland supporters would not benefit from the FSA's Football Embassy in Cagliari. The Embassy was the idea of Steve Beauchampé, who worked with FSA chair Craig Brewin on its launch. 'I ended up funding a lot of it,' admits Brewin now, 'which was never my intention. It's just that I had a Eurocheque book and we ran out of money. The FSA didn't want to fund it, so Steve raised the money from the private sector and the Football Trust.' The two chose the name because they kept hearing that football fans 'were expected to be ambassadors'.

Staffed by Beauchampé, Brewin and other FSA volunteers, this temporary supporters' consulate was housed in a rented office above a shop during England's spell on Sardinia. Under the positive banner of being 'pro-fan' rather than explicitly 'anti-hooligan', it existed to help with accommodation and travel plans, observe police tactics, build relationships with the local community and represent supporters through whatever obstacles they faced. Crucially, the Embassy also sought to show the world that the majority of England followers were not intent on throwing plastic chairs and starting fights. For England's knockout stage fixtures the Embassy relocated to the mainland. In all, it helped 2000 fans and gave 300 press interviews, each one hacking away at stereotypes of English supporters. The FSA ran another Embassy in Malmo for the 1992 Euro Championships, and has done so at every tournament featuring England since. Truly one of the FSA's greatest legacies, the concept was subsequently adopted by a number of nations for international tournaments.

Beauchampé reported on the Embassy for *Tired and Weary* fanzine (*Off the Ball* ceased publication in 1989). He sensed a dark disappointment among the gathered press and local hooligans that not many England fans seemed interested in scrapping or indeed throwing furniture. 'Undoubtedly,' he wrote, 'the attitude of our media, police intelligence officers and government ministers contributed to the problem. For six months Italians had read how they were to be invaded by a marauding army and the hard Sards believed the hype. The number of English headcases rarely got above 100 and was more often around 0.' Back home, 'The English press generally kept strictly to their preconceived stereotypes, taking the line: no aggro, no story – any aggro, front page story'.

Pre-tournament media hyperbole inspired severe tactics from the Italian police. From behind their visors, they saw every England fan as a hooligan. No matter the nature or extent of an incident, their response seemed to be the same, wrote Beauchampé: 'Fire teargas, baton charge and strike with rifle butts first, then don't ask questions later.'

A correspondent for Blackburn Rovers fanzine *Many Miles from Home* spent five weeks at the tournament. Police attitudes manifested on arrival, with 'Passports checked against blacklists and comparisons with mugshots of "wanted" men'. Sardinians had been 'whipped into a state of paranoia over the "English Invasion".' In the light of multiple provocations such as 'the pre-conceived media hype and the harassment by the Italian police . . . coupled with the constant niggling from the ubiquitous scooter-riding teenagers,' continued *Many Miles from Home*, 'the behaviour of the English fans was exemplary.'

In Swindon Town fanzine *Bring the Noise*, Irishman Mike Lyne reported on his country's opening Group F fixture with England. Moving from town to stadium 'resembled a military operation' with police helicopters whirling above. Fans were then 'Marched in convoy across the car park,' wrote Lyne, and 'the supposed policy of strict segregation became farcical as Irish and English fans met along converging walkways, shook hands, wished each other well, and took photographs for the family album.'

Not many aspects of supporters' experiences tally with the romantic, technicolour Italia '90 of Schillaci's eyes bulging and Gazza's dripping as portrayed now. The World Cup that ushered in modern football did not look from the terrace like it did on the telly. Another fan account, in *Off the Shelf*, recounted a dreadful experience laced with disorganisation and living costs tripling from one week to the next. Within stadiums, areas reserved for £150 Category 1 seats were easily accessible to those who had bought far cheaper tickets. Even worse, the beer contained no alcohol. In Port Vale fanzine *The Memoirs of Seth Bottomley*, another English traveller to Italy, Phil Sherwin, reported that fans were searched three times upon entering stadiums. 'They literally went through everything,' wrote Sherwin, 'at one stage tipping my bag of Opal Fruits out onto the floor to make sure I wasn't concealing a micro sub-machine gun within. One supporter had all his English coinage taken away.'

Those were minor hassles compared to the horrendous treatment meted out to fans before England's game with the

Netherlands on 16 June. According to Steve Beauchampé, 'Several hundred fans were set upon by the security forces in a revenge attack on anyone English following an earlier stone throwing incident by a different group of fans.' All of them were kettled on the forecourt of a petrol station on the outskirts of Cagliari as they attempted to reach the match. Many were 'brutally beaten and some were robbed (cameras, cash, match tickets)'.

Rodney, Rodney! published a lengthy eyewitness report by FSA delegate John Tummon. 'The bruise on my left shoulder has gone away now,' wrote Tummon, 'but the memory of how I got it will take some shifting, as it will for the hundreds of others who were beaten with rifle butts and riot sticks and then held like prisoners of war.' Officers, he continued, 'sank to such depths of cowardly violence against innocent and peaceful people that they do not deserve to be called a police force, not even a bad, inefficient or corrupt police force'.

Following trouble in the coastal resort of Rimini, prior to their quarter-final tie with Belgium in Bologna 247 England supporters were arrested by police, transferred to the airport and deported. The arrests seemed to target supporters randomly. Many of the 247 had not even been in Rimini. 'In one case,' wrote Craig Brewin of the FSA in its newsletter, 'police walked into a restaurant and asked if there were any English people present. They were told they were being taken into protective custody.' One of the deported had been on a family holiday rather than in Italy to watch football. Leaving his hotel to buy cigarettes, he had been detained and sent back to England. 'The first his wife knew was when she received a telephone call from Gatwick,' continued Brewin. 'It is also believed that the plane was hired three days before the deportations and the numbers rounded up were simply to make it a full plane load.' A Rimini Defence Fund was launched by the FSA to pay the innocent deported fans' legal costs and hold the Italian authorities to account, its details carried in appeal messages across hundreds of fanzines.

Fanzines pre-emptively countered other aspects of what became the orthodox narrative of the tournament that changed football. No god was untouchable. In Ireland, following the tournament Shelbourne fanzine *From Home to Home* was mystified by the veneration of manager Jack Charlton and his team. An autumn 1990 article found there to be 'something very eerie' about the team's parade from Dublin Airport to College Green. It was 'sinisterly reminiscent of the Nuremberg rallies in Germany with Adolf Charlton surrounded by his Goebbels-like henchmen! Sieg heil for der Fuhrer Charlton!'

The article moved on to Charlton's agricultural playing style: 'If that's how football should be played, well then you can shove it up your arse with a wire brush and Dettol!' The gentle Geordie himself – or 'Wor Neckie Charlton' – was 'a boorish ignoramus, content to lock himself away inside his pompous aura of infallibility'. Overall, 'The only winners during Italia '90 were the fascist capitalist pig bankers and the scumbag leeches in the travel industry who bled an incredibly gullible public for every last penny'. It did not quite meet with the image of an ecstatic Ireland unified by soccer as depicted in Roddy Doyle's *The Van* and elsewhere.

England's own deity also had his atheists. As the Gazza duvet covers flew out of Argos and Index, *The Spur* took a critical view of the player who made it acceptable for men to cry in public. In mid-1991, writer James Loxley dispelled several myths as perhaps only a Spurs fan could, having watched the part-beguiling, part-infuriating Gascoigne over three years. While recognising many 'spectacular' moments in Italy, Loxley observed the homecoming and 'assumed the Pope had declared Gazza to be the reborn Christ'. Spurs fans had seen 'the glory punctuated by serious outbreaks of crap. And said nothing. We saw the petulant kid sticking his elbows into opponents who had the temerity to play better than him. We had to endure two disgusting 45s and an unspeakable sub-karaoke LP. We had to watch our hero endorsing an aftershave distilled from the sewage of Sellafield.

We had to live with the fact that the man we idolised had as much credibility as Woodpecker Cider, extra sweet.'

Now, after Gascoigne's 'abysmal' behaviour and tackle during the 1991 FA Cup Final against Nottingham Forest, and with the Geordie bound for Rome, Spurs fans had turned. On the night of the Wembley final, Loxley had been in a pub with fellow supporters, watching match highlights. Gazza's 'tackles and his departure on a stretcher were greeted with jeers'.

No one and nothing was sacred in fanzine pages. Yet for all their writers' views from the front line at home and abroad, the effects of Italia '90 on how football and its followers were perceived had been profound. Its glow, however, should not detract from the endeavours of fanzine contributors, who had begun their own missionary work years earlier, after all. *Grorty Dick* summarised this position in the summer of 1990. 'The jolt of England's World Cup glory has acted like a jet-powered shot of hormone replacement therapy for our once decrepit national game,' said an editorial, 'removing – at a stroke – the sags and wrinkles of its wizened public image. Suddenly garbed in the timeless fashion of success, football is trendy again – suitable for primetime family viewing and edging out the weather as the number one in the bus stop chat chart.' However, the West Bromwich Albion fanzine emphasised, the 'groundwork of positivism' had been 'laid by fanzines and the FSA in the years since Heysel' and had now 'translated into a euphoric return to Europe' for English clubs.

Within this brave new world, there were, too, other achievements towards which fanzines made an enormous contribution. Little wonder they were now attracting widespread attention.

38p per minute

This is Leyton Orient Clubcall on 0898 thirty pence a minute! Yes! Leyton Orient Clubcall. Yo! This is Clubcall. You have dialled Leyton Orient Clubcall. Yes congratulations - it's time for a crappy ten minute jingle before we tell you what goodies we have for you today (or yesterday maybe).

Yes, we have perhaps five minutes of chit chat and news from Orient, some completely banal and boring, some quite interesting, you never know, so You'll have to hang on and wait and see on Leyton Orient Clubcall on 0898 - 38p a minute, in case we tell something you might well expect to hear on local radio if you had a decent service or read in the local press, but we'll make sure we get the news first, and you must pay 38p a minute for the privilege - a total of £1.50/£2, or even £10 a week! Make sure you pay your bill. What? You're phoning from work, and you work for British Telecom? Bastard. Leyton Orient Clubcall on 0898. Oh, sod it.

Later on we will hear from Frank Clark on the exciting build up to our big match against Stockport County next Saturday. That will be really interesting, later on on Clubcall.

But, first of all, last Saturday the O's suffered a home defeat against some mediocre 4th division run of the mill team - an unlucky defeat for the O's, but we could still win the league if we win all our remaining games. We spoke to Terry Howard.

Clubcall: Ooh Terry Howard, what about our promotion chances then?

Terry: You know what I mean?

Clubcall: Now we speak to John Sitton. John, a couple of wicked tack - les last week. You certainly don't take prisoners, do you?

John: Er, yeah, like...

Terry: You know what I mean?

Clubcall: Alan, another fine performance from yourself. Are you pleased with your form this season?

Alan: Well, I'm quite middle class really and I have a bit of a posh voice and never say "know what I mean" or "yeah, like" but I do sometimes throw in the odd soccer cliche, at the end of the day.

Clubcall: Now a word from Paul Ward. Paul you're out injured at the moment and John Sitton is the current captain. Now, do you think you can win your place back when you're fit again?

Biffa: Awa, awa! Are yuz takin' tu me? Whaddye takin' aboot? How, ye must be soft - like that southern softie Sitton! A've seen berra and tuffer tacklin' in bloody kindergarten. Leave me alurn, will ya. Are yuz lookin' at me, like? Spill my pint?

Clubcall: Thankyou Paul. Now, Peter Wells. How do you feel playing for the reserve team at the moment?

Peter: I'll have a pint of lager please.

Terry: What time is Rainbow on?

Clubcall: Now, the O's have an exciting Capital League match at Wealdstone next Wednesday. That's the 2nd XI at Wealdstone. Should be really exciting, and on Saturday, we have 4th division action at Carlisle. If you can't make that, then ring 0898 something or other for live commentary at our cheap off peak rate - only 25p a minute! It might be cheaper to actually travel 1st class on B.R. and go and watch the real thing, but never mind. What about Saturday - how do you see it going, Terry? And what's your favourite colour?

Terry: Know what I mean? If you were constantly asked the same stupid questions, what can you do? Recite some poetry or what?!

Clubcall: Yes, thankyou. We are providing a service which the punters want. Now, Frank, what about Saturday's game?

Frank: Eeh, well, er - beep, crackle, burr - Hello there, my name is Sue, let me tell you about the first time I -

PUT THAT BLOODY PHONE DOWN!

*All the characters in this pathetic article are fictitious and any resemblance to actual persons, living or dead, is purely coincidental. Ha ha ha.

Voice of the Valley

NO 1
FEB 88
30p

The only INDEPENDENT Charlton mag

MESSAGE TO OUR SUPPORTERS

CHARLTON ATHLETIC

On March 26....

LET'S GO HOME

ABSOLUTELY NO CONNECTION WITH CASC OR CAFC

CHAPTER 17: END OF THE GOLDEN AGE AND FOOTBALL IN FASHION

We sat down and said, 'This is the end of it, really, isn't it?' because they just wanted to sanitise it and make it mainstream. And they wanted to be a little bit edgy by bringing us into the fold. The edge was lost at that point.

— ANDY GROOM, EDITOR OF *THE PETERBOROUGH EFFECT* FANZINE

On 21 September, 1985, Charlton Athletic defeated Stoke City at The Valley. The atmosphere as the game kicked off was gloomy, hushed, reflective; like that of a wake before the bar opens. Two weeks earlier, each Addicks supporter attending a game against Crystal Palace had been handed a piece of paper carrying glum tidings: their club was leaving home to become a lodger at Selhurst Park. Their exile was indefinite and the club had no intention of returning.

At half-time during the Stoke game, some fans climbed onto the pitch. They were applauded until one group attempted to snap a crossbar, provoking chanted pleas for their removal. The asset stripping could wait until after the final whistle. At that juncture, 'Grown men and women grabbed any souvenirs they could lay their hands on,' said Darren Risby in *Valiants' Viewpoint*, 'from pieces of turf to ripping out seats. One lad climbed a floodlight in protest. Events could have got ugly when a rightly boisterous 400-strong demo, of potential lynch-mob proportions, developed on the ruined pitch. Feelings ran so high because ordinary people loved their club.'

It was a familiar tale – an impoverished board with little regard for the heartstrings of fans. Rick Everitt was there that day against Stoke, as always. He can be seen in pictures of the post-match bounty grab, holding up a banner protesting against the club's move. It was, he reflects now, 'the culmination of a period where the club was in a very, very poor state. So although the particular circumstances were extraordinary, the fact that there was a crisis wasn't unexpected.' Charlton's exodus was not driven by maladministration alone. Palace chairman Ron Noades 'passionately advocated' the move, continues Everitt, setting up a company named Selhurst Valley Limited that would theoretically facilitate co-ownership of the Eagles' stadium. In 1985, Noades had declared, 'I believe we will see ground-sharing by six more teams… It will always work.'

Everitt immediately lobbied for Charlton's return home, and in October 1986 a supportive petition in the local *Mercury* newspaper ignited an organised campaign. Alongside fellow activists, he also strived to form a viable business case for the move. Then he realised that the campaign needed a focal point, a place to chip away, organise and gather momentum. It needed a fanzine.

Everitt launched *Voice of the Valley* issue 1 in January 1988. Its first cover blared a simple message: LET'S GO HOME. An evocative editorial led the way and provoked the goosebumps: 'There are weeds three feet high where once Derek Hales claimed goalscoring records. The goalmouths are choked with greenery more suffocating than any offside trap . . . Nails driven into the doors of rusting turnstiles might as well be driven into supporters' hearts . . . The smell of hamburgers is displaced by the smell of neglect. The floodlights never pierce the evening gloom. The theatre of our dreams is dark.'

'It was really striking how it was received,' says Everitt of those early days, 'fans were not used to people speaking in their voice and reporting their views.' Enthusiasm flowed from fellow supporters grateful to have their thoughts staring back at them, and to read of how, by acting together, they might help their team get home. Although attendances at Selhurst Park fell to the 6000 mark, 2500 of them were buying *Voice of the Valley*.

The fanzine's campaign was bolstered by Everitt's position from 1989 as the *Mercury*'s Addicks correspondent. In its pages, he was able to give sympathetic coverage and cover each seemingly monumental setback from an informed position. Then, in 1990, a momentous decision: the campaign would stand 60 candidates – covering every ward – in that May's local elections.

The Valley Party masterminded an impressive, organised and energetic crusade driven by the fanzine and a considerable activist base. One activist, Richard Hunt, worked in advertising and was able to negotiate 30 prime billboard sites declaring: Vote Valley. Everitt's *Mercury* role meant another space for reaching thousands with Vote Valley slogans. Support also flowed from other clubs' fanzines and their supporters, including local rivals Palace and Millwall. Vote Valley campaigners experienced unlikely solidarity at the Den during a canvass of the turnstiles.

Although no Valley Party councillors were elected, their candidates split the vote in several wards with significant consequences. The head of the planning committee, serial blocker of blueprints to redevelop The Valley, was ousted. In all, 14,838 votes were won, more than those cast for the Liberal Democrats and Greens combined. Soon, council attitudes began to change, and after much to-ing and fro-ing, and the securing at last of solid finance, in 1992 the Addicks moved home.

It was widely felt that *Voice of the Valley* had played a central part in this victory. Beyond giving fans the distraction of typical fanzine content, it had retained focus and heart, firing on the campaign in its doomiest months. Everitt is too modest to say as much, but will concede that it certainly 'created shared consciousness. It allowed people to understand that what they thought was what other people thought. And that they weren't the outliers. It was the club or the media that were the outliers.'

Despite fanzines' resolute contributions to supporter culture in the early 1990s, and a boom in new titles, some within the movement felt that it had lost direction. In the introduction to his second book of fanzine highlights, *Get Your Writs Out!*, editor Martin Lacey suggested that 'Standards have declined. The unwritten code of the pioneering fanzines that being "alternative" meant being self-consciously anti-racist, anti-sexist, anti-homophobic has been seriously breached by a minority.' Instead of 'humorous disrespect', the new wave of fanzines had begun to write about other clubs with 'pointless provocation'. Breaching a cardinal rule of the early, trailblazing fanzine movement, many new titles made tidy profits. Some had been founded by ambitious editors driven by motives far removed from the unpaid DIY days of the 1980s. Steve Moss of the artful *Blow Football* fanzine felt similarly. Writing in Lacey's book, he decried the recent 'decline of a large part of the fanzine world into an orgy of poor writing, pathetic slagging off of its rivals and their supporters, and copying ideas – in short, everything that fanzines were supposed to be about blowing away'.

Late in 1991, *Five to Three* – a Welsh production that despised the 'awful' word 'fanzine' – lamented that publications were 'definitely on the decline'. Many, declared an editorial, were now 'glossy efforts full of match reports', and 'As the list of current "fanzines" in *WSC* lengthens, so the entire structure weakens and one of these days it's all gonna crash to the ground.'

Taking his own discontent further, Manchester City supporter Phill Gatenby founded *This Charming Fan*, a two-issue fanzine of 500 copies lamenting the movement's decay. Fanzines had, said Gatenby, departed from their dissenting origins as 'political pressure groups, dealing with the politics of government legislation or club politics'. In tandem, a new prime minister – John Major – had arrived, claiming to be 'a friend of football', and celebrities had begun to attach themselves to the game. 'All of a sudden,' Gatenby continued, 'the fan has shifted from the

80s yob to the 90s "new fan, new man" label.' With little to moan about, fanzines had lurched into bland territories, with many now resembling matchday programmes and cosying up to their clubs. The spread of Amstrad PCs professionalised design but also made it less human. Like punk, ran the argument of Gatenby and others, the movement had been subsumed into the mainstream. Fanzines had been so successful at rebranding football supporters as witty and cultured that now others wished to join them. No longer did anyone have to whisper their love of the game in polite company.

Andy Lyons feels this trendifying of fandom began even before World Cup '90. From 1989, he and other *When Saturday Comes* staff members were regularly courted by television networks and production companies keen to develop shows that would effectively be fanzines on screen. Then, after the Italian tournament BBC2's Janet Street-Porter made contact. 'They'd received several pitches for programmes about football fan culture,' remembers Lyons, 'some of which had enclosed copies of *WSC*. And none of them had told us. So she thought she'd ask us to have a look at these pitches and see what we thought.' Street-Porter's vision was for a programme named *When Saturday Comes*, with Lyons et al as researchers. However, he adds, 'We thought that didn't sound like such a good idea, because if it wasn't very good, then it would kill us off. We'd be the magazine of the failed TV show. In the end that became *Standing Room Only*.'

Over four series, screened from 1991 to 1994, *Standing Room Only* – some of us can still whistle the theme tune – co-opted the fanzine ethos, and indeed occasionally showed issue covers. Elsewhere, through fanzines themselves television and radio researchers asked for contributions from readers. In 1990, BBC producer Nick Patrick wrote to various titles advertising a new radio show named *Bob Hatton Rattle*. 'By building on the foundations laid by yourselves and other fanzines,' he wrote, the show would 'provide an entertaining alternative to existing football programmes.' Producers did not always credit the influence of the fanzine movement. In the summer of 1994, BBC2 aired an evening of football programming under the umbrella title of *Goal TV*. As *WSC* noted in August of that year, 'Given that the whole evening used fans' experiences as its principal source of material, the complete absence of references to fanzines was nothing short of astonishing.'

The Peterborough Effect's Andy Groom views the conventional media's adoption of fanzines as 'almost the beginning of the end. I remember getting invited to Central TV and Anglia TV and I had a slot on the local radio station on a Friday. And we sat down and said, "This is the end of it, really, isn't it?" Because they just wanted to sanitise it and make it mainstream. And they wanted to be a little bit edgy by bringing us into the fold. The edge was lost at that point.' Local and national outlets, whether broadcast or print, began to run features with names such as 'Fans' Eye View' and 'FanZone'. Suddenly, deafness cleared, snobbery fell away and editors could not get enough. At its best, this fresh output gave those who had loved fanzines from the start further creative joy; no football phone-in has come close to Danny Baker's inspired *606*. At its worst, it gave us David Mellor inexplicably presenting the same show.

Among this changing scene, 1992 saw the publication of Nick Hornby's *Fever Pitch*, an unprecedented and sublime rendering of a supporter's obsessive nature. 'Although Nick Hornby's often credited with making football respectable for the middle-classes and making it cool,' argues Adrian Goldberg, 'he walked into the space that had been created by the fanzines. The fanzines laid the ground for a literature of football. And I bear him no ill will. He's a fantastic writer. But I think fanzines helped to create the environment and the readership for something different about football.'

Not all fanzine writers enjoyed the book. An anonymous Preston North End contributor in *Deepdale Rudge* attributed its success as stemming 'solely from his [Hornby's] membership of the literary establishment' and accused the Berkshire-raised author of being 'a trophy hunter'. In *Dial M For Merthyr*, Taffy

Fox picked apart one particular aspect: 'I disagree venomously with *Fever Pitch*, in which the author says that football fans always prefer a 4-0 victory to a 3-2 comeback win. Total toss, call me old-fashioned but football is all about emotion and having it stretched and thrown like a particularly tough Stretch Armstrong is pure delight!' Revisiting the article now, Taffy Fox (Jonny Owen) laughs: 'Reading this is like looking at an old photo of yourself – you see you but you see a different you. As a 54-year-old I would say I'd prefer a 4-0 win now. . . maybe it's an age thing and the rollercoaster is too much. Give me a steady drive now!'

For his part, in a 1995 *WSC* article, Hornby recognised that while his book's publication 'coincided exactly with the formation of the Premier League', it was quite clear which event 'had the most bearing on the way that the game has changed over the last couple of years. If there are more families at football now, and more directors' boxes, and more giant screens and less noise, then it is not because I wrote a book and a lot of Southern softies loved it; it is because Alan Sugar, David Dein and the rest wanted it that way.'

From *Fever Pitch* and similar works derived a new fan stereotype, defined by Mike Ticher as 'that sort of fanatical identification to the nth degree with your team'. Andy Lyons noted the same rebranding of supporters and feels it was represented in the way that 1990s football television programmes 'required people in the audience to wear a football shirt, because in this new image football fans are fanatics who wear the shirts and they name their kids after players and they paint their houses in the colours of the team. That became another easy archetype and of course it was never as simple as that.'

One such show was BBC2's *Fantasy Football League*, presented by David Baddiel and Frank Skinner. First airing on 11 January, 1994 in a post-pub 11.15 p.m. berth, team managers included Andrew Ridgeley, Peter Cook and Mandy Smith. In a matter of years, celebrities had gone from keeping any affection for football in the closet to demanding their agents sealed slots on the bandwagon. London football fanzine *Tales from the Riverbank* was not impressed: 'Not only has every newspaper latched on to the idea of producing their own leagues, but now even the BBC has stooped low enough to have a television programme dedicated to Fantasy Football. It is presented by two second rate student comedians.'

Fantasy Football was, says Andy Lowe of *The Tricky Tree*, the moment fanzine culture was comprehensively purloined by the mainstream. 'That's when you lose the ethos and what it was actually about in the first place. It goes from being that underground movement into the mainstream and people just take it and do their own thing with it. Now we're watching David Baddiel blacked up as Jason Lee and we're going, "Hold on a minute, what? What's that? That's not funny."' As Tom Davies puts it, 'Suddenly we were almost sick of people hyping football rather than putting it down.'

Yet the hype machine was only just revving up.

British Broadcasting Corporation,
New Broadcasting House,
PO Box 27
Oxford Road
Manchester M60 1SJ

STANDING ROOM ONLY

Dear Fanzine Editors,

TV's only programme for the "football fan", is looking for new reporters to front some of our film packages. If you fancy your chances, read on....

We're keen to build on our links with the fanzines and reflect more fanzine culture in our programme. If you're an editor who's got what it takes, all you have to do is this:

1. Think up a topical idea for a five minute film package on **STANDING ROOM ONLY**.

2. Put pen to paper and explain how you would pursue and angle the story, who you would interview (with at least two interviewees) and what you'd expect them to say. Then write your own narrative, introduction and conclusion linking the interviews.

3. Finally, construct a running order of six items for **STANDING ROOM ONLY**, including humorous and personality-based features.

4. Finished?! Send it off to Dele Oniya, **STANDING ROOM ONLY**, at the above address to arrive by Tuesday 25th August 1992. Please include your curriculum vitae, a recent photo and your daytime and evening telephone number with your application.

Remember to give information about the visual content and the kind of pictures you would use.

STANDING ROOM ONLY will be shortlisting outstanding candidates to be screen-tested at the BBC in Manchester in late August. If you're successful there is the prospect of fronting your own special reports on the show, which goes on air on September 7th 1992.

The CROOKED SPIREITE

no.6
Sep.'88
30p.

UNFETTERED BY THE TRUTH

It's Pinocchio!

Inside:

FULHAM FIX- MORE LIES! pp.4&5
the truth behind the slur: p.25

SCOTTISH CUP ◦ FSA ◦ EURO '88

CHAPTER 18: HELLO PREMIER LEAGUE, GOODBYE TO ALL THAT

The Premier League has come into being and I for one think that it will be a bit of a flop. The reason being that it won't earn the kind of dosh the big clubs expect.

– *MI WHIPPET'S DEAD*, ROTHERHAM UNITED FANZINE

They had wanted it for years, the unseen suits. A Super League, smaller in form than the existing Division One, and possibly with no relegation so that their clubs' monopoly could not be disturbed by piffling lesser teams. Television would be integral, and an opening up of sponsorship. Everything was for sale and there was hardly a mention of mere fans.

Various incarnations were proposed and defeated until the Premier League sidled into view and shone pound signs in the suits' eyes. In 1986, big club chairmen reluctantly reversed a proposed Super League scheme in exchange for a greater share of the revenue distributed to smaller clubs. Two years on, more discussions prompted the spectre of a 12-club division in which teams would face each other four times over each season. Television money had been split between the Football League's 92 clubs; now the dirty dozen would take it all. Another proposal decreed that Super League membership would depend on stadium size, with a minimum capacity set at 20,000.

A 'Big Five' – Arsenal, Everton, Liverpool, Spurs and Manchester United – steered much of this plotting. Fanzines attached to smaller clubs who acquiesced reacted angrily. 'It was a disgrace and an embarrassment when the club grovelled to the Big Five and tagged along in their Super League wake,' said West Ham's *Never Mind the Boleyn*. 'Who takes these decisions and on whose behalf? Did anyone ask you what sort of football you wanted to see at Upton Park? Of course not – we're only the ones who keep the club alive, pay the wages, etc etc.' *Off the Ball* revealed another leaked scheme in autumn 1988. Once more, a 'Big Five' had concocted the ploy – a European Super League in which England's elite would be joined by the cream of Scotland, the Netherlands, Spain and Italy.

In August 1991, *Speke from the Harbour* – an Everton fanzine based in Northern Ireland – polled its readers with the question, 'Do you agree with the concept of a Super League?' Ninety per cent of respondents said 'No'. *Speke*'s editorial pleaded that the club refuse to become part of 'an elitist grouping. We should be doing everything in our power to stop it going ahead. The problem is how? Whilst politicians are elected by the votes of the people they represent, football club directors have no mandate from the supporters . . . none of them are answerable to the fans.'

Momentum was with the directors. Supported by Graham Kelly of the Football Association ('the thinking man's dung beetle', according to *A Load of Bull* fanzine), they announced their intention to leave the Football League and join a new Premier League. The reaction of writer CTP in Watford fanzine *The Yellow Experience* spoke for many: 'So those treacherous bastards that masquerade as the game's custodians have finally crawled out from under their stones, betraying all and sundry for the lure of television's millions.' In hoarding money, continued the article, the Premier League clubs had demonstrated that they 'do not care about *us* because at this stage they cannot see any further than the huge, enormous pound signs glistening in their greedy little minds. . . Without the lifeline, frayed and tattered as it is already, the smaller clubs will go to the wall, they will die.'

Also in opposition was the FSA and numerous player reps in the Professional Footballers' Association trade union. Rumours of a players' strike circulated. In November 1991, writer Ed Horton sent letters to 60 fanzines to muster support. The Premier League, he insisted, was not 'inevitable. There is one group of people who will be seriously affected by a shake-up of the football industry – and have the power to change it. That's the players . . . A players' strike can stop the Premier League.' Horton's stance was perceptive; six months after his letter, players voted overwhelmingly to strike, in theory forcing the postponement of fixtures. Negotiations, though, saw their action abandoned. 'The strike tends to confirm what we knew all along,' said Stockport County fanzine *The Tea Party*, 'players have got far more integrity than the greedy sods who are behind the Premier League.'

To fanzines, it was obvious prior to deals even being settled that the coming of any Super or Premier League would mean television companies dominating clubs and ignoring fans. In a 1990 issue of Derby County fanzine *Mutton Mutineer*, Simon Woodward wrote of their 'new-found powers to manipulate fixtures. The roles of Master and Servant are sadly obvious. Consequently, an unsightly scramble for T.V. money has developed and the doctrine of win at all costs has proliferated. . . A league tailored for T.V. is on the horizon.'

Upon the Premier League's arrival in August 1992, fanzines were far from entertained by Sky Television's inflatable sumo wrestlers and grinning cheerleaders. In *The Tea Party*, Mike Cochrane despaired at 'hysterical' presenter 'Richard Whatever His Name Is' and predicted that 'the whole Sky football thing will collapse. About 700,000 people on average are watching the Sky games, compared with around 2 million watching Channel 4's Italian football.' It was a sentiment echoed in Rotherham United fanzine *Mi Whippet's Dead*: 'The Premier League has come into being and I for one think that it will be a bit of a flop. The reason being that it won't earn the kind of dosh the big clubs expect.'

A correspondent in Doncaster Rovers' *Raise the Roof* had decided to experience Sky's new-fangled Monday Night Football for a fixture between Coventry City and Spurs: 'We got there early, only to find a giant matchball in the centre circle, and both teams trying to do their pre-match warm-ups, hindered by about seventy dancers. . . Then a large-bellied figure in Spurs colours waddled on to the pitch. Was it Gazza returning to his old club for the evening? No, it was BSKYB's own Bart Simpson, making a nuisance of himself during the warm-up by knocking over the Spurs keeper Ian Walker.'

Fanzines quickly perceived the shifting of money towards the top of the game. While there had always been an elite, funds had trickled downwards and the consensus was that all clubs were part of the same biosphere. Now, the detached Premier League seemed to care little for the pyramid. The day after the new division's first round of fixtures, precarious finances saw fourth tier Maidstone United resign from the Football League and implode. Aldershot had folded not long previously, and fanzine writers perceived a troubling trend. In the *Preston Pie Muncher*, Steve Brennan defined the Premier League clubs' attitude to teams like his own as: 'To hell with the likes of Aldershot and Maidstone and even our good selves, the 22 clubs who resigned from the Football League are up there on their own laughing their socks off.' In what now feels a case of forlorn hope, Spurs fanzine *A View from the Shelf* called for 'the boycotting of games and not wilting to the ever-increasing demands of Sky. Let us show that it is not money that decides the future of football.'

One solo refusenik was Andy Zaltzman. Writing in a 1993 issue of *Over the Moon* fanzine, the comedian and cricket statistician recorded how he had become 'pissed off with the greedy, selfish, narrow-minded attitude of the Premier League clubs'. Instead, Zaltzman had embraced his local club, Gillingham, and on '8th January 1993, at approximately 9.30 pm . . . discovered for the first time why football is so universally popular. When Gillingham made victory certain with a fourth goal in the last minute against Rochdale, I was overwhelmed with exhilaration, delight and any similar emotions you can find in your Thesaurus.' Further, if the game continued to 'treat its followers and the smaller clubs with such disrespect' it 'could lose much of its appeal, and many of its fans'.

No matter the whims and yearnings of fanzine writers such as Zaltzman, the Premier League was immovable. Its inexorable, headlong rush towards absolute power was underway. With heavy irony, fanzines had played their part in its success by helping make the game a more attractive, marketable proposition. 'The Premier League benefitted from the change in culture that fanzines helped bring about, 100%,' believes Adrian Goldberg. 'And I don't think fanzine culture has received enough credit for the beneficial changes that happened in football in the 1990s. Too often it's said "1992 Premier League comes along and that changes football." But supporters changed football through fanzine culture and the fanzine movement.'

Beneath the Sky gloss remained the grime. The experience of going to matches did not instantly improve the moment Simple Minds' 'Alive and Kicking' jangled onto our screens. There were still incidents to report, struggles for fanzines to wage, ideas worth fighting for.

Although by the first season of the Premier League fences had been removed at Anfield, Old Trafford, White Hart Lane and elsewhere, many remained. Now less terrifying with their spikes amputated and heights reduced, nonetheless they left many of us watching wondering what we had done wrong. Often, the grounds where they were still in place were those of lower division and non-league clubs starved of funds to undertake modifications. Even in 1994, Llama in *Dial M For Merthyr* was dreaming of their being removed at Penydarren Park: 'The place is like a bloody fortress, without a satisfactory reason. . . So come on and dismantle the damn things.'

Neither had all police forces entirely ceased regarding all supporters as hooligans. In April 1992, *The Fox* reported on the visit of Leicester City to Prenton Park. There, specialist officers had stood at the away turnstiles 'Protecting and Serving the public by grabbing surprised looking people round the neck and enquiring if they had had a drink . . . No-one arrived at the ground in anything like a drunken state, and there isn't a law, yet, that says you can't have a drink if you are going to a football match.' Their work continued for some time, leaving 'Astonished people walking around, minus three or four mates who had been dragged off, wondering what they had done to have their evening ruined.' Inside the ground, the officers continued to intimidate fans by staring solidly at them. Leicester equalised, with some supporters clinging to the fence in celebration, a common sight. Their actions, however, were 'obviously an uprising of insurgents designed to damage the very fabric of society' and were 'dealt with as such by our eager friends'.

At the same time, in Derby County fanzine *Hey Big Spender* a correspondent reported being kept behind a police line while officers ignored 'bottle and coin throwing'. The next sentence could have been plucked from any fanzine over the previous six or seven years: 'I am getting heartily sick of being treated as some lower form of life because I choose to spend my leisure hours following my football team around the country.' At Derby's own Baseball Ground, early in 1993 Dave Stringer of *The Tea Party* had witnessed throwback crushing while venturing to watch Stockport County in the FA Cup. Complaining he was suffering on a 'grossly overpopulated' terrace, a police officer and steward told him to return there. Then, 'stewards and police attempted to close the gates to this area of terracing. This blocked the only means of escape supporters had from this dangerous situation.' Finally, the gates were reopened and some Stockport fans allowed onto the pitch before being moved. We can probably imagine what passed through their minds for a few minutes.

Nor had violence around stadiums been completely eradicated. Late in 1992, Simon Wright of *Grorty Dick* wrote to his counterpart at Burnley fanzine *Who Ate All the Pies?*,

Dave Cooper. A number of Wright's fellow Baggies – including fathers with their young sons – had been 'systematically attacked and beaten'. Cooper responded that 'The behaviour of some of the Burnley fans that day was vile enough to make me feel ashamed of being associated with them through common support of the same club'.

A few months later, Manchester City supporters invaded the Maine Road pitch during an FA Cup quarter-final with Spurs. The mood outside the stadium afterwards was febrile. Juliette Wills wrote in *The Spur* of being suddenly marooned with one other friend amid volatile City fans: 'I'd hidden my scarf, but they soon spotted a lone Spur decked out in his colours and proceeded to beat him to bits on the pavement in front of us. There was nothing at all we could do – two of us against fifty of them? No chance! All we could do was to get onto the bus and get the hell out.' Having emerged from the darkest hours of the 1980s, it was thoroughly depressing for any fanzine contributor to find that some fans wished to turn out the lights again.

These blazes of violence, though, were undoubtedly rarer than they once had been. All the same, they gave the tabloid press an opportunity to fall back into their castigation of football supporters. England fans were of particular use in this pursuit. Issue 10 of *Bamber's Right Foot*, a Torquay United fanzine, carried a first-hand article from a fan who had been in the Netherlands for England's 2-0 defeat in October 1993 – Graham Taylor's infamous 'Do I Not Like That?' match. Having watched among the hostility of baying youths and chain-smoking orange-scarved police officers, the article's author returned to his travel coach. Four supporters were now missing, but the police forced the bus to depart before their return. On boarding a ferry at Calais, English newspapers were purchased to 'find out how the game and the fans behaviour' was being reported. The Torquay writer was incredulous: '"1,400 arrested", really? "Fans burn down stadium!" – *Daily Mirror*. What a load of rubbish. I've come home from some of these games before, but the reporting for this was the pits. Any old cobblers to sell a few extra copies.' In fact, only

20 had been formally arrested, and six charged. The spirit of Moynihan's calculator lived on if you followed the Three Lions.

If lesser-craved morsels of old football still stank out the game, there was one aspect that changed remorselessly in the early years of the Premier League. Throughout the divisions, our cherished homes changed forever, for better or worse. Although Lord Justice Taylor's all-seater demands were slowed or slackened, his report meant wholesale redesigns, rising prices at the gates and a change in match atmosphere. It also shaped games in a more pleasant direction. Where a 1986 father would probably choose against taking his daughter to watch their team together, now she had a season ticket next to him.

Yet many clubs had begun replacing crush barriers with minibars before Hillsborough and Taylor. The Kenilworth Road scheme showcased an aspect of redevelopment resolutely unpopular with fanzines: the executive box, coming to a ground near you to coincide with whatever sparkling Super League could be connived. In *Wise Men Say*, Eric Williams objected to boxes' necessary reduction of the turnstile loyal, and their defacing of grand old stadiums. Aesthetics had been 'ruined' at Villa Park where the 'beautiful Trinity Road Stand has never looked the same since the club installed executive boxes, whilst Highbury's bank of boxes is totally out of character with the rest of the ground. The clock has even been moved onto the top of this monstrosity.' Arsenal fanzines seemed to agree. In its 1989 redevelopment, the club, said the *Arsenal Echo Echo*, had 'put good old business sense ahead of tradition and, most Clock Enders would claim, ahead of the fans'.

North London rivals Spurs seemed determined to exchange their fans' beloved Shelf – an unusual if traditional terrace in the second tier of the East Stand – for similarly glassy facilities. Fanzines and the FSA led the charge against the plot, driving the Left on the Shelf (LOTS) campaign. Doug Cheeseman,

Spurs fan and art editor at *WSC* for a decade from 1989, wrote in *The Spur* of how 'The directors are prostituting the club's traditions and the fans' interests once again by pandering to the sponsors before the supporters . . . This is a football club becoming a Thatcherite vision of mock comfort and sterility.' In a letter to the same fanzine, Christopher Johnson supposed that the club now wished to 'fill the ground with 25,000 or so rich businessman types and Scandinavians, and so gradually price us out of White Hart Lane altogether'. Loudly uniting and employing tactics such as the lobbying of Haringey Council, LOTS won a concession against this seemingly inevitable development – a diminished 'Shelf' area for 3000 fans in front of the executive boxes.

The concerns of top-flight fans were echoed down the divisions. Fanzine contributors knew their grounds would have to change – they, after all, stood to benefit most from football becoming a safer watch. That change, though, did not have to mean the executive embrace and rising ticket prices. As early as March 1988, Swindon Town fanzine *Bring the Noise* acknowledged that, in the aftermath of the Bradford fire, the club's Shrivenham Road end would have to be demolished. Its wooden floors and seats were perilous enough, but in 'strong winds it is apparently likely to come tumbling down around our ears'. Dissent arose over rumours of the new stand including executive boxes. 'I fail to see the justification for these abominations at any soccer ground,' said one writer. 'After all, if people wish to watch sport in warmth and comfort over lunch or whatever, they may as well stay at home in front of the bloody TV.' Further, 'It would certainly strike me as immoral if on a cold rainy winter's day the privileged lounged around in luxury, while the stalwarts cultivated their pneumonia on a soaking Stratton Bank.'

A contemporary issue of Reading fanzine *Elm Park Disease* also identified this trend: 'Private boxes, reduced facilities and the sheep-like treatment of supporters tend to indicate that football clubs are not interested in paying customers through the turnstiles. What they now want are cigar smoking, cologne wearing local businessmen, who wear tatty sports jackets and expensive Sheepskin overcoats.'

By the time 1992 came around, all-seater grounds, their stands often peppered with executive boxes, had become much of football's inescapable fate. In March, general fanzine *Each Game as it Comes* highlighted that ticket prices had already begun to climb, a phenomenon that would only worsen. 'We've had to put up with a lot over the years,' reflected an editorial, 'and it is a great tribute to the game of football that attendances have actually been going up over the past few years. But for many this could be the final straw, if only because they are not well off enough to pay the increased entrance fees.'

Beyond the executive box land grab, beloved ground features were razed. Their losses were mourned in fanzines, many of which from the 1990s took on new narrative roles as curators of history and nostalgists. While football clubs seemed determined to bomb the past, fanzines sought to preserve stadium subtleties, artefacts and entire stands in written form.

Floodlights, their pylons increasingly usurped by bulbs fixed to new stands' roofs, were frequently mourned. In late 1991, Dave Rowley regretted 'the passing of Wolves' greatest asset – The Molineux Floodlights'. He also highlighted the practical implications of clubs' pylon destruction; how else would away supporters locate grounds in the dark?

The following September, Quincy Wagstaff of Bristol City fanzine *Bounty Hunter* cooed and sighed over Ashton Gate's floodlights. Their dismissal was a 'wanton, mindless act of vandalism . . . We just cannot come to terms with the fact that those four mighty, majestic towers of glory, splendour and, um, electricity, are simply no longer there.' When approaching the ground, the lights' absence created an 'overwhelming' sense of 'emptiness and loss'. For a night match, 'The great sheets of light that those four soaring towers of steel threw down onto the ground took your breath away.' Now, Ashton Gate melted in with the rest of the skyline.

The incremental changing of grounds gave way to the substantial. Entire, adored stands were annihilated. In 1995, to mark the passing of Turf Moor's colossal Longside terrace, *Forever and a Day* fanzine printed a special supplement edition. Writer Dave Burnley would miss the 'mass migrations from the Longside to the Bee Hole End as the game reaches a conclusion, resembling thousands of iron filings being drawn to a huge magnet represented by the exit' and 'traditional celebrations of scoring a goal Longside-style, the manic leaping up and down'. Gone too would be the 'orgasmic standing ovation at the Opera House', all of it lost to seating's staid atmosphere.

At least Burnley were losing only a terrace. In those middle years of the decade, many fans lost their entire homes. Until the seat rush, few clubs had moved across the entire century, which in itself said much about our stadium stock. Indeed, only Scunthorpe United in 1988, St Johnstone (1989) and Walsall (1990) had relocated in recent times; now directors and local councillors scrambled to find outskirt sites, dragging clubs from their urban origins. Fans were rarely asked about this flitting – to where it should be, or how they would like their new homes to look. Smashed by the wrecking ball within a few nineties' years were the Victoria Ground and Roker Park, the County Ground and Burnden Park. 'I can't believe that today's game is really the last at Ayresome Park,' wrote Robert Nichols in the 1995 *Fly Me To The Moon* issue commemorating Middlesbrough's last fixture at the old ground, 'that after today it will all be consigned to history.'

A year previously, a writer in Huddersfield Town fanzine *A Slice of Kilner Pie* had expressed similar sadness at departing Leeds Road for the all-seater McAlpine Stadium. Once more, regret flowed about being bereft of terraces, 'Those crude concrete steps behind the goal where supporters from every imaginable background gather in a united cause.' Lost would be the tradition of people taking up their spots on the concrete while being 'free to move when they want, watch the game from where they want, do what they bloody well want without some bastard steward asking them to "Sit down mate".' Goal celebrations – never, ever the same when seated – would also be missed, their 'fits of reckless arm waving, head-banging' made impossible. 'You see,' continued the article, 'like so many other lower division grounds, Leeds Road was a shithole. But it was our shithole and a mighty fine one at that.'

In common with a mood shift from grief to excitement after Middlesbrough fans migrated to the Riverside Stadium, experiencing the McAlpine fuelled a switch in mood. 'With its sweeping curves and banana trusses ... reaching out into the northern skies', the stadium would 'breathe fresh life into a comatose giant,' continued the *Kilner Pie* article. 'We had to get out, start anew ... rebuild for the future and whilst seating the old stadium was an option, its costs and the implications of the Taylor Report would've crippled us.'

All-seater stadiums did not entirely sweep away the presence of danger. Crude adaptations – terraces with plastic seats effectively strapped onto them – were rarely comfortable and occasionally hazardous. Even new-build stands troubled some. In the first issue of Liverpool fanzine *Red All Over the Land (RAOTL)*, John Pearman – editor then and still now – described a half-time crush at Newcastle's recently-renovated St James' Park. Stairways became blocked in either direction, wrote Pearman: 'I am not trying to say that the ground presents the possibility of another Hillsborough and I apologise immediately to anyone who may feel slighted by the comment. What I am trying to say is that this is an all-seater stadium built in the wake of Hillsborough and I do not believe that it is totally safe.' Had someone fallen on the steps, matters may have proceeded in a more frightening manner. 'I am fast coming to the conclusion that all-seater stadiums are nothing more than silk purses covering pig's ears,' added Pearman.

Fanzines' early warnings that all-seater, corporate-heavy stadiums would mean price rises were also being realised. While Manchester United were arriving as *the* footballing machine of the 1990s Premier League, several of their fanzines cautioned against the changing nature and noise of Old Trafford. *Red Issue* was particularly vehement, and so too *Red Attitude* ('Red,

Anti-Fascist and Proud'). At the start of the 1994/95 season, editor Dave protested that working-class supporters had already been nudged from the stadium in favour of a quieter, more wadded breed: 'You're more likely to find yourself sat next to a company director these days than a kid with a job on a building site or factory floor. Let's face it, company directors generally don't sing their hearts out for the lads.' Warming to the theme, the problem was, he continued, the 'middle-class wankers who buy expensive tickets and add nothing to the atmosphere'.

Early the following season in *United We Stand* (*UWS*), Rob Pattinson reacted to a letter issued by the club telling supporters that 'we must not swear, we must not stand up, we must not smoke, we may not get pissed. This is where football has gone wrong.' Until recently, continued Pattinson, 'a football match was one of the only places that you could do all this in comfort, without anyone else around you thinking you were some sort of demented baboon.' With assistance from the local FSA, United fanzines including *Red Issue* and *UWS* created the Independent Manchester United Supporters Association. It would, in the words of a *Red Issue* article, campaign to reverse the 'destruction of the atmosphere at Old Trafford' and curb rises in ticket prices. It was, according to a *UWS* editorial, 'a voice which fans can channel their energy into.'

Good and bad, the game had changed. Money and glamour were terms foreign to British football when the fanzine movement started out. Now, any fanzine editor wishing to continue printing had to find a place within the modern landscape that they had helped to create. Not all of them chose to do so. Their work was done.

ENDINGS AND NEW BEGINNINGS

Robert Nichols will be by his lamppost; I can see him without looking. He is always there when there is a new fanzine on sale. His cries of 'Fly Me to the Moon!' and 'Fanzine!' are part of the musicality of matchday, mingling with shouts advertising the official programme and jackpot draw. The nose catches sizzling burger wagon onions, the ears these fleeting anthems, and we feel enormously grateful to be here, closing in on kick-off.

I buy issue 659 from him, and as usual he takes my coins without examining them. 'Record Breaker' say capitalised words over the roundel advertising the fanzine's £2 price. A few months ago, it was realised that *FMTTM* is now the highest-numbered fanzine remaining, having overtaken Stoke City's much-missed *Oatcake* at number 656. With my friend Paddy, who designs the fanzine's covers, we stand chatting mostly about life, and occasionally about Middlesbrough Football Club.

I watch as tens and then hundreds and then a thousand or more match-goers gallop by en route to 3 p.m. For some of them, buying the fanzine remains a habit, part of the ritual like a lucky scarf or entering via the same turnstile. Chatting with Rob is usually a segment of their routine too. 'You see the same people and you speak to them,' he says, 'and some might say the same thing to you, maybe ask for the match prediction. There's always a guy that'll only buy it off me. It's unlucky if he buys it off anybody else.' When he is standing at the lamppost, we feel as though all is right in the world, until the match starts at least.

Still, it is a struggle to sell pieces of paper in 2025. Many have given up the fanzine habit. Many more never even cultivated it. Plus, finances are difficult when the product costs almost as much as the postage stamp that conveys it to subscribers. Today, there is a rare boom. Rob has nearly sold out. Boro are playing Wrexham and scores of their followers are buying souvenirs of this rare visit to Teesside. It is very possible that some of them think *FMTTM* is the programme. 'I've never had as many away fans buy copies since the eighties,' adds the gleeful editor, 'and thankfully none of them have spotted that I've spelt "Wrexham" wrong on the cover.'

Print fanzines live on, reports of their murder by time and the internet exaggerated. Their numbers are vastly reduced – 75 as this book went to print – but there are other Robs by other lampposts. Over the last 30 years, a couple of dozen titles have survived the ravages of message boards and social media. In that time, they have waged important campaigns and, importantly, entertained. New fanzines have joined them. From both groups, editors and contributors have straddled mediums old and young to create modern online profiles for traditional print publications.

If we are optimistic – and wasn't this movement founded on the idea of change being possible and there being better days ahead? – there may even be the basis for a print renaissance as increasing numbers of people seek solace away from screens. There is calm in fanzines' considered, knowingly dated output and delight in their grains and scents. Their authenticity has never waned, surely an increasingly attractive attribute as Artificial Intelligence strides on unchecked.

Specific to football, as more clubs cease producing programmes and paper tickets, perhaps the fanzine can fulfil that universal need for a physical record of matchday, clenched in 20 or 30 years to act as a paper time machine and whirr us back to some sacred victory or heart-crunching defeat. As Scott Sumner of *4000 Holes* says, 'Who would have ever thought that the fanzine would outlive the programme?'

There are other reasons for a renewed fanzine movement. As in the 1980s, football clubs once more control the stories told about them through their own media operations. Social media accounts, podcasts and fan TV attempt to plug the gap but seem increasingly cacophonous as they do so. Or, they are mired in tactics and transfer talk where some of us crave pie reviews and a time when football conversation was less, well, *serious*. The ego of the one-team content producer sits in contrast to the cross-club solidarity of the early fanzine editor; the reactionary X post about a performance meaning a manager *must* be sacked contrasts with the fanzine piece gradually thought out and weaved down a page once calm has descended.

'The nature of fan media is all about reaction,' says Glen Wilson, editor of Doncaster Rovers fanzine *popular STAND*. 'Who is the loudest, the angriest, the most annoyed, to the point where the sort of reaction that perhaps you'd have only seen in *Ripping Yarns* years ago now greets an unlucky one-nil defeat. It's really unhinged, away from the reality I know of watching sport and I watch it with considered people. Because football fans aren't that unhinged minority. They're much more considered, much more world weary.'

Indeed, occasionally fanzine editors who helped give supporters a voice may watch Fanalysis on Sky TV and wish they hadn't bothered.

Producing a paper fanzine is, of course, far more onerous than shouting into a microphone. Every summer, Robert Nichols and others estimate the hours they will spend and the money they won't make over the approaching season. Nichols recalls the turn of the century as being the era he became aware that the scene he had first known while inviting people in nightclubs to stapling parties was slipping away. '*When Saturday Comes* stopped doing their listings pages and it felt like things were slowing down,' he says. 'You started to see fewer fanzines being sold at away grounds, and you realised that you didn't really have a vast amount of interaction with that many editors anymore.'

At the same time, the dwindling of print numbers and the emergence of a generation unwilling to pay for football media brought regular existential doubt: 'Your sales are down. You're aware that ever since the first couple of years, you've been on a decline. And then you're slowly but surely realising that one fanzine after another is stopping and that people are getting older. I remember the Man City guys, old guys that were selling it at the Riverside. And I said to myself, "I'm never going to still be doing this when I've got grey hair." Well, look at me!'

Mike Harrison of *The City Gent* would understand. 'I have this love-hate relationship with the *City Gent* because whilst it's a hobby, I'm bound to keep it going. Who's going to take over? There isn't anybody to take over. I haven't got anybody to pass it on to. We haven't got any youngsters involved on the editorial side, although we have had young writers go on to forge successful careers in the regional and national press.' Yet, says the energetic Harrison, there will always be a fanzine while there are writers and contributors: 'It's part of the social fabric of the game in Bradford. It can be a lonely job sitting here writing away and thinking. But I also think there is something magical about starting with a blank sheet of paper, then mapping it all out and slowly the *City Gent* begins to form.'

Reflecting, he adds: 'As we get older maybe all we have is our memories. The fact is that those are nice things to have. I hope that some younger readers might find their dad's or granddad's *City Gents* in the loft somewhere and start reading them and thinking, "Wow, that's really interesting." I think there's enough of us still going that believe in little printed pieces of social history to keep going.'

Harrison's version of Rob's lamppost is a specific parcel of limestone wall close to Valley Parade. Such was his readers' need for fanzine escapism and connection in a lonely time that when Covid restrictions temporarily lifted in June 2020, he announced via social media that during the coming football-bereft Saturday he would stand in his usual spot selling *The City Gent*. 'About 40 people turned up! How bonkers is that? They came for a catch-up, and we had our two-metre distanced chat. I was really pleased that we did that, because I think most other fanzines just took a break.'

Over the Pennines, Scott Sumner continues to sell *4000 Holes* at Ewood Park, where 'the steady stream of trade at the ground on matchdays really ensures sustainability'. While young readers are difficult to persuade, an older cohort remain. 'Maybe it's retaliation against the modern mood that "everything's online" as there are so many social media accounts, blogs and websites that it's sometimes hard to know what is reputable,' thinks Sumner. 'A hard copy fanzine hopefully has more gravitas, especially if the name has been around since 1989 like ours has. I enjoy putting together something which you can hold in your hand.'

While many fanzines have become more tranquil in tone through the years, *4000 Holes* has remained militant in its opposition to Rovers' 'invisible and immovable' owners, the Venkys. However, their many 'satirical and sarcastic front covers and articles' have 'gone unnoticed by the club powers and wouldn't have any impact anyway'. Long gone are the days of directors threatening libel.

Steering a fanzine even older than *FMTTM* or *4000 Holes* is Aynsley Taylor, the tenth editor of *The Leyton Orientear*. 'I recognise how precious this thing is because of the tradition, the heritage, the age of it,' he explains. 'There's part of the job that is protecting something that has been around for a long time, is venerable.' Pleasantly bucking a trend, *Orientear* sales have increased in recent years. As with all three previously mentioned senior titles, there remain collecting customers who were there for issue 1. Taylor is unceasingly grateful to them and for the goodwill of sellers who continue to stand on each corner of Brisbane Road stadium in the hard cold of a football winter. Although he worries that we live in 'an increasingly post-literate society', there remains hope that 'these things will come back round again'. He cites the example of his 16-year-old daughter:

'She and her friends like physical media, they like objects, they like CDs, they like vinyl. Obviously, they're distracted by TikTok and Instagram so it's not as straightforward as it sounds, but it's not dying. I don't think it will die. We shouldn't give up, we *mustn't* give up.'

Across London, Dave Thomas is in his 39th year of editorship. *A Kick Up the R's*, he presumed, 'would last for six months, and then I would just lose interest in things'. Now, 'I can't give it up. I'm not allowed to give it up because my readers and people who buy it religiously won't allow me.' As with Nichols at his lamppost and Harrison next to the wall, he feels 'part of the furniture, part of the matchday experience. People get in touch if I'm not there, through illness or whatever – "It's not the same without you." And people still say to me, "Yeah, I can hear you at the other end of the street shouting." I think it's got an endless future because it retains the principles of a fanzine.'

Sunderland's *A Love Supreme*, meanwhile, has survived and prospered through what Martyn McFadden calls 'unintentionally diversifying' – building on the trust around the print product to run a supporters' bus, publish books, produce music and sell merchandise, all from a shop opposite the Stadium of Light. 'It's so hard when you've a generation that read screens and not pages,' adds McFadden. 'People read more about football now than they did when the fanzines were starting, but there's so many outlets where you just flip through your phone. You don't need to buy a magazine. And there's a generation of people under 30 who've just grown up not buying magazines or newspapers.'

At 80 years old, John Pearman is the country's most senior fanzine editor. He started *Red All Over the Land* in 1995. 'It was all word processors and floppy disks by then,' he recalls in 2026, 'no need for glue!' Issue 1 landed in November of that year – 'We were playing Everton at home. It rained, and we lost 2-1 but we sold 400 copies.' Taking up the crusading ethos of earlier fanzines, over the years *RAOTL* campaigned vigorously for the victims of Hillsborough and their families. Even as Liverpool gathered yet more trophies in recent seasons, *RAOTL* continued to question club policies, from ticket prices to the perceived prioritisation of high-spending 'tourist' supporters over traditional fans.

Despite a loyal readership, however, Pearman suspects the fanzine's decline is hovering near. 'A lot of people say to me, "Well, if you go, then something's gone, matchday's changed forever." I don't deny that,' he says, 'But I'm 80 now. To stand outside Anfield on a cold, miserable day, and you've sold 20 copies in two and a half hours – you feel a bit fed up.' Ironically, as those day trippers unversed in fanzine culture arrive, Pearman is faced by a problem known to the earliest fanzine sellers four decades ago. 'People come walking past,' he adds, 'and they're saying, "What's that?"'

What, then, of *When Saturday Comes*, now a cultural archive of four decades of fandom? Deputy editor Ffion Thomas feels that by adhering to many of its founding principles, it will remain a vital publication for a certain type of supporter. The magazine, she feels, will always matter because 'We've balanced holding authorities to account and issuing criticism where it is due with championing the good that football does in communities and celebrating the bonds and relationships that come about as part of being a match-going supporter, in particular, at all levels of the game'. Writers approach their topics with a sense of 'solidarity and openness, not partisanship, and our readership understands and embraces that. They want to read across the game about the emotional aspects that we all share, but also where isolated issues that might affect one club can often broaden into a wider significance or threat, as we've seen many times.'

Each month an envelope arrives through my letterbox and drags me homewards. I grew up in York; my mum may well have pushed my buggy past the WI headquarters as Kettlewell and Ormston thrust the handle of the Gestetner. This modern package comes from the city and each time I see the editor's tiny scrawl whispering my name and address I am transported. For half an hour, having spilled its ingredients, I will read about York City. Occasionally, I swear I can smell Bootham Crescent on its breath.

Y Front resembles an old fanzine but isn't. Michael Miles – its address-scrawling editor – intended it to replicate some of the titles he fell in love with in the late 1980s. Its look – bright card covers, Courier font, grainy photocopied images – adds to the sense of travel it furnishes me with, now throwing me to the past. 'There's some wonderful fanzines out there,' says Miles. 'Some of them are glossy. The Hollywood sort of fanzines. I never wanted that. I always wanted the organic, even down to using a typewriter font. I wanted it to look as if it was handmade. And it is handmade because I put them all together myself.' To add to the throwback thrill, free gifts such as City stickers or old programmes usually also fall from the package. 'I always loved the buzz of a free gift with a comic,' says Miles, 'a plastic gun or one of those polystyrene aeroplanes. So that was something I always wanted to bring in to *Y Front*.' Fittingly, dipping into my *Y Front* envelopes rewards me with the boyhood thrill of lunging into a new box of Kellogg's cereal for a toy. Miles is not alone in offering such bounties; neatly-designed stickers fall from the pages of many a modern fanzine and make titles visible on lampposts and away end seats across the country.

In the spirit of his *Terrace Talk* idols, Miles began production on a work computer and photocopier, back in 2016. Then a caretaker in a primary school, his employers allowed him use of their facilities, although unlike many a pioneer, he funded his own paper and ink. 'It was just something that I've always wanted to do,' he continues, 'so I read up about it.' Miles produced *Y Front's* pages initially by cutting images with a Stanley knife and glueing them onto the paper. After photocopying, he would 'go into the kitchen at school and they had a big, long silver table where they used to prepare the food and I used to line up all the pages. I'd be doing this at 8, 9 o'clock at night.' The Yorkshireman would soon learn some rudimentary computer skills and buy a 'great lump of a photocopier' for £50 ('Mind, I've spent £1000 on parts, repairs and servicing)'. Each monthly issue is, he confesses, 'a real ball-ache of a job. But I'll never change. It's a proper fanzine. I've had people offer to print it for me, but when I put it together, I own it.'

Another among the newer wave of fanzine editors is Barry Crossan, a Dubliner at the helm of Shelbourne's *Red Inc.* since 2014. A more modern production than *Y Front*, the colour fanzine was founded by Shels' Reds Independent supporters' group in 1999 as a place for protest against boardroom decisions. 'There was a void to be filled there, and a space for fans to be able to express their opinion,' says Crossan. Modern-day relations with the club's owners are much improved, although 'We're always remaining vigilant because you never know when the next cock-up is around the corner. And it's important to be able to get that down on paper and to write honestly and freely.' Selling outside Shels' wonderful Tolka Park ground and to countries across the globe via post, *Red Inc.* is in fine fettle. 'Everything was supposed to kill fanzines,' says Crossan. 'It was radio phone-ins, the internet, message boards, social media. Fanzines survive because by their nature, football fans are nostalgic for physical products. They love having a paper magazine rolled up and putting it in their back pocket. It reminds them of when they went to their first game with their granddad or their dad.'

Further, says Crossan, they offer a home for nuanced reflection that 'doesn't compete with social media or immediate new media but complements it in a different way. It has a different role.' Or, as Richard Bellis, co-founder with brother Neil of Chester fanzine *The Blue & White* phrases it, 'Fanzines used to be the main alternative football media. That's not the case anymore. There's now so much noise, so much bullshit. The job of the fanzine is to provide something you can't get elsewhere, something considered that can't be clipped for social media.'

Crossan and the Bellis brothers helped Darren Norton as he sought to establish a fanzine for non-league North Ferriby

United in 2016, a common endeavour among editors past and present. *View From the Allotment End* (*VFTAE*) quickly became a campaigning organ against United's owners, who would within three years lead the club to the abyss. Then, the fanzine played a vital part in its rebirth. 'Darren got me banned from North Ferriby, in old club form,' says present editor Matthew Kempson. 'I was selling the fanzine, Darren had put in an article calling the previous owners "shithouses" which I think was, to be fair, a perfectly acceptable phrase. And Darren wasn't there. I was selling outside the ground, got a tap on the shoulder and ultimately, I was escorted off the premises and was told that I'd been given an indefinite ban. As it turned out, our fanzine lasted longer than the club.'

VFTAE remains fiercely independent, though from a position of 'critical support'. Norton adds, 'We have to be careful in what we say about certain things, because when your crowds are about 350, 400 and 100 people are reading the fanzine, word gets out to the 300 that aren't reading the fanzine.' In common with many modern titles including *The Blue & White*, all *VFTAE* profits are donated to charitable causes or the club. Fanzines are helping again, and that goes for mutual assistance too. There exists between many editors a resolute community, members of which know each other's pains and sometimes fill one another's pages.

Far removed from the classic design principles of *Y Front*, Brighton & Hove Albion fanzine *Dogma* offers another model for flourishing. 'We decided early on, after playing around with a more DIY, old-fashioned ethos,' says co-editor James William, 'that *Dogma* couldn't just be a printed version of the internet. It had to do its own thing and be worthy of the paper that it's printed on.' Artfully crafted and printed quarterly on high-specification paper, *Dogma* is resolutely, purposefully 'different to what's currently out there in fan media. The articles that we publish are long-reads, broad in scope. They don't tend to focus on the detail of the week-by-week stuff, which the internet serves well. The idea is that it sits on your coffee table and has longevity and feels like something that you own and cherish. It's a kind of experiential thing.' Within *Dogma*'s finely-honed pages dwell words of substance, many of them iconoclastic in the decades-old fanzine tradition. While Brighton & Hove Albion have been understandably lauded for their tremendous footballing progression in recent years, the fanzine readily criticises missteps by the club or modern supporter trends such as leaving matches preposterously early.

In her work as a university fashion lecturer, Liverpudlian Jacqui McAssey has witnessed a blossoming of youthful interest in such cherished objects including 'zines, as those born this century tend to label their own creations. She perceives a shift in recent years that could represent the seeds of a renaissance. 'A lot of younger people I work with,' she says, 'have their online self and their real self. That real self is increasingly offline and embracing tactile, tangible things. That's why some of them have started their zines. They're not doing football ones yet, but I'm optimistic that'll follow.'

McAssey knows football fanzines well. Pioneering a 2010s movement to document women at football matches through interviews and photographs, she was determined that its main output 'would be a fanzine. I always wanted to be in print, always wanted it to be the type of thing you can roll up, take into a game, take home again.' *Girlfans* fanzine began publication in 2013 and each issue since has showcased magnificent photography of female supporters in England and Scotland. 'For the first issue, we printed them and then distributed them at Anfield to some people who I'd photographed and then to others who were complete strangers. And it started from there,' she adds. While McAssey's project illuminates the issues football-loving women confront, it is more than anything a celebration of fandom, its diversity and what she calls 'the spectacle of matchday'.

Cherishing fanzines of all vintages and purposes is Peter Slater. For two years he has been compiling The List – a spreadsheet aimed at capturing the title of every football fanzine published in these isles, currently sitting at 1816 but rising –

and writing weekly blogs about his work. He was part of a unit of volunteers who helped research what became *Voice of the Fans*, an award-winning 2025 fanzine exhibition based in Leeds Central Library in partnership with the British Library. Slater calls himself 'Just basically a retired guy, filling his time'. In many eyes, he is performing God's work, curating this previously uncatalogued, unrepresented area of fandom and social history. When asked whether fanzines remain important, his opinion matters: 'Absolutely. They still have a vital place.'

For Barry Crossan, the fanzine voice will remain relevant by being activist, following the lead of continental publications. 'In Germany,' he says, 'fanzines were at the forefront of resistance against certain changes like to the 50+1 rule. Obviously, that's ultra-led, so they're quite militant. But it's the fanzine that can give that direction.' Ffion Thomas agrees that fanzines will always have an essential function because 'fans will always need to challenge and hold clubs and authorities to account, and we need an independent media to do that'. Of further importance, the fanzine is a 'documentation and preservation of genuine fan culture and fan voices, not the interpretation that you get from Sky Sports or betting companies or even clubs themselves of what a fan is and does, that sort of sanitised view that you get in a TV advert'.

Blue & White co-editor Richard Bellis concurs that a fanzine's ability to let supporters 'define what being a football fan is for themselves remains very important'. Whereas in the early years, that meant resisting the stereotyping of fans as criminals, now it is 'more about resisting commercialism. It used to be: "We need to control these people because they're hooligans." Now, it's: "We need to control these people so we can extract as much money from them as possible." And I think that's where fanzines push back.'

In Brighton, James William foresees in the *Dogma* audience a positive future: 'I reject the idea that fanzines are nostalgic exercises. A significant chunk of our demographic are under 25. They're the most active in terms of their engagement with our social stuff. I think our readership is incredibly broad and it's not just blokes that bought fanzines in the 80s.' Dogma's social interaction – online, but also via murals across town – has created a community that wants to indulge in print. 'There's nothing inherently retro about having nice things in your life,' he adds.

Michael Miles' determination that fanzines prosper is more succinct: 'Even if sales fall down to 100 issues, if 100 people enjoy it, then I'll keep going.'

When the great Rogan Taylor reviewed the early years of the fanzine movement in 1990, he labelled its effects 'enormous'. It had been, he told *The Fox*, 'like a mini proletarian revolution'. The 'bouncy boys behind the goal' were now involved, whereas before 'nothing had ever been written for them'. It was a 'clear indication that they wanted to do more than jump up and down behind the goal'. Unity and potential had been awoken.

Glancing backwards 36 years after Taylor did, his former FSA colleague Craig Brewin salutes fanzines' role in encouraging 'people to protest and not accept that they had no control. They connected people and started conversations.' Pragmatically, Brewin cautions that, as an example, 'Charlton didn't get back to the Valley because people wrote about it. It was a political campaign and a business proposal.' However, 'a fanzine gets the message across and has a supporting role.'

Of further value was the FSA's assistance in helping fanzine contributors become part of media companies' contacts lists. Interactions with local or national broadcasters and newspapers demonstrated that many football fans were articulate, decent and – contrary to their portrayal throughout the 1980s – human. That image was reinforced as people within the media and wider public experienced physical fanzines at their creative, roaring best. As Mike Ticher says, 'Fanzines changed the idea of what most fans are like. And that became the mainstream way of thinking about them.'

The media, governing authorities and football clubs gradually understood that supporters' voices mattered in a game on the cusp of monumental change. The years of ignoring were ending. In turn, fans – many of them fanzine editors or contributors – became emboldened, pioneering supporter involvement in the direction and running of the game. Rob Bagchi sees a lineage to modern campaigns as a 'fanzine diaspora' began 'the fightback in terms of fan ownership and other things. There is a middle-aged audience there that is committed to being activists because of what fanzines achieved.'

Fanzines also helped football supporters' self-identity, instilling solidarity over shared irritants and indeed joys. 'They made fans see that they had a collective sensibility,' says *WSC* writer Harry Pearson. 'They were a fringe thing, but it was a big fringe. They gave you a sense that what you thought about the game was actually shared by lots of other people, and the way you talked about the game was the way that other people talked about it. They gave fans a collective voice and showed that there was actually a collective identity of fans.'

Pearson further reflects that fanzines helped win material gains for supporters: 'A lot of the things that fanzines campaigned for came into being. Of course, that could well have been a mixture of the pressure of fanzines and the people who read fanzines then subsequently going into higher positions in football. Either way, the clubs started to listen to fans because of fanzines.'

The police stopped hitting people so much. Stadium facilities improved. Fanzine food and toilet reviews ceased to be so scathingly funny, a sign that something had shifted. Gains cannot be credited entirely to fanzines, but even the miserly would confess that they pushed and harassed and changed the conversation at least.

Their conversing was, as we have seen, often erudite and occasionally incendiary. That was a consequence of giving blank pages to the great unheard masses that dwelled behind the goal. Those pages did not fill themselves. Anyone was encouraged to have a go, expressing themselves as never before and feeling the rush of seeing their words or pictures in print. It created a deluge, legions of writers and illustrators who hitherto were dispossessed of the confidence or know-how to create. 'I often think about this PO Box we had for our mail,' smiles Archie MacGregor of *The Absolute Game*. 'Every time I went to that box, it felt like Christmas Day because you just didn't know what was going to be there. Letters, articles, anything.'

In MacGregor's Scotland and beyond, their ink spilled from the page and influenced mainstream writing. 'I think it was all part of that movement that changed sports writing,' says Bagchi, who observed fanzines' literary influence close-up at Sportspages and then as a journalist. 'It made newspapers up their game and be more understanding of where fans were coming from. It changed the way that broadsheet football writing was, and it brought a lot of great books in its wake.'

Speaking from among bundles of fresh eBay fanzine acquisitions, Peter Slater is unequivocal: 'This movement changed fandom. At both the local and the national level, it drove protest. The history of protest is so crucial to this country and fanzines were a really, really important part of that in the national sport.'

Much of that movement's spirit now seems absent despite the ills supporters could be decrying: Fixtures spread over a weekend, with away fans compelled to travel hundreds of miles for hellish kick-off times; clubs quasi-owned by repressive governments; extortionate match tickets; facial recognition software being used by the police to profile supporters; fans singing 'Is this is a library?'; VA-bloody-R.

Perhaps it is time to dust those cobwebs from the typewriter.

TITLE WINNERS

From *Brian Moore's Head Looks Uncannily Like London Planetarium* (Gillingham) to *Mr Bismark's Electric Pickelhaube* (Meadowbank Thistle), fanzine titles continue to conjure delight. Here are ten favourites with less-obvious origin stories:

***53 Miles West of Venus* (Preston North End)**
In April 1987, Preston midfielder Les Chapman scored a winner which won his side promotion. Asked after full-time how he felt, he invoked the title of a B-52s single, elatedly claiming to be '53 miles west of Venus'.

***Can I Bring My Dog?* (Dundee United)**
When in 1993 the Tangerines faced a UEFA Cup away tie against Brøndby of Denmark, supporters' club members queried logistics around their two-day coach journey. One question, asked completely seriously, soon became a fanzine title.

***Fly Me To The Moon* (Middlesbrough)**
In the late 1980s, Boro manager Bruce Rioch was asked: 'If you had to travel to the moon, who would you take with you?' His answer was Tony Mowbray, a legendary club captain. For many years, *FMTTM* covers carried lunar cartoons of the pair.

***Hello Albert* (Chester City)**
Sealand Road, Chester's old home, boasted one of football's first public address systems. From as early as 1931, local lore claims, the announcer would begin his shift with the message, 'Hello Spion Kop! Hello Albert!' Albert was, apparently, a veteran fan.

***Mudhutter* (Wigan Athletic)**
At some point in the murky past, Latics fans began singing 'We come from Wigan/and we live in mudhuts', a local bikers'

standard from the 1960s. The line is met by the response 'Ooh-ah, ooh-ah, you should be a Wiganer!' Perfect for a fanzine title.

***On Cloud Seven* (Hull City)**
'Well, Colin, how does it feel to be back at Hull City?' asked a BBC Humberside reporter of recently-returned manager Colin Appleton in May 1989. '... er,' answered Appleton, 'I'm on cloud seven really.'

***The Deranged Ferret* (Lincoln City)**
Another lower division manager with a unique way with words, Colin Murphy told *Saint & Greavsie* that in a recent game his players had run around like 'deranged ferrets'. It is not clear whether this was a compliment.

***The Memoirs of Seth Bottomley* (Port Vale)**
'Seth Bottomley' was a made-up footballer – a spoof stalwart right-half from the good old days invented for a fanzine title. So ingrained did the name become, one *Memoirs* ... editor claimed he had heard a fan lament that a current Vale midfielder 'couldn't hold a candle to Bottomley.'

***War Of The Monster Trucks* (Sheffield Wednesday)**
In 1991, Wednesday defeated Manchester United in the Rumbelows Cup final at Wembley. Any Owl back in the White Rose county wishing to watch their team celebrating was in for a shock. On full-time, Yorkshire Television switched away from the national stadium and instead screened a 1986 recording of *War of the Monster Trucks*.

***Wendy Who?* (St Johnstone)**
Another chant-inspired title. '*Knock Knock – Who's there?*' began this terrace ditty at Saints' old Muirton Park home. '*Wendy*', came the answer, met quickly with a '*WENDY WHO?*', and then finally: '*Oh Wendy Saints, Oh Wendy Saints, Oh Wendy Saints go marching in ...*'

IMAGE CAPTIONS

Page IX: Cover, *Fly Me to the Moon* #63, Middlesbrough fanzine. Credit: *Fly Me To The Moon* (1991, author's collection).

Page XVI: Cover, *Terrace Talk* #5/7, York City fanzine. Credit: Nik Curry (1986, author's collection).

Page 12: Cover, *City Gent* #1, Bradford City fanzine. Credit: *City Gent* (1984, kindly supplied by Mike Harrison).

Page 24: Cover, *Dial M For Merthyr* #16, Merthyr Tydfil fanzine. Credit: *Dial M For Merthyr* (1991, author's collection).

Page 38: Cover, *Off the Ball* #9, general fanzine. Credit: *Off the Ball* (1987, author's collection).

Page 55: Stop-a-Gob spoof advert from *Here We Go Again* #3, Bolton Wanderers fanzine. Artist unknown (1991, author's collection).

Page 56: Cover, *The Occasional Terrorist* #2, Tooting & Mitcham United fanzine. Credit: Tim Megone (1989, author's collection).

Page 70: Cover, *When Saturday Comes* #1, general fanzine. Credit: When Saturday Comes Ltd. (1986, author's collection).

Page 84: Cover, *4000 Holes* #1, Blackburn Rovers fanzine. Credit: Scott Sumner (1989, private collection of Peter Slater).

Page 94: Cover, *AWOL* #3, Meadowbank Thistle fanzine. Credit: © Meadowbank Thistle Brake Club (1987, private collection of Peter Slater).

Page 107: Copyright apology from *Friday Night Fever* #3, Tranmere Rovers fanzine. Creator unknown (1989, author's collection).

Page 107: *When Saturday Comes* appeal for sellers from *The Memoirs of Seth Bottomley* #5, Port Vale fanzine. Creator unknown (1989, author's collection).

Page 107: Juma printers advert from *Football Supporter*, FSA newsletter. Credit: Juma Printing & Publishing (1990, author's collection).

Page 108: Cover, *Two For Joy* #3, Chorley fanzine. Credit: Mike Hindley, Dave Hindle, John Singleton (1988, author's collection).

Page 122: Sportspages advert from *Football Supporter*, FSA newsletter. Creator unknown (1990, author's collection).

Page 132: Cover, *Wise Men Say* #8, Sunderland fanzine. Credit: Jim Fox, Dave Hillam, Mike Hillam, Keith Nixon (1989, author's collection).

Page 146: Cover, *Fly Me to the Moon* #15, Middlesbrough fanzine. Credit: *Fly Me To The Moon* (1989, author's collection).

Page 162: Cover, *A Kick Up The R's* Hillsborough Special, Queens Park Rangers fanzine. Credit: *A Kick Up The R's* (1989, author's collection).

Page 176: Rough Guide to Easter Road from *Hibs Monthly* #24, Hibernian fanzine. Credit: Colin Leslie (1989, author's collection).

Page 189: Meat pie and Bovril cartoon from *Mutton Mutineer* #2, Derby County fanzine. Creator unknown (1990, author's collection).

Page 189: Spoof Wembley advert from *4 Bleats to the Baah* #8, Tamworth fanzine. Creator unknown (1991, author's collection).

Page 190: Cover *United Colours of Football*, anti-racism fanzine. Credit: FSA/Adam Brown/Gareth Evans (1994, author's collection).

Page 205: Piece of Brechin City hedge given free with *Tomato Soup and Lentils* #1, Arbroath and Leeds United fanzine. Creator unknown (1990, NLS collection).

Page 205: Policeman cartoon from several titles including *View From the Tower* #2, Blackpool fanzine. Creator unknown (Date unknown, author's collection).

Page 206: Cover, *Football Supporter*, FSA newsletter. Credit: FSA (1990, author's collection).

Page 219: Spoof ClubCall script from *The Leyton Orientear* #28, Leyton Orient fanzine. Credit: Gary Winch (1989, author's collection).

Page 220: Cover, *Voice of the Valley* #1, Charlton Athletic fanzine. Credit: Rick Everitt (1988, author's collection).

Page 229: Advert for *Standing Room Only* contributions from *When Saturday Comes* #67. Creator unknown (1992, author's collection).

Page 230: Cover, *The Crooked Spireite* #6, Chesterfield fanzine. Credit: Stuart Basson (1988, author's collection).

BIBLIOGRAPHY

Books

Goldberg, Adrian, *Where's The Money Gone?: The Battle For The Soul Of English Football* (Byline Books, 2025)
Inglis, Simon, *The Football Grounds of England and Wales* (Harper Collins, 1983)
Lacey, Martin, *El Tel Was a Space Alien* (Juma, 1989)
Lacey, Martin, *Get Your Writs Out: Another Dose of the Alternative Football Press* (Juma, 1990)
Shaw, Phil, *Whose Game is it Anyway?: The Book of Football Fanzines* (Argus Books, 1989)
Various authors, *Foul: Best of Football's Alternative Paper, 1972-1976*, editor Mike Ticher (Simon & Schuster, 1987)
Various authors, *When Saturday Comes: The Half-Decent Football Book* (Penguin, 2005)

Fanzines

This list of around 180 titles encompasses fanzines used in the main text of the book. In addition, circa 500 other titles were viewed, though are here omitted for the sake of space.

Absolute Game, The (General)
Against the Tide (for female supporters)
Another Wasted Corner (Liverpool)
Arsenal Echo Echo, The (Arsenal)
AWOL (Meadowbank Thistle)
Ayresome Angel (Middlesbrough)
Balls (General)
Bamber's Right Foot (Torquay United)
Bayview Bulletin (East Fife)
Beyond the Boundary (Oldham Athletic)
Blow Football (General)
Blue Print (Manchester City)

Blue & White (Chester)
Bobbing Along (Cardiff City)
Boleyn Scorcher, The (West Ham United)
Bolton Wanderers Worldwide (Bolton Wanderers)
Born Kicking (for female supporters)
Bountyhunter (Bristol City)
Brian (Nottingham Forest)
Brian Moore's Head Looks Uncannily Like London Planetarium (Gillingham)
Bring the Noise (Swindon Town)
Cappielow Bugle (Greenock Morton)
Cheers (Meadowbank Thistle)
Chelsea Independent, The (Chelsea)
City Gent, The (Bradford City)
Crooked Spireite, The (Chesterfield)
Crying Time Again (Hamilton Academical)
Cumberland Sausage, The (Carlisle United)
Dalymount Roar, The (Bohemians)
Depleated (Luton Town)
Deranged Ferret, The (Lincoln City)
Dial M For Merthyr (Merthyr Tydfil/Merthyr Town)
Deepdale Rudge (Preston North End)
Dogma (Brighton & Hove Albion)
Dons Outlook (Wimbledon)
Each Game as it Comes (General)
Eagle Eye (Crystal Palace)
Electric Blue (Manchester City)
Elm Park Disease (Reading)
Elmslie Ender, The (Wealdstone United)
Everywhere & Nowhere (Sheffield Wednesday)
Exceedingly Good Pies (Rochdale)
Falkirk Unofficial Fanzine, The (Falkirk)
Filbo Fever (Leicester City)
Fingerpost (West Bromwich Albion)
Five to Three (General)
Flashing Blade (Sheffield United)
Flippin' Heck Ref, That Was a Foul Surely (Waterlooville)
Floodlight (Colchester United)
Fly Me To The Moon (Middlesbrough)

Follow, Follow (Rangers)
The Football Pink (LGBT)
Forever and a Day (Burnley)
For Fox Sake (Leicester City)
4000 Holes (Blackburn Rovers)
Fox, The (Leicester City)
Foxy Ferret (Carlisle United)
From Behind Your Fences (Boston United)
From Home to Home (Shelbourne)
Get A Grip, Ref! (Scunthorpe United)
Get Into Them (hooligan)
Girlfans (female supporters)
Gooner, The (Arsenal)
Grorty Dick (West Bromwich Albion)
Gull's Eye (Brighton & Hove Albion)
Hail-Hail (Celtic)
Hanging Sheep (Leeds United)
Hello Albert (Chester City)
Here We Go Again (Bolton Wanderers)
Hey Big Spender (Derby County)
Hibs Monthly (Hibernian)
Hit the Bar (General)
Hull, Hell and Happiness (Hull City)
Imperfect Match, An (Arsenal)
Interesting, Very Interesting (Derby County)
In the Loft (Queen's Park Rangers)
Jackmail (Swansea City)
Jolly Potter (Stoke City)
Just Another Wednesday (Sheffield Wednesday)
Kick Up the R's, A (*AKUTR's*) (Queens Park Rangers)
Killie Ken (Kilmarnock)
King of the Kippax (Manchester City)
A Large Scotch (Shrewsbury Town)
Leyton Orientear, The (Leyton Orient)
Light at the End of the Tunnel (Dartford)
Lion Roars, The (Millwall)
Load of Bull, A (Wolves)
Love Supreme, A (Sunderland)
Mag, The (Newcastle United)

Many Miles From Home (Blackburn Rovers)
Marching Altogether (Leeds United)
Marlon's Gloves (Burnley)
Memoirs of Seth Bottomley, The (Port Vale)
Mission Impossible (Darlington)
Mission Impossible (Torquay United)
Mi Whippet's Dead (Rotherham United)
More Dead Wood Than the Mary Rose (Portsmouth)
Mud, Sweat and Beers (Watford)
Mutton Mutineer (Derby County)
My Eyes Have Seen the Glory (Tottenham Hotspur)
Never Mind the Boleyn (West Ham United)
Never Mind the Danger (Norwich City)
No One Likes Us (Millwall)
Normid Nomad (Bolton Wanderers)
Northern Light (Aberdeen)
Not the View (Celtic)
Oatcake (Stoke City)
Off The Ball (General)
Off the Shelf (Tottenham Hotspur)
One Nil Down, Two One Up (Arsenal)
Only the Lonely (Airdrie)
On the Terraces (West Ham United)
Out of Court (Bournemouth)
Over the Moon (anti-fascist)
Over the Moon (Kent/general)
Over the Wall (Albion Rovers)
Pie, The (Notts County)
Peterborough Effect, The (Peterborough United)
PNE View, The (Preston North End)
Poppies at the Gates of Dawn (Kettering Town)
Preston Pie Muncher (Preston North End)
popular STAND (Doncaster Rovers)
Proclaimer, The (Hibernian)
Raging Bull (Oxford United)
Railway Ender (Ayr United)
Raise the Roof (Doncaster Rovers)
Reclaim the Game (FSA)
Red All Over the Land (Liverpool)

Red Attitude (Manchester United)
Red Inc. (Shelbourne)
Red Issue (Manchester United)
Red News (Manchester United)
Rodney, Rodney! (General)
Rub of the Greens (Plymouth Argyle)
Saddle Sore (Walsall)
Shankill Skinhead, The (Manchester United)
Sing When We're Fishing (Grimsby Town)
Slice of Kilner Pie, A (Huddersfield Town)
Sound of the Shay, The (Halifax Town)
South Riding (Barnsley)
Speke from the Harbour (Everton)
Spur, The (Tottenham Hotspur)
Square Ball, The (Leeds United)
Taking the Biscuit (Reading)
Tales from the Potting Shed (Preston North End)
Tales from the Riverbank (London)
Terrace Talk (York City)
Tea Party, The (Stockport County)
There's a Store Where the Creatures Meet (St Mirren)
There's Only One F in Fulham (Fulham)
This Charming Fan (General)
Through the Wind and Rain (Liverpool)
Tired and Weary (Birmingham City)
Tricky Tree, The (Nottingham Forest)
Two For Joy (Chorley)
United Colours of Football (FSA)
United We Stand (Manchester United)
UTD/United (joint Dundee United/West Ham United)
Valiant's Viewpoint (Charlton Athletic)
View from the East Bank, A (Sheffield Wednesday)
Voice of the Valley (Charlton Athletic)
View From the Allotment End (North Ferriby)
View from the Shelf, A (Tottenham Hotspur)
Walking Down the Halbeath Road (Dunfermline)
Watch the Bluebirds Fly (Cardiff City)
Web, The (Queen's Park)
What a Load of Cobblers (Northampton Town)

When Saturday Comes (General)
When Skies Are Grey (Everton)
When Sunday Comes (Liverpool)
When the Hoodoo Comes (Dundee United)
Who Ate All the Pies? (Burnley)
Win on the Plastic (Preston North End)
Wise Men Say (Sunderland)
Yellow Experience, The (Watford)
Y Front (York City)
You Wot! (Torquay United)

Interviewees

Adrian Goldberg
Andy Groom
Andy Lowe
Andy Lyons
Archie MacGregor
Aynsley Taylor
Barry Crossan
Colin McPherson
Craig Brewin
Darren Norton
Dave Wallace
Dave Thomas
Ffion Thomas
Frank Ormston
Glen Wilson
Graham Ennis
Harry Pearson
Iain Campbell
Jacqui McAssey
James Brown
James William
Jim Cooke
John Pearman
Jonny Owen
Mark Evans
Martin Lacey
Martyn McFadden
Matt Kempson
Michael Miles
Mike Harrison
Mike Kettlewell
Mike Ticher
Neil Forsyth
Paul Hawksbee
Peter Holmes
Peter Slater
Richard Bellis
Rick Everitt
Rob Bagchi
Rob Nichols
Scott Sumner
Simon Wright
Tom Davies

Websites

footballfanzineculture.blog
footballfanzinesarchive.wordpress.com
Times Digital Archive via Gale/NLS
wsc.co.uk/digital-edition

REFERENCES

No major inquiry into the Heysel disaster was ever held: *When Saturday Comes: The Half-Decent Football Book* (Penguin, 2005) and 'Liverpool still torn over night that shamed their name', *Guardian* article by Paul Kelso, 2 April, 2005.

One estimate gave the attendance figure at 112,000, more than 10 per cent over capacity: *WSC* magazine, issue #8 (June/July 1987).

BBC Head of Sport Jonathan Martin opined that 'Football rates itself too highly ... It does not have a God-given right to appear on the BBC.' quoted in *The Times* newspaper, 15 February, 1985.

In the autumn of 1987, it was reported that sports minister Colin Moynihan ... was planning the forced breathalysing of travelling fans as they queued outside grounds: Various fanzines including *Balls*, issue #2 (November 1987) and *Champion Hill Street Blues* issue #1 (March 1988) reported that the tests were proposed for fans as they waited to enter grounds. Newspaper coverage (for example *The Times* 20 October, 1987) and House of Commons debate suggested the tests were proposed for inside grounds: https://hansard.parliament.uk/Commons/1987-11-04/debates/2f01dd40-ec3e-49c1-8467-5b4dd489530e/Environment [accessed 30 March, 2026]

Bournemouth's scheme created members' only terraces and coincided with the installation of new steel fences and CCTV cameras: *Out of Court*, issue #1 (Sept/Oct 1988) and issue #2 (Nov/Dec 1988).

Torquay United barred away fans and before matchdays local police threatened to arrest anyone in possession of a visiting club's local accent: *Terrace Talk* volume 7 issue #5 (winter 1987/88) and *Off the Ball* issue #16 (January 1989).

It was, wrote John Peel, 'an impudent farrago of music, football and social irresponsibility.': Foreword to *Whose Game is it Anyway?: The Book of Football Fanzines*, compiled by Phil Shaw (Argus Books, 1989)

Ernie Clay was the Cottagers' owner who sold Fulham's home to Bulstrode, profiting a reported £6m in the process: *WSC* magazine, issue #7 (April/May 1987). In *The Times* on 26 February, 1987, Jimmy Hill said Clay 'picked up over £5m'.

The Sir Norman Chester Centre for Football Research made a 'conservative' estimate that 'over one million' fanzines were sold over season 1988/89: '*Football Fanzines Survey*', Sir Norman Chester Centre for Football Research, University of Leicester (1989).

Subsequently, *Gull's Eye* was the first fanzine to be sued for libel, with editor Peter Kennard and writer Ian Hart defendants: *Gull's Eye* issue #30 (October 1990) and #34 (February 1991).

Strenuously trying to justify the new measures, sports minister Moynihan released what the tabloids called a 'League Table of Terror': Various fanzines reproduced coverage, including *Dial M For Merthyr* issue #1, *On the Terraces* issue #11 and *Crooked Spireite* issue #10. The original figures were released by the UK government in July 1988.

The cause of most deaths and injuries at Valley Parade that day, wrote Popplewell, had been locked exits and turnstiles, which prevented escape: *Interim Report, July 1985*, Cmnd 9585 (this report contains most detail about the Bradford tragedy). *Committee of Inquiry into Crowd Safety and Control at Sports Grounds Final Report, Chairman: Mr Justice Popplewell* (London: HMSO Cmnd 9710, 1986).

A further, prescient incident unfolded at Loftus Road in January 1988: *WSC* magazine, issue #15 (May 1988).

Then in January 1990 the Hillsborough Stadium Disaster Inquiry published its findings: Chapter 15, *The Hillsborough Stadium Disaster, 15 April 1989 Inquiry by the Rt Hon Lord Justice Taylor, Final Report* (London, Home Office, January 1990).

... Lord Taylor's recommendation that stadiums should become all-seater. Within days of the report's publication, the government announced that his proposal would be passed into law: A House of Lords debate on the Hillsborough inquiry report, 29 January, 1990, included reference to government responses: https://hansard.parliament.uk/lords/1990-01-29/debates/f28f69fc-caa7-488c-907a-435a5d87eb58/HillsboroughDisasterInquiryReport [accessed 13 April, 2026]

Crystal Palace player Ian Wright noticed the effect *Marching Altogether* was having: 'We went to Leeds the other week. It was brilliant. They've got a thing down there petitioning against the noises and racial abuse black players take': Interview on *Great Britain United*, Channel 4 documentary, September 1991.

ACKNOWLEDGEMENTS

To spend day after day leafing through football fanzines was heavenly, but all researchers rely on dedicated staff to indulge them – heartfelt thanks go to Dr Alexander Jackson, Curator at the National Football Museum (NFM) and Paul Dudman, Archivist at the University of East London (UEL). The former helped me access the Manchester Metropolitan University fanzine collection, held at the NFM's Deepdale archives. The latter assisted me in accessing the *When Saturday Comes* club fanzine archive, held at the UEL's Docklands library.

I am, once again, deeply grateful for the support and faith in my words of my agent David Luxton, and his DLA colleague Rebecca Winfield – both of whom suggested this book as an idea a number of years ago. At Bloomsbury, it was wonderful to work with my editor Charlotte Croft again, and with her excellent colleague Caroline Hewlett. Thanks also to Jenni Davis for her diligent copy editing and Susan McCann for her fantastic proofing.

I am forever indebted to all of the fanzine editors and contributors who allowed me to interview them for this book and who were endlessly helpful afterwards. In keeping with the fanzine movement they created, their words were always interesting and often funny. The encouragement and assistance of Peter Slater (footballfanzineculture.blog) – not least in proofreading the first draft of the book – are enormously appreciated. A special mention too for Robert Nichols, whose fanzine changed my life.

Finally, on the other side of every writer's closed door are people who know when to leave that writer alone with their keyboard and when to knock with tea (brewed for precisely three-and-a-half minutes) and Orange Club biscuits. Without you two, nothing is possible.

Purveyors of Creative Derision Since 1989
THE INDEPENDENT MAGAZINE OF BERWICK RANGERS F.C.
SEASON 89-90
The Fanzine of Blackburn Rovers Supporters
SEPTEMBER, 1989
"A Northern Horde of uncouth Garb and Strange Oaths"
Issue no. 1
50p
Issue 64
DIAL M FOR MERTHYR
The board employ new stewards to look after the "Merthyr Youth Crew"
£2
An independent Fanzine of Merthyr Town FC
ICE CREAM SPECIAL
ELECTRIC BLUE
Nº6
50p
THE ONLY CITY 'ZINE TO COME FROM MANCHESTER
WARNING: THIS IS NOT THE PROGRAMME
THE MEMOIRS OF SETH BOTTOMLEY
" It's not the programme it's that book thing ! "
7·00
£1.00
VIEW FROM THE ALLOTMENT END
NORTH FERRIBY F.C. INDEPENDENT FANZINE
ISSUE 25
£2.50
Associate Member FSA
All profits to:
HOME START Hull
When Saturday Comes
The Half Decent FOOTBALL Magazine
June 1989 No. 28
Hillsborough: Unanimous Verdi
It wasn't our fault
It wasn't our fault
It wasn't our fault
TERRACE TALK
Vol.5 No.4 December 1985 20p
TERRACE TALK
No.4 December 1985 20p
O'S A PRETTY BOY?
d off as a pimple on my backside, doctor".
THE CITY GENT
HILLSBOROUGH DISASTER APPEAL SPECIAL ISSUE
All profits from the sale of this publication will be donated to the Appeal Fund
The Voice of Bantam Progressivism
at least 50 pence
A LOV SUPREM
OUR TEAM, OUR MAGAZI
FALLING IN LOVE AGAIN !
INSIDE:
•THE GARY BENNETT INTERVIEW
•ASK YOUR DAD
•BATMAN!
•LOTS OF LETTERS
•PIES AND BOVRIL